Grade 1

Addison-Wesley Mathematics

Robert E. Eicholz   Phares G. O'Daffer   Randall I. Charles
Sharon L. Young   Carne S. Barnett   Charles R. Fleenor

Stanley R. Clemens   Gloria F. Gilmer   Andy Reeves
Freddie L. Renfro   Mary M. Thompson   Carol A. Thornton
Joan E. Westley

♠ Addison-Wesley Publishing Company

Menlo Park, California ▪ Reading, Massachusetts ▪ New York
Don Mills, Ontario ▪ Wokingham, England ▪ Amsterdam ▪ Bonn
Sydney ▪ Singapore ▪ Tokyo ▪ Madrid ▪ San Juan ▪ Paris
Seoul, Korea ▪ Milan ▪ Mexico City ▪ Taipei, Taiwan

Program Advisors

John A. Dossey   Professor of Mathematics
Illinois State University, Normal, Illinois

Bonnie Armbruster   Associate Professor, Center for the Study of Reading
University of Illinois, Champaign, Illinois

Karen L. Ostlund   Associate Professor of Science Education
Southwest Texas State University, San Marcos, Texas

Betty C. Lee   Assistant Principal
Ferry Elementary School, Detroit, Michigan

William J. Driscoll   Chairman, Department of Mathematical Sciences
Central Connecticut State University, New Britain, Connecticut

David C. Brummett   Educational Consultant
Palo Alto, California

Multicultural Advisors

Bill Bray
James Hopkins
Marsha Muhammad

Moyra Contreras
Carol Artiga MacKenzie
Margarita Perez

Barbara Fong
Gloria Maldonado

Jeanette Haseyama
Mattie McCloud

Contributing Writers

Betsy Franco
Ann Muench
Sandra Ward

Mary Heinrich
Gini Shimabukuro
Judith K. Wells

Penny Holland
Marny Sorgen

Marilyn Jacobson
Connie Thorpe

Executive Editor

Diane H. Fernández

Cover Photo Credit: Steven Hunt/The Image Bank

ISBN: 0-201-44510-7

3 4 5 6 7 8 9 10 11 12 -WC- 96 95 94 93

Contents

Chapter 4 Understanding Subtraction

Chapter 5 Addition Facts: Count Ons and Zeros

Chapter 6 Addition Facts: Sums to 12

Chapter 7   Measurement

Chapter 8   Subtraction Facts: Count Backs, Zeros, and Doubles

Chapter 9   Geometry

Chapter 10   Subtraction Facts to 12

Chapter 11   Place Value

Chapter 12 Number Relationships and Counting Patterns

Chapter 13 Money

Chapter 14 Time

Chapter 15 Addition Facts: Sums to 18

Chapter 16 Addition and Subtraction Facts to 18

Chapter 17 Understanding 2-Digit Addition and Subtraction

Chapter 18 Extending Number Ideas

Resource Bank and Glossary

Dear Girls and Boys,

What will you do inside this book?

You will talk about numbers.

You will find patterns.

two   **four**   **six**

2   4   6

You will write numbers and math words.

You will work in groups or with a partner.

You will see how math can be used everyday.

You will learn about shapes and measuring.

You will do many things during math.

You will think about math and have fun. We know you will like your book.

From your friends at Addison-Wesley.

1
Classification, Patterns, and Numbers to 9

Workmat

Theme: Pets

Classification

Ring what belongs.

1.

2.

3.

4.

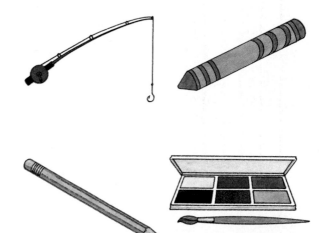

My Pattern Book

Color to continue the pattern.

Dear Family:
Ask your child
to tell how he or
she chose what
color to use.

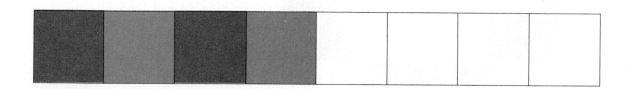

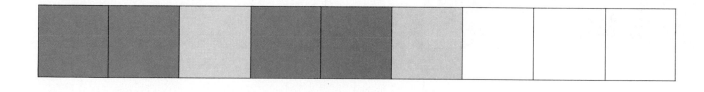

Color to continue the pattern.

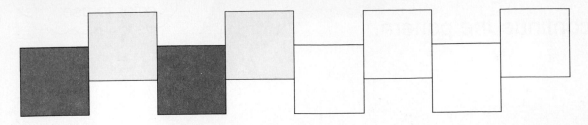

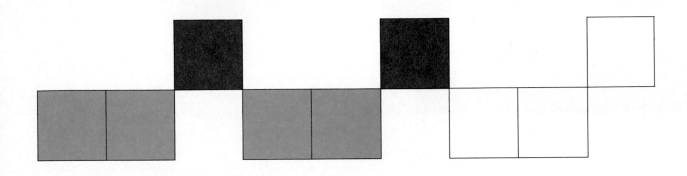

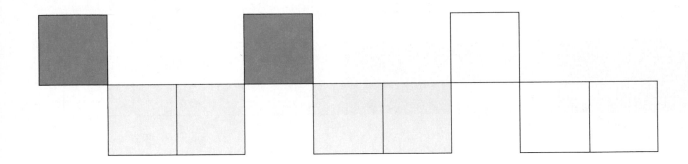

Color your own pattern.

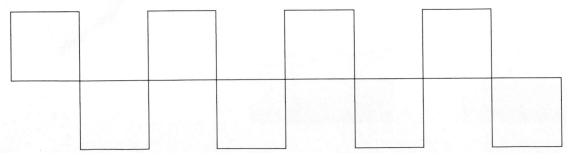

Introduction to Problem Solving

Listen to the story.

UNDERSTAND
FIND DATA
PLAN
ESTIMATE
SOLVE
CHECK

Using Critical Thinking

Tell how each car is different from
the one before.
Draw and color the next car.

1.

2.

3.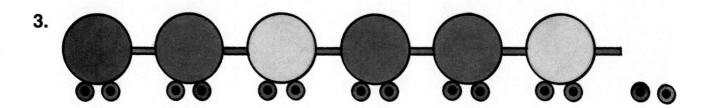

4. Draw and color a one-difference train.

Problem Solving
Finding Data from a Story

UNDERSTAND
FIND DATA
PLAN
ESTIMATE
SOLVE
CHECK

Listen to the story.
Tally the pets.
Write the number for each tally.

PET PARADE

🦎		🐦		🐹
				3				
🐐		🐸		🐈

Problem Solving Strategy
Look for a Pattern

UNDERSTAND
FIND DATA
PLAN
ESTIMATE
SOLVE
CHECK

Navajo Weaver

Listen to the story.
Draw what comes next in the pattern.
Talk about the patterns you see.

1. Jenny's rug

2. Steph's rug

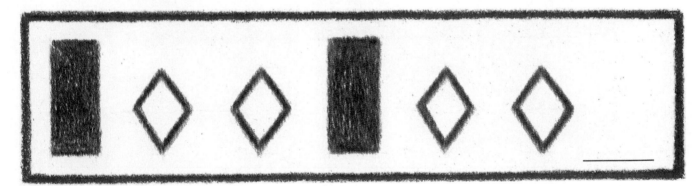

3. Make your own rug pattern.
   Ask you partner what comes next.

Name _____

WRAP UP

MATH WORDS

Ring what belongs. Tell why.

1.   7   ‖‖ |

2. |¢

3. 4   ‖‖

4.   2   ‖|

MATH REASONING

Write the missing numbers.
Talk about the pattern.

5.

2, _____, _____, 4, _____, _____, _____

Name _____

POWER PRACTICE/TEST

1. Ring what belongs.

2. Ring what comes next.

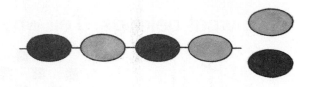

3. Write numbers to continue the pattern.

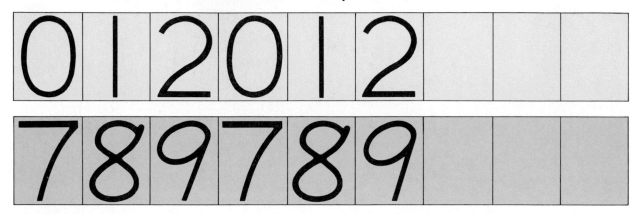

Write how much money.

4.  _____ ¢

5.  _____ ¢

6. Connect the dots in order. Start at ★.

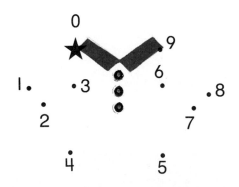

Write the missing numbers.

7. **8.**

ENRICHMENT
Identifying Patterns

Continue the pattern.
Talk about the patterns you see.

1.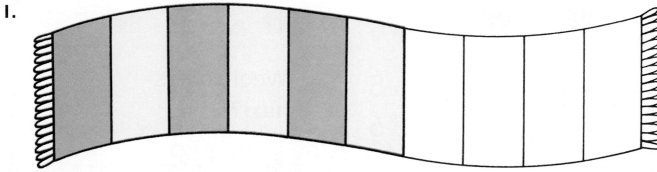

2.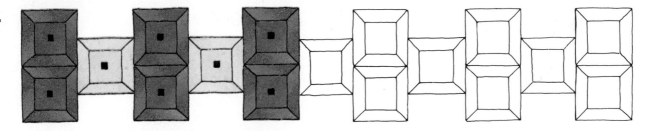

3. Color to make your own pattern.

4. Draw and color a pattern you see.

Cumulative Review

Name _____

How many are there?

1.
○ 3
○ 4
○ 5

2.
○ 5
○ 6
○ 7

3.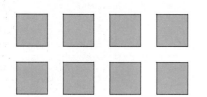
○ 8
○ 9
○ 10

4. How much money is there?

○ 4¢
○ 7¢
○ 8¢

5. Choose which one belongs.

○ △
○ ◯
○ ▢

6. What comes next?

1, 2, 1, 2, 1, _____
○ 2
○ 1
○ 3

7. Choose the number that is right after.

| 5 | 6 | 7 | |
○ 9
○ 4
○ 8

8. Choose the number that is right before.

| | 7 | 8 | 9 |
○ 6
○ 8
○ 5

9. Ted saw 卌 I .

He saw 卌 III .

How many did Ted see?
○ 7
○ 8
○ 9

2
Numbers to 20 and Graphing

Workmat

Theme: Deep Blue Sea

Numbers 10 to 12

Use counters.

Ten   **Ones**

1. Fill the 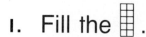.

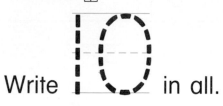

Write **10** in all.

2. Fill the ▦.
   Put down 1 extra counter.

Write **11** in all.

3. Fill the ▦.
   Put down 2 extra counters.

Write **12** in all.

WRITE ABOUT IT

1 dozen eggs

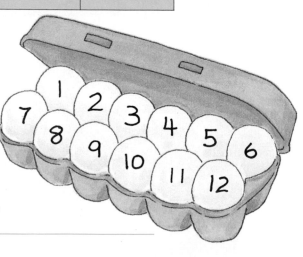

4. Count all the eggs.
   Write the number and the word.

_____ eggs in a **dozen**.

     Chapter 2

Problem Solving
Understanding the Operations

UNDERSTAND
FIND DATA
PLAN
ESTIMATE
SOLVE
CHECK

Listen to the story. Use counters to show it.
Write the answer.

1. the story

    _____

    _____ seals

2. the story

    _____

    _____ fish

3. the story

    _____

    _____ crates

4. the story

    _____

    _____ gulls

ESTIMATION

I need ⊂▭⊃.

About how many will fit?
Ring what you think.
Use objects to check.

I.

about 3 5 10

2.

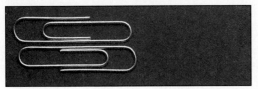

about 4 8 10

3.

about 3 6 10

4.

about 3 6 10

5.

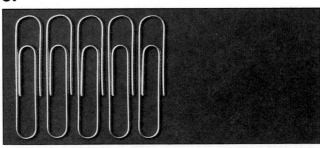

about 3 8 10

Making and Reading Graphs

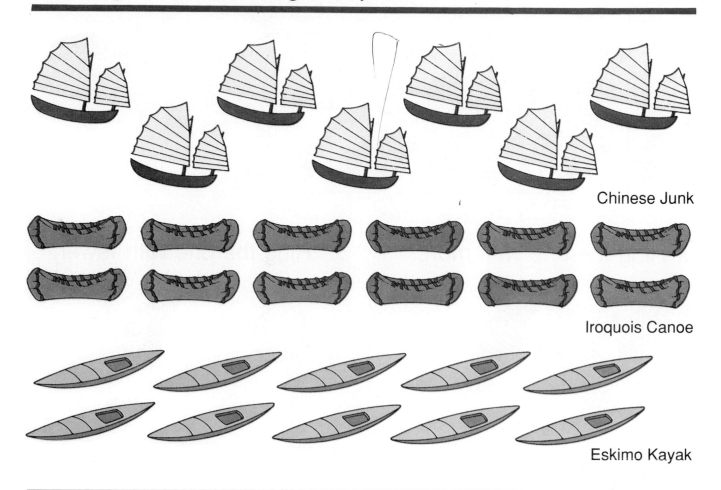

Chinese Junk

Iroquois Canoe

Eskimo Kayak

Count the boats.
Color a box for each boat.

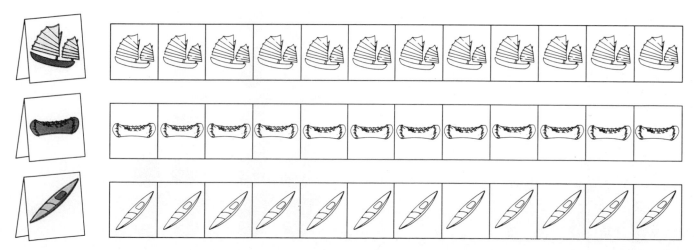

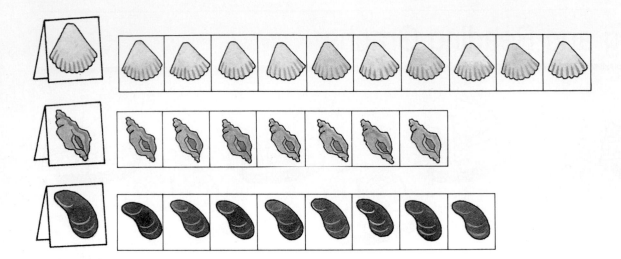

1. Ring the one with more.

2. Ring the one with fewer.

POWER PRACTICE/QUIZ

Ring 10. Write the number in all.

1.

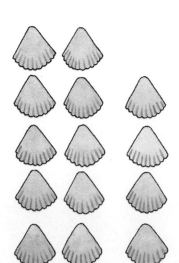

_____

_____

2.

_____

_____

Name _____

Graphing and Comparing Numbers

A class counted the sea animals they saw.

 卌 || or 7

 卌 ||| or 8

 卌   or 5

 卌 | or 6

Sea Animals We Saw

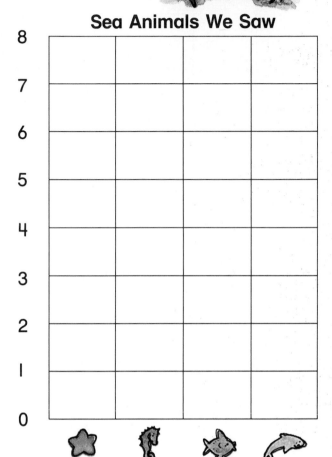

1. Color the graph to show how many the class saw.

_____

2. How many more than ? _____ more

_____

3. How many fewer than ? _____ fewer

_____

4. How many more than  ? _____ more

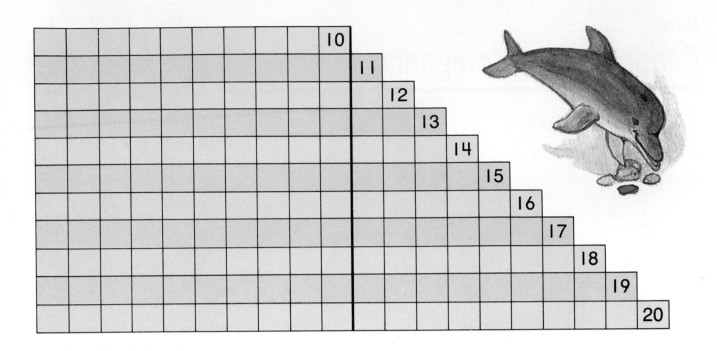

Ring the number that is greater.

1. 10 (14)
2. 17 13
3. 14 18

Ring the number that is less.

4. 16 13
5. 12 19
6. 15 11

FIND THE DATA

7. **Data Hunt** Ask 8 friends the question.
Show their answers on the graph.

aquarium

zoo

Do You Like the Aquarium or the Zoo Better?

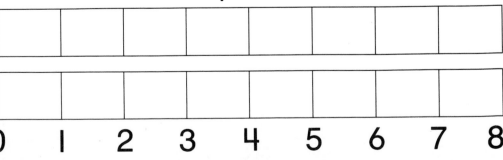

0 1 2 3 4 5 6 7 8

Order to 20

| 8 | 9 | 10 | 11 | 12 | 13 | 14 | 15 | 16 | 17 | 18 | 19 | 20 |

When you count on, the number that is **less** comes **before.**

When you count on, the number that is **greater** comes **after.**

Write the numbers.

1. before   between   after

11   12   ☐

2. before   between   after

☐   18   19

3. before   between   after

8   ☐   10

4. before   between   after

☐   16   17

5. before   between   after

18   19   ☐

6. before   between   after

13   ☐   15

Write the missing numbers.

1.

14, ___, ___, 17, ___, ___, 20

2.

___, 10, 11, ___, 13, ___, 15

3.

13, ___, ___, 16, ___, ___, 19

4.

___, ___, 12, ___, ___, 15, ___

MIXED REVIEW

5. Write numbers to continue the pattern.

1, 3, 5, 1, 3, 5, 1, 3, ____, ____, ____

6. Connect the dots in order.
Start at 0.

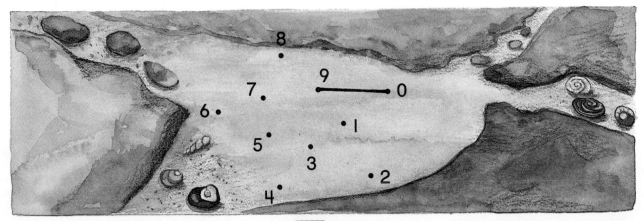

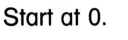

Problem Solving
Retelling a Story

Listen to the story.
Write the number you hear.
Retell the story with a number you pick.
Write your number.
Ring the number that is greater.

1.

number
you
hear _____

your
number _____

2.

number
you
hear _____

your
number _____

3.

number
you
hear _____

your
number _____

Problem Solving Strategy
Act It Out

UNDERSTAND
FIND DATA
PLAN
ESTIMATE
SOLVE
CHECK

Listen to the story.

Act it out.

Paste fish to show the story.

WRAP UP

MATH WORDS

1. Ring the numbers that come after 12.

 15 10 13 9 20 11

2. Ring the numbers that come before 15.

 19 12 14 16 18 10

3. Ring the numbers that come between 12 and 16.

 13 11 17 15 18 14

MATH REASONING

I have 14¢.

I have 18¢.

I have 16¢.

Is each sentence correct? Ring **yes** or **no.**

4. All have more than 12¢.   yes   no

5. All have less than 17¢.   yes   no

6. One has less than 15¢.   yes   no

POWER PRACTICE/TEST

Ring 10. Write how many in all.

1. 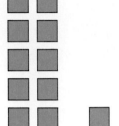 _____

2.  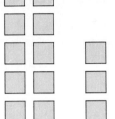 _____

3.  _____

4.  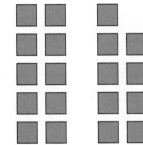 _____

5. Write how much money.

 _____ ¢

6. Count. Write how many. Ring the number that is greater.

 _____ _____

7. Write the missing numbers.

 12 13 ___   15 ___ 17   ___ 19 20

ENRICHMENT
Reading Number Names

Connect the red dots in order.
Start at zero. Count on. Connect
the blue dots in order. Start
at ten. Count back.

0	zero	6	six
1	one	7	seven
2	two	8	eight
3	three	9	nine
4	four	10	ten
5	five		

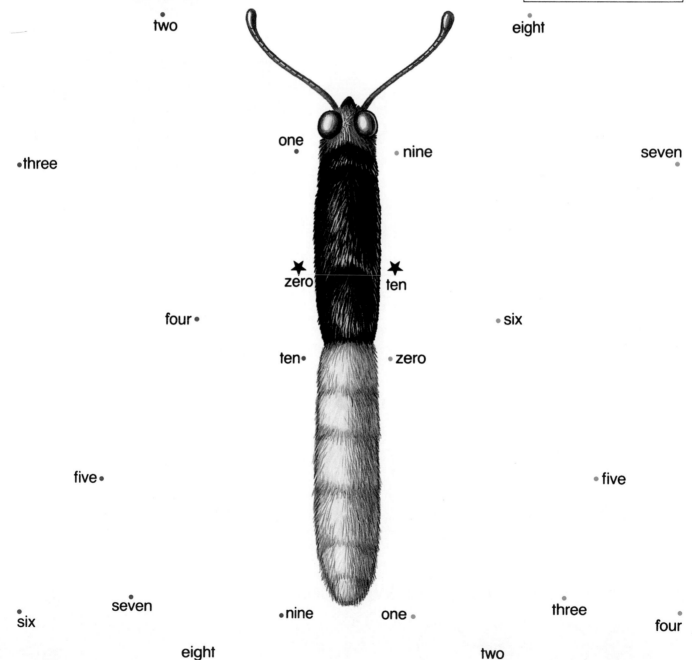

two

eight

one

nine

•three

seven

★
zero

★
ten

four •

• six

ten•

• zero

five •

• five

seven

three

six

•nine

one •

four

eight

two

CUMULATIVE REVIEW

How many are there?

1.
- ○ 5
- ○ 6
- ○ 4

2.
- ○ 7
- ○ 8
- ○ 9

3.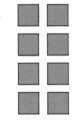
- ○ 10
- ○ 11
- ○ 12

4.
- ○ 16
- ○ 15
- ○ 17

How much money is there?

5.
- ○ 3¢
- ○ 5¢
- ○ 7¢

6.
- ○ 11¢
- ○ 12¢
- ○ 13¢

7. Choose the number that comes after.
- ○ 11
- ○ 10
- ○ 6

7, 8, 9, ____

8. Choose the number that comes before.
- ○ 15
- ○ 19
- ○ 14

____, 16, 17, 18

9. Ana is making a 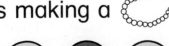. What comes next?

- ○
- ○
- ○

3
Understanding Addition

Workmat

Theme: At the Circus

Addition

Use counters.
Put some in a pile.
Put some more in the pile.
Find how many in all.

Put in 3.
Put in 2.
There are
5 in all.

1. _____ + _____   _____
    put in   put in   in all

2. _____ + _____   _____
    put in   put in   in all

3. _____ + _____   _____
    put in   put in   in all

4. _____ + _____   _____
    put in   put in   in all

PROBLEM SOLVING

5. Tell your partner an addition
    story about putting counters
    into a box. Use counters to
    show the story. Draw it here.

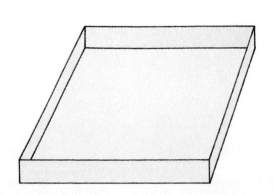

My Addition Book

Dear Family:
Ask your
child to read this
book to you.

Paste some animal punchouts to tell a story.

Write the number sentence.

Paste $\boxed{+}$ or $\boxed{=}$.

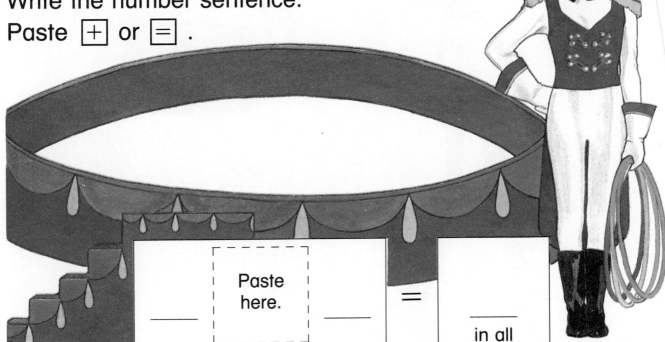

___ ___

Paste
here.

___ ___ = ___

in all

___ + ___

Paste
here.

___

in all

| ___ | Paste here. | ___ | = | ___ in all |

| ___ + ___ | Paste here. | ___ in all |

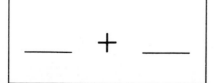

Different Ways to Show a Sum

Work with a partner.

Share 5 cubes of one color.

Share 5 cubes of a different color.

Put some cubes of one color on the circus train.

Finish the train with cubes of the other color.

Color to show what you did.

Write the number sentence.

I.

_____ + _____ ::::: _____

sum

2.

_____ + _____ ::::: _____

sum

3.

_____ + _____ ::::: _____

sum

4.

_____ + _____ ::::: _____

sum

Use two colors.
Show different ways to make a sum of 7.
Write the number sentences.

1.    _1_ + _6_ = _7_

2. 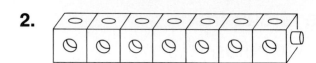   ___ + ___ = _7_

3.     ___ + ___ = ___

4.   ___ + ___ = ___

POWER PRACTICE/QUIZ

1. Write the number sentence.

___ + ___ = ___   ___ + ___ = ___

2. Draw ◯ to show the numbers.
   Write the sum.

   1 + 2 = ___   2 + 2 = ___

Problem Solving
Understanding the Operations

UNDERSTAND
FIND DATA
PLAN
ESTIMATE
SOLVE
CHECK

Listen to the story.
Use counters to show it.
Answer the question.
Write the number sentence.

1. the  story

$4 + 2 =$ ____

____ elephants in all

2. the  story

$1 + 5 =$ ____

____ dogs in all

3. the  story

$2 + 3 + 2 =$ ____

____ chimps in all

Chapter 3

Probability

Guess what you will spin. Color to show
your guess. Use your spinner.
Color to show your spin.

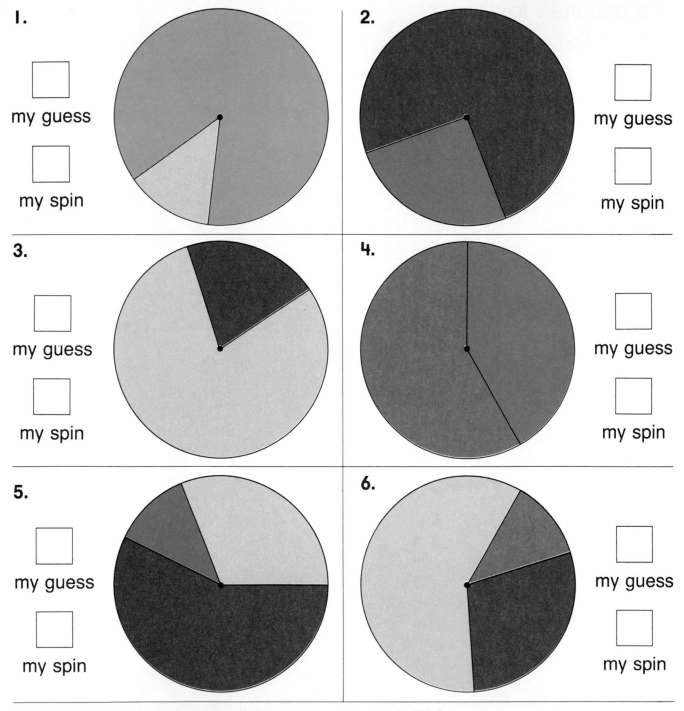

1.

my guess

my spin

2.

my guess

my spin

3.

my guess

my spin

4.

my guess

my spin

5.

my guess

my spin

6.

my guess

my spin

7. How many times did you guess right?
Tell how you decided what to guess.

Adding in Horizontal and Vertical Forms

1 + 2 = 3

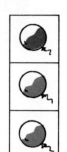
$$\begin{array}{r} 1 \\ + 2 \\ \hline 3 \end{array}$$

Use two colors. Color what you see.
Add.

1. 1 + 3 = ___

$$\begin{array}{r} 1 \\ + 3 \\ \hline \end{array}$$

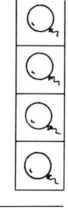

2. 1 + 1 = ___

$$\begin{array}{r} 1 \\ + 1 \\ \hline \end{array}$$

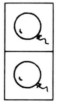

3. 3 + 2 = ___

$$\begin{array}{r} 3 \\ + 2 \\ \hline \end{array}$$

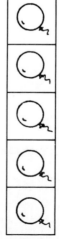

Write what you see. Add.

1.

$$\begin{array}{r} 3 \\ +\ 4 \\ \hline 7 \end{array}$$

2.

$$\begin{array}{r} \\ +\ \\ \hline \end{array}$$

3.

$$\begin{array}{r} \\ +\ \\ \hline \end{array}$$

4.

$$\begin{array}{r} \\ +\ \\ \hline \end{array}$$

5.

$$\begin{array}{r} \\ +\ \\ \hline \end{array}$$

6.

$$\begin{array}{r} \\ +\ \\ \hline \end{array}$$

7.

$$\begin{array}{r} \\ +\ \\ \hline \end{array}$$

8.

$$\begin{array}{r} \\ +\ \\ \hline \end{array}$$

9.

$$\begin{array}{r} \\ +\ \\ \hline \end{array}$$

MIXED REVIEW

Write how much money.

10. _____ ¢

11.  _____ ¢

12. Write the numbers before and after.

_____ , 14, _____

13. Write the number between.

18, _____ , 20

Money Sums

Game   **Spinner**

Work with a partner.
Take turns.
Spin.
Take that many
pennies.
Find the sum.

1. _____ ¢ + _____ ¢ = _____ ¢
    spin   spin   sum

2. _____ ¢ + _____ ¢ = _____ ¢
    spin   spin   sum

3. _____ ¢ + _____ ¢ = _____ ¢
    spin   spin   sum

4. _____ ¢ + _____ ¢ = _____ ¢
    spin   spin   sum

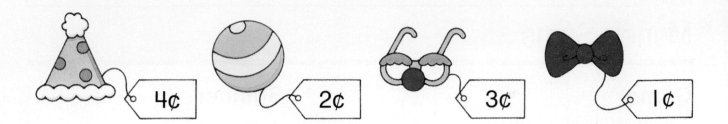

Write how much money to pay.

1. _____ ¢ + _____ ¢ = _____ ¢

2. _____ ¢ + _____ ¢ = _____ ¢

3. _____ ¢ + _____ ¢ = _____ ¢

PROBLEM SOLVING

4. You will spend

Ring what you can buy.

Problem Solving
Acting Out the Story

UNDERSTAND
FIND DATA
PLAN
ESTIMATE
SOLVE
CHECK

Listen to the story.
Act it out.
Write the number sentence.

1.

_____ + _____ = _____

_____ monkeys in all

2.

_____ + _____ = _____

_____ seals in all

3.

_____ + _____ = _____

_____ horses in all

4.

_____ + _____ = _____

_____ lions in all

UNDERSTAND
FIND DATA
PLAN
ESTIMATE
SOLVE
CHECK

Problem Solving Strategy
Use Objects

Flo

Cut out the clowns. Listen
to the first story. Use the clowns
to act it out. Listen to the second
story. Paste the clowns to show it.

Jo

Paste here.

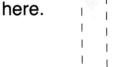

Paste here.

Mo

Paste here.

Paste here.

Paste here.

WRAP UP

MATH WORDS

Ring the ones that make the same sum.

1.

2.

3.        

MATH REASONING

4. Make two number sentences.
   Use all the numbers.

 +  =

  +   =

Name _____

POWER PRACTICE/TEST

Draw ● to show the number.
Write the sum.

1.

$3 + 2 =$ ___

2.

$4 + 1 =$ ___

3. Use two colors. Show two different
ways to name a sum of 6. Write
the number sentences.

___ + ___ = ___

___ + ___ = ___

Add. Write the turnaround fact.

4.

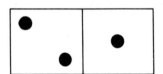

$2 + 1 =$ ___

___ + ___ = ___

Write what you see. Add.

5.

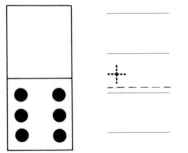

6.

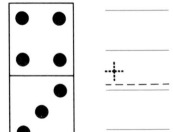

7.

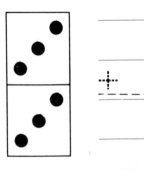

8. Add.

$3¢ + 2¢ =$ ___ ¢

$2¢ + 4¢ =$ ___ ¢

ENRICHMENT
Probability

Which spinner should you use to
spin each? Ring the spinner.

1. always yellow

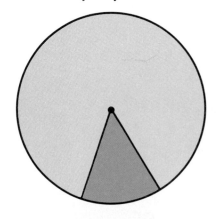 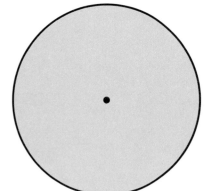 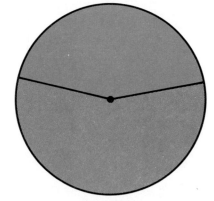

2. never yellow

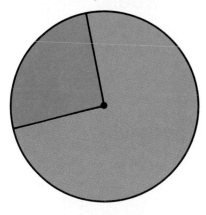 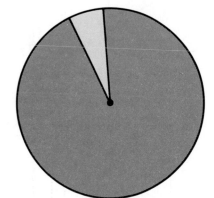 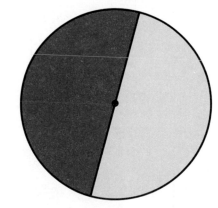

3. sometimes yellow

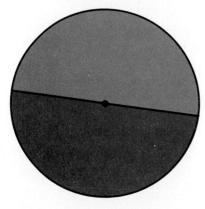 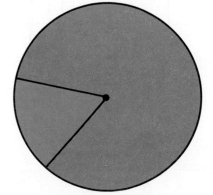 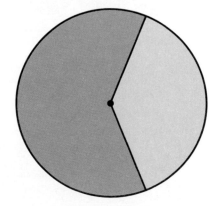

CUMULATIVE REVIEW

How many are there?

1.
- ○ 15
- ○ 16
- ○ 14

2.
- ○ 9
- ○ 8
- ○ 10

3.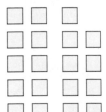
- ○ 19
- ○ 18
- ○ 20

4. How much money is there?
- ○ 7¢
- ○ 15¢
- ○ 16¢

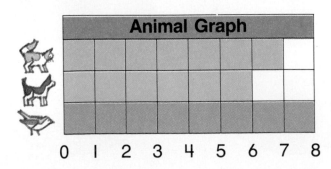

5. What number comes after?

14, 15, ____
- ○ 11
- ○ 17
- ○ 16

6. What number comes before?

____, 9, 10
- ○ 6
- ○ 11
- ○ 8

7. What number comes between?

14, ____, 16
- ○ 13
- ○ 15
- ○ 17

8. Which is greater than 16?
- ○ 15
- ○ 17
- ○ 14

9.

Animal Graph								

0 1 2 3 4 5 6 7 8

How many dogs are there?
- ○ 7 dogs
- ○ 8 dogs
- ○ 6 dogs

Chapter 3   Cumulative Review

5
Addition Facts
Count Ons and Zeros

Workmat

Theme: Folk and Fairy Tales

Name _____

Counting On 1 or 2 and Zero Addition Facts

Ring the greater number.
Add 0 or count on.
Check with counters.

1. $2 + \widehat{(5)} = \underline{7}$

2. $7 + 1 = \underline{}$

3. $5 + 0 = \underline{}$

4.
$$\begin{array}{c} 1 \\ +4 \\ \hline \end{array} \qquad \begin{array}{c} 1 \\ +9 \\ \hline \end{array} \qquad \begin{array}{c} 2 \\ +6 \\ \hline \end{array} \qquad \begin{array}{c} 8 \\ +0 \\ \hline \end{array} \qquad \begin{array}{c} 4 \\ +2 \\ \hline \end{array} \qquad \begin{array}{c} 0 \\ +5 \\ \hline \end{array}$$

5.
$$\begin{array}{c} 2 \\ +3 \\ \hline \end{array} \qquad \begin{array}{c} 0 \\ +4 \\ \hline \end{array} \qquad \begin{array}{c} 7 \\ +2 \\ \hline \end{array} \qquad \begin{array}{c} 4 \\ +1 \\ \hline \end{array} \qquad \begin{array}{c} 1 \\ +8 \\ \hline \end{array} \qquad \begin{array}{c} 6 \\ +1 \\ \hline \end{array}$$

6.
$$\begin{array}{c} 1 \\ +2 \\ \hline \end{array} \qquad \begin{array}{c} 5 \\ +1 \\ \hline \end{array} \qquad \begin{array}{c} 2 \\ +8 \\ \hline \end{array} \qquad \begin{array}{c} 7 \\ +0 \\ \hline \end{array} \qquad \begin{array}{c} 7 \\ +1 \\ \hline \end{array} \qquad \begin{array}{c} 0 \\ +9 \\ \hline \end{array}$$

FIND THE DATA

7. Ask classmates if they like cats. Tally here. Did more classmates like or not like cats?

Like Cats	Do Not Like Cats

Counting On with Turnaround Facts

Count on to add. Start
with the greater number.
Write the turnaround fact.

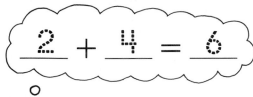

$4 + 2 = \underline{6}$

$\underline{2} + \underline{4} = \underline{6}$

two ways,
same sum

1. $2 + 3 = \underline{5}$ and $\underline{} + \underline{} = \underline{}$

_____

2. $8 + 2 = \underline{}$ and $\underline{} + \underline{} = \underline{}$

_____

3. $5 + 1 = \underline{}$ and $\underline{} + \underline{} = \underline{}$

_____

4. $2 + 6 = \underline{}$ and $\underline{} + \underline{} = \underline{}$

_____

5. $4 + 2 = \underline{}$ and $\underline{} + \underline{} = \underline{}$

_____

6. $1 + 9 = \underline{}$ and $\underline{} + \underline{} = \underline{}$

Chapter 5

1. Count on to add. Draw lines to match the turnaround facts.

$$\begin{array}{r} 6 \\ +2 \\ \hline \end{array} \qquad \begin{array}{r} 2 \\ +9 \\ \hline \end{array} \qquad \begin{array}{r} 2 \\ +6 \\ \hline \end{array} \qquad \begin{array}{r} 9 \\ +2 \\ \hline \end{array}$$

Add. Ring if the sum matches the red number.

2.	10	$9 + 2$	$9 + 1$	$8 + 2$	$1 + 9$
3.	8	$2 + 6$	$1 + 7$	$5 + 2$	$6 + 2$
4.	9	$9 + 0$	$7 + 2$	$2 + 4$	$2 + 7$

SHOW WITH COUNTERS

5. Add. Use counters to check.

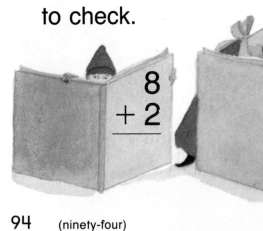

$$\begin{array}{r} 8 \\ +2 \\ \hline \end{array} \qquad \begin{array}{r} 1 \\ +5 \\ \hline \end{array} \qquad \begin{array}{r} 9 \\ +2 \\ \hline \end{array}$$

Counting On 3

Work in a group. Use your spinner.
Spin. Write that number on the bag.
Count on 3¢. Write how much in all.

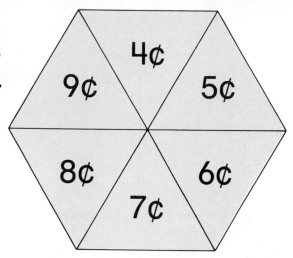

  7¢

_10_ ¢
in all

1.   _____ ¢

_____ ¢
in all

2.   _____ ¢

_____ ¢
in all

3.   _____ ¢

_____ ¢
in all

4.   _____ ¢

_____ ¢
in all

5.   _____ ¢

_____ ¢
in all

6.   _____ ¢

_____ ¢
in all

same as

Add.

1.

5¢
+ 3¢
8¢

2¢
+ 5¢
7¢

2.

1¢
+ 5¢
6¢

3¢
+ 5¢
8¢

3.

2¢	2¢	3¢	4¢	7¢	0¢
+ 6¢	+ 9¢	+ 0¢	+ 3¢	+ 2¢	+ 5¢

4.

7¢	5¢	3¢	2¢	4¢	6¢
+ 3¢	+ 1¢	+ 6¢	+ 8¢	+ 0¢	+ 2¢

PROBLEM SOLVING

5. I spent 10¢. Ring what I bought.

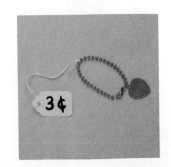

More Practice, page 414, set C

Counting On 1, 2, or 3

Start with the greater number. Count on fast.

$$8 \quad ⑨$$
$$+ 1$$
$$\overline{9}$$

$$2$$
$$+ 6 \quad (7, 8)$$
$$\overline{8}$$

$$9 \quad (10, 11, 12)$$
$$+ 3$$
$$\overline{12}$$

Add. Look at the sums.
Continue the pattern.

1.

$$\begin{array}{r} 6 \\ +2 \\ \hline \end{array} \qquad \begin{array}{r} 3 \\ +6 \\ \hline \end{array} \qquad \begin{array}{r} 5 \\ +3 \\ \hline \end{array} \qquad \begin{array}{r} 2 \\ +7 \\ \hline \end{array} \qquad \begin{array}{r} 7 \\ +1 \\ \hline \end{array}$$

2.

$$\begin{array}{r} 8 \\ +1 \\ \hline \end{array} \qquad \begin{array}{r} 3 \\ +7 \\ \hline \end{array} \qquad \begin{array}{r} 2 \\ +7 \\ \hline \end{array} \qquad \begin{array}{r} 8 \\ +2 \\ \hline \end{array} \qquad \begin{array}{r} 1 \\ +8 \\ \hline \end{array}$$

3.

$$\begin{array}{r} 4 \\ +2 \\ \hline \end{array} \qquad \begin{array}{r} 2 \\ +6 \\ \hline \end{array} \qquad \begin{array}{r} 1 \\ +5 \\ \hline \end{array} \qquad \begin{array}{r} 3 \\ +5 \\ \hline \end{array} \qquad \begin{array}{r} 3 \\ +3 \\ \hline \end{array}$$

4.

$$\begin{array}{r} 4 \\ +3 \\ \hline \end{array} \qquad \begin{array}{r} 3 \\ +8 \\ \hline \end{array} \qquad \begin{array}{r} 5 \\ +2 \\ \hline \end{array} \qquad \begin{array}{r} 2 \\ +9 \\ \hline \end{array} \qquad \begin{array}{r} 1 \\ +6 \\ \hline \end{array}$$

Add.

1.

$$\begin{array}{r} 3 \\ +7 \\ \hline \end{array}$$
$$\begin{array}{r} 1 \\ +3 \\ \hline \end{array}$$
$$\begin{array}{r} 0 \\ +4 \\ \hline \end{array}$$
$$\begin{array}{r} 4 \\ +1 \\ \hline \end{array}$$
$$\begin{array}{r} 8 \\ +0 \\ \hline \end{array}$$
$$\begin{array}{r} 7 \\ +3 \\ \hline \end{array}$$

2.

$$\begin{array}{r} 6 \\ +3 \\ \hline \end{array}$$
$$\begin{array}{r} 0 \\ +5 \\ \hline \end{array}$$
$$\begin{array}{r} 7 \\ +2 \\ \hline \end{array}$$
$$\begin{array}{r} 0 \\ +3 \\ \hline \end{array}$$
$$\begin{array}{r} 2 \\ +9 \\ \hline \end{array}$$
$$\begin{array}{r} 8 \\ +2 \\ \hline \end{array}$$

3.

$$\begin{array}{r} 7 \\ +0 \\ \hline \end{array}$$
$$\begin{array}{r} 9 \\ +3 \\ \hline \end{array}$$
$$\begin{array}{r} 5 \\ +2 \\ \hline \end{array}$$
$$\begin{array}{r} 6 \\ +1 \\ \hline \end{array}$$
$$\begin{array}{r} 2 \\ +3 \\ \hline \end{array}$$
$$\begin{array}{r} 4 \\ +2 \\ \hline \end{array}$$

POWER PRACTICE/QUIZ

1. Ring the greater number.
Write the sum.

$$\begin{array}{r} 4 \\ +2 \\ \hline \end{array}$$
$$\begin{array}{r} 1 \\ +6 \\ \hline \end{array}$$
$$\begin{array}{r} 3 \\ +2 \\ \hline \end{array}$$
$$\begin{array}{r} 2 \\ +9 \\ \hline \end{array}$$
$$\begin{array}{r} 8 \\ +1 \\ \hline \end{array}$$
$$\begin{array}{r} 5 \\ +1 \\ \hline \end{array}$$

2. Add. Write the turnaround fact.

$3 + 7 =$ ___

and

___ $+$ ___ $=$ ___

$5 + 2 =$ ___

and

___ $+$ ___ $=$ ___

$2 + 8 =$ ___

and

___ $+$ ___ $=$ ___

Problem Solving
Understanding the Operations

UNDERSTAND
FIND DATA
PLAN
ESTIMATE
SOLVE
CHECK

Listen to the story. Use counters to
show it. Write + or − in the ◯ .
Finish the number sentence.

The Walking Fish,
Vietnamese Tale

1. 2 ◯ 3 ═ ___

___ fish

2. 2 ◯ 4 ═ ___

___ fish

3. 4 ◯ 1 ═ ___

___ fish

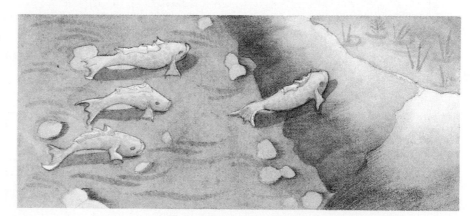

Informal Algebra

Work with a partner. Listen to the story.
Use counters to show it.
Write the numbers in the boxes.
Ring the greater sum.

1. the ▨ story

   3 + ☐

   3 + ☐

2. the ▨ story

   7 + ☐

   7 + ☐

3. the ▨ story

   6 + ☐

   6 + ☐

4. the ▨ story

   4 + ☐

   4 + ☐

Fact Practice and Probability

Toss two number cubes. Add the numbers.
Mark the sum on the graph.

$$4 + 3 = \underline{7}$$

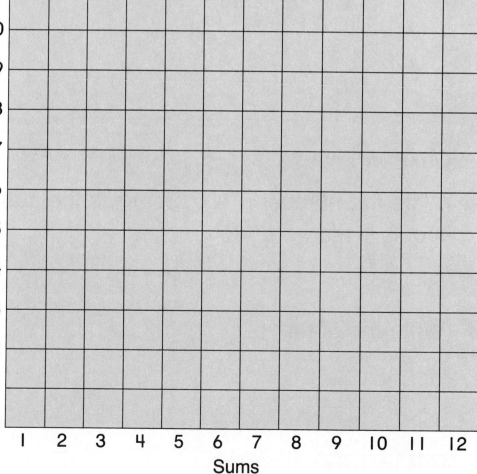

Put x in the box.

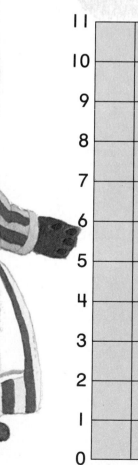

Which Sums Are More Likely?

Sums

Add.

1. $3 + 6 = \underline{9}$ $4 + 2 = \underline{}$ 6, 7, 8, 9

2. $9 + 3 = \underline{}$ $0 + 9 = \underline{}$

3. $7 + 1 = \underline{}$ $5 + 2 = \underline{}$

4.
$\begin{array}{r} 3 \\ + 4 \\ \hline \end{array}$
$\begin{array}{r} 6 \\ + 0 \\ \hline \end{array}$
$\begin{array}{r} 3 \\ + 8 \\ \hline \end{array}$
$\begin{array}{r} 5 \\ + 3 \\ \hline \end{array}$
$\begin{array}{r} 3 \\ + 0 \\ \hline \end{array}$
$\begin{array}{r} 2 \\ + 9 \\ \hline \end{array}$

5.
$\begin{array}{r} 5 \\ + 0 \\ \hline \end{array}$
$\begin{array}{r} 8 \\ + 2 \\ \hline \end{array}$
$\begin{array}{r} 4 \\ + 1 \\ \hline \end{array}$
$\begin{array}{r} 0 \\ + 7 \\ \hline \end{array}$
$\begin{array}{r} 3 \\ + 3 \\ \hline \end{array}$
$\begin{array}{r} 8 \\ + 0 \\ \hline \end{array}$

MIXED REVIEW

6. Write the number that is 1 more.

    5, _____

7. Continue the pattern.

    1, 1, 2, 2, 3, 3, _____, _____, _____

8. Write the number.

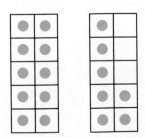 _____

 _____

Name _____

Fact Practice and Graphing

Add.

1.
$\begin{array}{r} 6 \\ +3 \\ \hline \end{array}$
$\begin{array}{r} 2 \\ +5 \\ \hline \end{array}$
$\begin{array}{r} 9 \\ +2 \\ \hline \end{array}$
$\begin{array}{r} 6 \\ +0 \\ \hline \end{array}$
$\begin{array}{r} 1 \\ +8 \\ \hline \end{array}$
$\begin{array}{r} 5 \\ +2 \\ \hline \end{array}$

2.
$\begin{array}{r} 9 \\ +0 \\ \hline \end{array}$
$\begin{array}{r} 7 \\ +2 \\ \hline \end{array}$
$\begin{array}{r} 3 \\ +6 \\ \hline \end{array}$
$\begin{array}{r} 0 \\ +7 \\ \hline \end{array}$
$\begin{array}{r} 8 \\ +2 \\ \hline \end{array}$
$\begin{array}{r} 3 \\ +6 \\ \hline \end{array}$

3.
$\begin{array}{r} 2 \\ +7 \\ \hline \end{array}$
$\begin{array}{r} 2 \\ +9 \\ \hline \end{array}$
$\begin{array}{r} 3 \\ +4 \\ \hline \end{array}$
$\begin{array}{r} 7 \\ +3 \\ \hline \end{array}$
$\begin{array}{r} 5 \\ +2 \\ \hline \end{array}$
$\begin{array}{r} 3 \\ +9 \\ \hline \end{array}$

4. Look above.   Tally sums of 7. _____

Tally sums of 9. _____   Tally sums of 11. _____

5. Color the graph to show the data.

How Many of Each Sum?

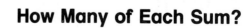

for sums of 7 | | | | | | | | |

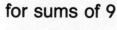

for sums of 9 | | | | | | | | |

for sums of 11 | | | | | | | | |

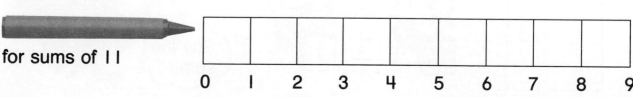

0   1   2   3   4   5   6   7   8   9

Add.

1. $3 + 3 =$ ___ $8 + 2 =$ ___ $0 + 6 =$ ___

2. $2 + 9 =$ ___ $9 + 3 =$ ___ $7 + 3 =$ ___

3. $5 + 3 =$ ___ $2 + 4 =$ ___ $0 + 8 =$ ___

4. $3 + 7 =$ ___ $2 + 8 =$ ___ $6 + 3 =$ ___

5. Look above. Tally sums of 6. _____

   Tally sums of 8. _____   Tally sums of 10. _____

6. Color the graph to show the data.

How Many of Each Sum?

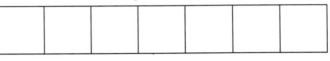

for sums of 6

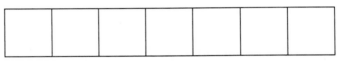

for sums of 8

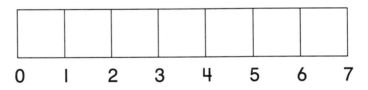

for sums of 10

0   1   2   3   4   5   6   7

USE MENTAL MATH

7. Work with a partner. Use punchout 🐝.
   Put one 🐝 on the ▢.
   Say the sum.

Say the sum.

Name _____

Problem Solving
Telling a Story

UNDERSTAND
FIND DATA
PLAN
ESTIMATE
SOLVE
CHECK

Tell a story about the picture.
Finish the number sentence for the story.

Liang and the Magic Paintbrush, Chinese Tale

1.

____ − ____ = ____

Why Mosquitoes Buzz in People's Ears, W. African Tale

2.

____ + ____ = ____

Three Billy Goats Gruff

3.

____ − ____ = ____

The Three Little Pigs

4.

____ + ____ = ____

Problem Solving Strategy
Guess and Check

UNDERSTAND
FIND DATA
PLAN
ESTIMATE
SOLVE
CHECK

Guess how many bikes and trikes are in each race. Write the number in the guess box. Cut out the bikes and trikes. Use them to check. Paste.

A bike has two wheels.

Bike and Trike Races

A trike has three wheels.

I.   **7 Wheel Race**

Guess	
Check. Paste Here.	

2.   **II Wheel Race**

Guess	
Check. Paste here.	

WRAP UP

MATH WORDS

Match the turnaround
facts. Write the sums.

1. $3 + 2 =$ ____ .

2. $2 + 4 =$ ____ .

3. $1 + 5 =$ ____ .

4. $4 + 1 =$ ____ .

5. $2 + 5 =$ ____ .

. $4 + 2 =$ ____

. $1 + 4 =$ ____

. $5 + 2 =$ ____

. $2 + 3 =$ ____

. $5 + 1 =$ ____

MATH REASONING

Finish the number sentences.
Use the numbers on
the balloons.

6. ____ $+ 0 =$ ____

7. ____ $+ 1 =$ ____

8. ____ $+ 2 =$ ____

POWER PRACTICE/TEST

1. Ring the greater number. Add.

$$\begin{array}{r} 5 \\ +2 \\ \hline \end{array} \qquad \begin{array}{r} 1 \\ +7 \\ \hline \end{array} \qquad \begin{array}{r} 6 \\ +0 \\ \hline \end{array} \qquad \begin{array}{r} 8 \\ +1 \\ \hline \end{array} \qquad \begin{array}{r} 0 \\ +9 \\ \hline \end{array} \qquad \begin{array}{r} 2 \\ +8 \\ \hline \end{array}$$

Count on to add.
Write the turnaround fact.

2. $6 + 2 =$ ____ and ____ $+$ ____ $=$ ____

3. $1 + 9 =$ ____ and ____ $+$ ____ $=$ ____

Count on 3¢. Write how much in all.

4.    ____

5.     ____

6. Add.

$$\begin{array}{r} 0 \\ +7 \\ \hline \end{array} \qquad \begin{array}{r} 9 \\ +2 \\ \hline \end{array} \qquad \begin{array}{r} 5 \\ +1 \\ \hline \end{array} \qquad \begin{array}{r} 4¢ \\ +3¢ \\ \hline \end{array} \qquad \begin{array}{r} 6¢ \\ +3¢ \\ \hline \end{array} \qquad \begin{array}{r} 8¢ \\ +1¢ \\ \hline \end{array}$$

7. Tom spent 8¢.
Ring what he bought.

  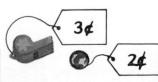

Name _____

ENRICHMENT
Missing Addends

Find how many must be in the bag to get the sum. Draw pictures to show it. Write the missing number.

1.

| 5 in all |

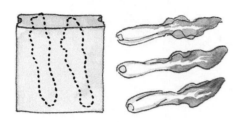

___2___ + 3 = 5

2.

| 3 in all |

1 + ___ = 3

3.

| 8 in all |

5 + ___ = 8

4.

| 7 in all |

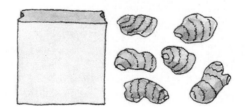

___ + 6 = 7

5.

| 10 in all |

___ + 7 = 10

6.

| 6 in all |

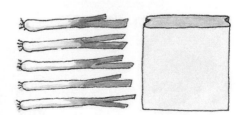

5 + ___ = 6

CUMULATIVE REVIEW

Add.

1.

$3 + 2 =$ ___

○ 6
○ 5
○ 4

2.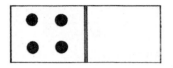

$4 + 0 =$ ___

○ 7
○ 4
○ 0

3.

$\begin{array}{r} 1 \\ + 3 \\ \hline \end{array}$

○ 5
○ 6
○ 4

4. $\begin{array}{r} 2¢ \\ + 1¢ \\ \hline \end{array}$

○ 4¢
○ 5¢
○ 3¢

Subtract.

5.

$6 - 2 =$ ___

○ 3
○ 4
○ 5

6.

$4 - 4 =$ ___

○ 4
○ 1
○ 0

7.

$\begin{array}{r} 7 \\ - 5 \\ \hline \end{array}$

○ 4
○ 2
○ 3

8.

$\begin{array}{r} 7 \\ - 2 \\ \hline \end{array}$

○ 4
○ 3
○ 5

9. Choose the question you would ask.

Three chimps are playing.
Two more join them.

○ How many chimps are left?

○ How many chimps are playing in all?

○ How many chimps go away?

6
Addition Facts
Sums to 12

Workmat

Theme: Crawling Critters

Small Doubles

Use cubes to show each double fact. Add and match.

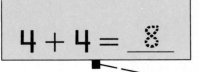

1.

$4 + 4 = \underline{8}$ $6 + 6 = \underline{}$ $5 + 5 = \underline{}$

Ring the double facts. Then add all.

2.

$\begin{array}{r} 5 \\ +5 \\ \hline \end{array}$ $\begin{array}{r} 3 \\ +4 \\ \hline \end{array}$ $\begin{array}{r} 2 \\ +2 \\ \hline \end{array}$ $\begin{array}{r} 1 \\ +7 \\ \hline \end{array}$ $\begin{array}{r} 6 \\ +6 \\ \hline \end{array}$ $\begin{array}{r} 4 \\ +4 \\ \hline \end{array}$

3.

$\begin{array}{r} 6 \\ +2 \\ \hline \end{array}$ $\begin{array}{r} 1 \\ +1 \\ \hline \end{array}$ $\begin{array}{r} 2 \\ +7 \\ \hline \end{array}$ $\begin{array}{r} 6 \\ +6 \\ \hline \end{array}$ $\begin{array}{r} 3 \\ +9 \\ \hline \end{array}$ $\begin{array}{r} 3 \\ +3 \\ \hline \end{array}$

4.

$\begin{array}{r} 6 \\ +6 \\ \hline \end{array}$ $\begin{array}{r} 3 \\ +6 \\ \hline \end{array}$ $\begin{array}{r} 5 \\ +5 \\ \hline \end{array}$ $\begin{array}{r} 2 \\ +8 \\ \hline \end{array}$ $\begin{array}{r} 4 \\ +4 \\ \hline \end{array}$ $\begin{array}{r} 5 \\ +2 \\ \hline \end{array}$

WRITE ABOUT IT

spider

5. Write the answer.

$4 + 4 = \underline{}$ is the _____ fact.

Sums of 10

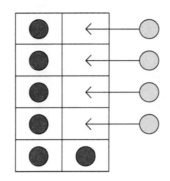

I start with 6.
I need 4 more
to make 10.

I will use counters to check.

$$\begin{array}{r} 6 \\ + 4 \\ \hline 10 \end{array}$$

Work with a partner.
Share 10 two-color counters.
Make sums of 10.
Use counters to check.

1.

$$\begin{array}{r} 6 \\ + \boxed{4} \\ \hline 10 \end{array}\qquad \begin{array}{r} 8 \\ + \boxed{} \\ \hline \end{array}\qquad \begin{array}{r} 3 \\ + \boxed{} \\ \hline \end{array}$$

2.

$$\begin{array}{r} 1 \\ + \boxed{} \\ \hline \end{array}\qquad \begin{array}{r} 5 \\ + \boxed{} \\ \hline \end{array}\qquad \begin{array}{r} 2 \\ + \boxed{} \\ \hline \end{array}$$

3.

$$\begin{array}{r} 4 \\ + \boxed{} \\ \hline \end{array}\qquad \begin{array}{r} 7 \\ + \boxed{} \\ \hline \end{array}\qquad \begin{array}{r} 9 \\ + \boxed{} \\ \hline \end{array}$$

Add. Ring sums of 10.

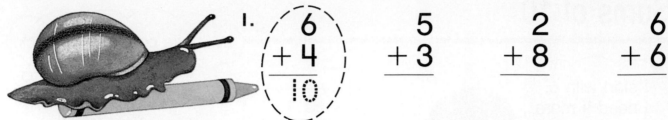

1.
$$\begin{array}{r} 6 \\ +4 \\ \hline 10 \end{array}$$ (ringed)
$$\begin{array}{r} 5 \\ +3 \\ \hline \end{array}$$
$$\begin{array}{r} 2 \\ +8 \\ \hline \end{array}$$
$$\begin{array}{r} 6 \\ +6 \\ \hline \end{array}$$

2.
$$\begin{array}{r} 2 \\ +6 \\ \hline \end{array}$$
$$\begin{array}{r} 4 \\ +4 \\ \hline \end{array}$$
$$\begin{array}{r} 6 \\ +3 \\ \hline \end{array}$$
$$\begin{array}{r} 2 \\ +9 \\ \hline \end{array}$$
$$\begin{array}{r} 3 \\ +7 \\ \hline \end{array}$$
$$\begin{array}{r} 3 \\ +9 \\ \hline \end{array}$$

3.
$$\begin{array}{r} 8 \\ +2 \\ \hline \end{array}$$
$$\begin{array}{r} 4 \\ +6 \\ \hline \end{array}$$
$$\begin{array}{r} 5 \\ +5 \\ \hline \end{array}$$
$$\begin{array}{r} 8 \\ +3 \\ \hline \end{array}$$
$$\begin{array}{r} 1 \\ +9 \\ \hline \end{array}$$
$$\begin{array}{r} 9 \\ +0 \\ \hline \end{array}$$

4.
$$\begin{array}{r} 0 \\ +8 \\ \hline \end{array}$$
$$\begin{array}{r} 7 \\ +3 \\ \hline \end{array}$$
$$\begin{array}{r} 2 \\ +5 \\ \hline \end{array}$$
$$\begin{array}{r} 2 \\ +7 \\ \hline \end{array}$$
$$\begin{array}{r} 9 \\ +1 \\ \hline \end{array}$$
$$\begin{array}{r} 3 \\ +4 \\ \hline \end{array}$$

PROBLEM SOLVING

5. Maria spent 10¢. What two things did she buy? Ring with 🖍.

6. Ali spent 12¢. What two things did he buy? Ring with 🖍.

Name _____

Fact Practice

Add.

Japanese Origami

3. $4 + 4 =$ _____

$0 + 2 =$ _____

2. $3 + 7 =$ _____

$6 + 6 =$ _____

$3 + 3 =$ _____

$3 + 8 =$ _____

1. $6 + 4 = \underline{10}$

$4 + 6 =$ _____

$9 + 1 =$ _____

$5 + 5 =$ _____

$0 + 0 =$ _____

$2 + 2 =$ _____

 4.
$\begin{array}{r} 5 \\ + 2 \\ \hline \end{array}$
$\begin{array}{r} 6 \\ + 2 \\ \hline \end{array}$
$\begin{array}{r} 7 \\ + 2 \\ \hline \end{array}$
$\begin{array}{r} 3 \\ + 4 \\ \hline \end{array}$
$\begin{array}{r} 5 \\ + 3 \\ \hline \end{array}$
$\begin{array}{r} 3 \\ + 6 \\ \hline \end{array}$

5.
$\begin{array}{r} 1 \\ + 6 \\ \hline \end{array}$

 The sums in make a number pattern.

6.
$\begin{array}{r} 9 \\ + 3 \\ \hline \end{array}$

7. Write the number pattern in .

_____ , _____ , _____ , _____ , _____ , _____

Ring the ways to make the sum.

1. 10 ⟩ $(5+5)$ $3+7$ $6+3$ $6+4$

2. 12 ⟩ $3+9$ $6+6$ $8+3$ $2+9$

3. 8 ⟩ $4+4$ $6+2$ $5+3$ $2+7$

4. 9 ⟩ $6+2$ $1+8$ $0+9$ $3+6$

5. 10 ⟩ $4+6$ $2+8$ $5+5$ $3+7$

Add.

6.

$$\begin{array}{cccccc} 2 & 3 & 3 & 6 & 3 & 1 \\ +3 & +3 & +8 & +6 & +6 & +5 \\ \hline \end{array}$$

MAKE AN ESTIMATE

7. Ring sums in ⭐6 that are close to 10.

8. Write another sum that is close to 10.

$$\begin{array}{c} \underline{} \\ + \\ \hline \end{array}$$

Name ____________________

UNDERSTAND
FIND DATA
PLAN
ESTIMATE
SOLVE
CHECK

Problem Solving
Understanding the Operations

Listen to the story. Use counters to show it. Finish the number sentence.

1. the  story

2 ◯ 4 = ____

____ lizards

2. the 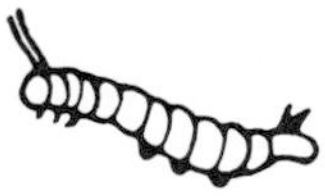 story

4 ◯ 2 = ____

____ caterpillars

3. the 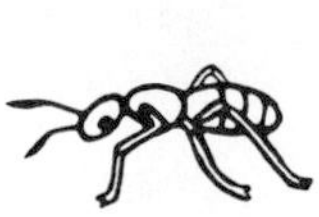 story

6 ◯ 6 = ____

____ ants

4. the  story

7 ◯ 3 = ____

____ grasshoppers

Mental Math

Use punchouts $\boxed{0}$ to $\boxed{12}$.
Show each clue.
Write the number.

Turn over cards you do not want.

$\overset{\bullet}{0}$ $\overset{\bullet}{1}$ $\overset{\bullet}{2}$ $\overset{\bullet}{3}$ $\overset{\bullet}{4}$ $\overset{\bullet}{5}$ $\overset{\bullet}{6}$ $\overset{\bullet}{7}$ $\overset{\bullet}{8}$ $\overset{\bullet}{9}$ $\overset{\circ}{}$ $\overset{\circ}{}$ $\overset{\circ}{}$

1.

I am less than $5 + 5$.

I am greater than $4 + 4$.

I am __9__.

less than
$5 + 5$

2.

I am greater than $6 + 4$.

I am less than $9 + 3$.

I am ____.

3.

I am the sum of a double.
I am greater than 9.
I am less than 12.
I am ____.

4.

I am on a 1 2 3 4 5 6 7 8 9 10 11 12.
I am less than $3 + 7$.
I am greater than 8.

I am ____.

5.

I am more than .
I am less than $6¢ + 6¢$.

I am ____ ¢.

Name _____

Doubles Plus One

I more than 5 + 5

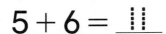

5 + 5 = 10

When an addend is I more than the other, think of a double to help.

Double the smaller addend and add I more.

5 + 6 = __   6 + 5 = __

Ring the double-plus-one facts.
Then add all.

1. (5 + 6) = ___   5 + 4 = ___   5 + 2 = ___

2. 0 + 5 = ___   4 + 5 = ___   5 + 5 = ___

3. 5 + 6 = ___   7 + 3 = ___   5 + 4 = ___

4. 6 + 4 = ___   3 + 1 = ___   4 + 1 = ___

5. 4 + 5 = ___   6 + 6 = ___   6 + 5 = ___

6. Tell a partner.
   How do doubles facts help you find
   doubles-plus-one sums?

Write the double that helps. Add.

1. $\begin{array}{r} 5 \\ +4 \\ \hline 9 \end{array}$ $\begin{array}{r} 4 \\ +4 \\ \hline 8 \end{array}$ $\begin{array}{r} 6 \\ +5 \\ \hline \end{array}$ $+$ ___ $\begin{array}{r} 4 \\ +5 \\ \hline \end{array}$ $+$ ___

Ring the double-plus-one facts.
Then add all.

2. $(5 + 6)$ = ___ $2 + 8$ = ___ $9 + 0$ = ___

3. $4 + 5$ = ___ $6 + 5$ = ___ $7 + 2$ = ___

4. $6 + 6$ = ___ $5 + 4$ = ___ $5 + 6$ = ___

5. $4 + 4$ = ___ $3 + 6$ = ___ $6 + 4$ = ___

FIND THE DATA

Data Bank (See page 398.)

6. How far is it from Tip's house to Rip's? ___ blocks

7. How far is it from Pip's house to Kip's? ___ blocks

8. How far is it from Flip's house to Pip's? ___ blocks

Fact Practice

Match.

1.

5 +4	3 +5	6 +6	6 +5	6 +4

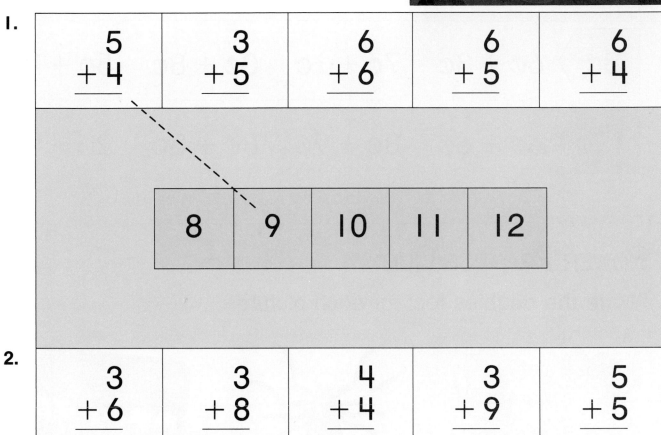

8	9	10	11	12

2.

3 +6	3 +8	4 +4	3 +9	5 +5

Add.

3.
7¢ +3¢	6¢ +2¢	1¢ +4¢	9¢ +3¢	6¢ +5¢	1¢ +6¢

4.
5¢ +4¢	0¢ +6¢	4¢ +3¢	8¢ +2¢	2¢ +5¢	2¢ +9¢

Cross out all the ways that
do not make the sum.

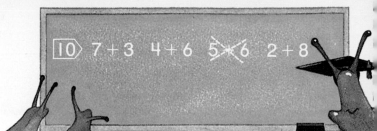

1.

| 10¢ | 7¢ + 3¢ | 4¢ + 6¢ | ~~5¢ + 6¢~~ | 2¢ + 8¢ |

2.

| 8¢ | 6¢ + 3¢ | 7¢ + 1¢ | 0¢ + 8¢ | 5¢ + 4¢ |

3.

| 12¢ | 6¢ + 6¢ | 3¢ + 9¢ | 8¢ + 3¢ | 2¢ + 9¢ |

POWER PRACTICE/QUIZ

1. Write the doubles fact for each picture.

   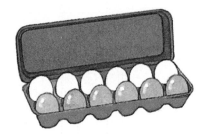

___ + ___ = ___   ___ + ___ = ___   ___ + ___ = ___

2. Add. Ring sums of 10.

$$3 + 5 \qquad 4 + 6 \qquad 7 + 3 \qquad 8 + 1 \qquad 5 + 5 \qquad 1 + 9$$

3. Add.

$5 + 4 =$ ___ $2 + 3 =$ ___ $6 + 5 =$ ___

Making 10, Adding Extra

Put in 7. Then put in as many of the 5 as you can.

Ten   Ones

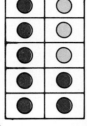

You have 10 and 2 extra. That makes 12.

$$\begin{array}{r} 7 \\ +\ 5 \\ \hline 12 \end{array}$$

Work with a partner.
Put counters in ⊞ for the
greater number. Then
put counters in for the
other number to make 10.
Put extra counters outside ⊞.

Ten   Ones

1. $\begin{array}{r} 7 \\ +4 \\ \hline \end{array}$ $\begin{array}{r} 4 \\ +7 \\ \hline \end{array}$

2. $\begin{array}{r} 5 \\ +7 \\ \hline \end{array}$ $\begin{array}{r} 7 \\ +5 \\ \hline \end{array}$

3. $\begin{array}{r} 8 \\ +4 \\ \hline \end{array}$ $\begin{array}{r} 4 \\ +8 \\ \hline \end{array}$

1. Draw ◯ to show the fact.
Finish the number sentence.

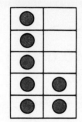   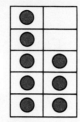   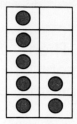

$7 + 5 =$ ___ $8 + 4 =$ ___ $7 + 4 =$ ___

Add.

2.
$\begin{array}{r} 8 \\ +4 \\ \hline \end{array}$
$\begin{array}{r} 5 \\ +2 \\ \hline \end{array}$
$\begin{array}{r} 6 \\ +5 \\ \hline \end{array}$
$\begin{array}{r} 8 \\ +3 \\ \hline \end{array}$
$\begin{array}{r} 4 \\ +7 \\ \hline \end{array}$
$\begin{array}{r} 3 \\ +5 \\ \hline \end{array}$

3.
$\begin{array}{r} 4 \\ +6 \\ \hline \end{array}$
$\begin{array}{r} 7 \\ +5 \\ \hline \end{array}$
$\begin{array}{r} 0 \\ +2 \\ \hline \end{array}$
$\begin{array}{r} 7 \\ +4 \\ \hline \end{array}$
$\begin{array}{r} 2 \\ +9 \\ \hline \end{array}$
$\begin{array}{r} 6 \\ +6 \\ \hline \end{array}$

4.
$\begin{array}{r} 5 \\ +7 \\ \hline \end{array}$
$\begin{array}{r} 5 \\ +6 \\ \hline \end{array}$
$\begin{array}{r} 2 \\ +8 \\ \hline \end{array}$
$\begin{array}{r} 4 \\ +4 \\ \hline \end{array}$
$\begin{array}{r} 8 \\ +4 \\ \hline \end{array}$
$\begin{array}{r} 5 \\ +5 \\ \hline \end{array}$

MIXED REVIEW

5. Subtract.

$5 - 2 =$ ___

6. Cross out. Subtract.

$3 - 2 =$ ___

7. Finish the fact family.

   $2 + 1 =$ ___ $3 - 1 =$ ___

   $1 + 2 =$ ___ $3 - 2 =$ ___

Adding Three Numbers

You can add down.

↓ $\begin{array}{r}\boxed{\begin{array}{c}3\\2\end{array}}\\+\;\underline{4}\\9\end{array}$

3 + 2 are 5 and 4 more make 9.

You can add up.

↑ $\begin{array}{r}3\\\boxed{\begin{array}{c}2\\4\end{array}}\\+\;\underline{}\\9\end{array}$

4 + 2 are 6 and 3 more make 9.

Add up or down.
Use counters to help.

1.

$\begin{array}{r}\boxed{\begin{array}{c}1\\8\end{array}}\\+\;\underline{1}\\\end{array}$
$\begin{array}{r}6\\\boxed{\begin{array}{c}1\\5\end{array}}\\+\;\underline{}\\\end{array}$
$\begin{array}{r}\boxed{\begin{array}{c}2\\2\end{array}}\\+\;\underline{4}\\\end{array}$
$\begin{array}{r}5\\\boxed{\begin{array}{c}2\\3\end{array}}\\+\;\underline{}\\\end{array}$
$\begin{array}{r}\boxed{\begin{array}{c}0\\9\end{array}}\\+\;\underline{1}\\\end{array}$
$\begin{array}{r}\boxed{\begin{array}{c}4\\5\end{array}}\\+\;\underline{3}\\\end{array}$

2.

$\begin{array}{r}5\\\boxed{\begin{array}{c}3\\3\end{array}}\\+\;\underline{}\\\end{array}$
$\begin{array}{r}\boxed{\begin{array}{c}3\\0\end{array}}\\+\;\underline{9}\\\end{array}$
$\begin{array}{r}\boxed{\begin{array}{c}6\\2\end{array}}\\+\;\underline{0}\\\end{array}$
$\begin{array}{r}2\\\boxed{\begin{array}{c}4\\3\end{array}}\\+\;\underline{}\\\end{array}$
$\begin{array}{r}\boxed{\begin{array}{c}5\\0\end{array}}\\+\;\underline{4}\\\end{array}$
$\begin{array}{r}\boxed{\begin{array}{c}1\\1\end{array}}\\+\;\underline{4}\\\end{array}$

3.

$\begin{array}{r}3\\3\\+\;\underline{4}\\\end{array}$
$\begin{array}{r}6\\2\\+\;\underline{3}\\\end{array}$
$\begin{array}{r}1\\5\\+\;\underline{3}\\\end{array}$
$\begin{array}{r}0\\4\\+\;\underline{2}\\\end{array}$
$\begin{array}{r}7\\2\\+\;\underline{1}\\\end{array}$
$\begin{array}{r}6\\1\\+\;\underline{0}\\\end{array}$

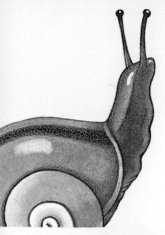

Add.

1.
$$\begin{array}{r} 4 \\ 1 \\ +\,0 \\ \hline \end{array}$$
$$\begin{array}{r} 5 \\ 4 \\ +\,2 \\ \hline \end{array}$$
$$\begin{array}{r} 5 \\ 1 \\ +\,4 \\ \hline \end{array}$$
$$\begin{array}{r} 4 \\ 0 \\ +\,5 \\ \hline \end{array}$$
$$\begin{array}{r} 3 \\ 1 \\ +\,5 \\ \hline \end{array}$$

2.
$$\begin{array}{r} 2 \\ 3 \\ +\,4 \\ \hline \end{array}$$
$$\begin{array}{r} 4 \\ 1 \\ +\,4 \\ \hline \end{array}$$
$$\begin{array}{r} 5 \\ 0 \\ +\,6 \\ \hline \end{array}$$
$$\begin{array}{r} 6 \\ 6 \\ +\,0 \\ \hline \end{array}$$
$$\begin{array}{r} 6 \\ 3 \\ +\,3 \\ \hline \end{array}$$
$$\begin{array}{r} 3 \\ 2 \\ +\,5 \\ \hline \end{array}$$

3.
$$\begin{array}{r} 4 \\ 4 \\ +\,2 \\ \hline \end{array}$$
$$\begin{array}{r} 2 \\ 2 \\ +\,5 \\ \hline \end{array}$$
$$\begin{array}{r} 3 \\ 3 \\ +\,6 \\ \hline \end{array}$$
$$\begin{array}{r} 5 \\ 1 \\ +\,5 \\ \hline \end{array}$$
$$\begin{array}{r} 2 \\ 4 \\ +\,2 \\ \hline \end{array}$$
$$\begin{array}{r} 4 \\ 2 \\ +\,5 \\ \hline \end{array}$$

TRY A CALCULATOR

4. Guess one number that could go in all the boxes.

$$\boxed{} + \boxed{} + \boxed{} = 12$$

my guess ____

Use a to check your guess.

Write the correct number in each box.

Name _____

Problem Solving
Showing Data

| UNDERSTAND |
| FIND DATA |
| PLAN |
| ESTIMATE |
| SOLVE |
| CHECK |

Draw more or cross out to show the story.

1. Ed has 6.
   Bay has 6.

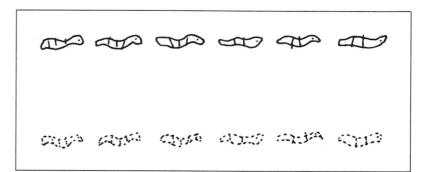

2. Fay had 8.
   She lost 2.

3. Bill has 4.
   Ty has 2.
   Clara has 4.

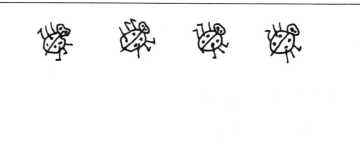

4. Li-Chen
   had 7.
   She gave
   away 3.

Problem Solving Strategy
Make a Table

UNDERSTAND
FIND DATA
PLAN
ESTIMATE
SOLVE
CHECK

Use the table to answer the question.

1. How much do 3  cost?

lizards 2¢ each

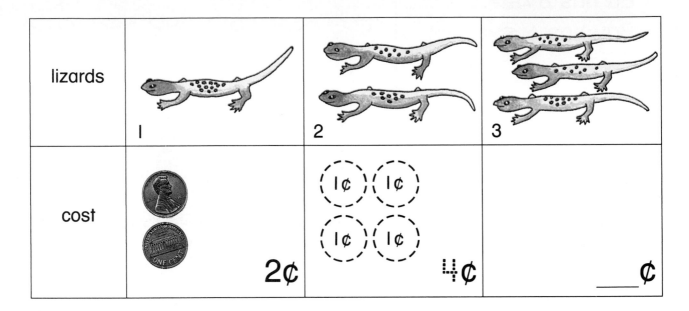

lizards	 1	 2	 3
cost	2¢	4¢	____¢

2. How much do 3 🪱 cost?

worms 3¢ each

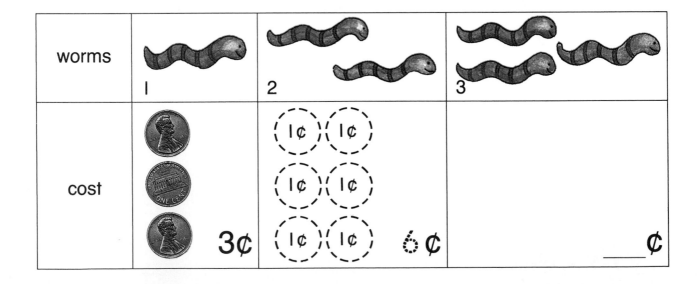

worms	 1	 2	 3
cost	3¢	6¢	____¢

WRAP UP

MATH WORDS

Ring examples of each.

1.	doubles	$5 + 3$	$4 + 4$	
2.	doubles plus one		$3 + 4$	$6 + 5$
3.	sums of 10	$6 + 4$		$3 + 7$

MATH REASONING

Ring the fact that has the greater sum. Tell how you know.

4. $4 + 4$ or $5 + 5$ 5. $3 + 3$ or $2 + 2$

6. $3 + 4$ or $3 + 3$ 7. $2 + 2$ or $2 + 3$

8. $2 + 3$ or $2 + 4$ 9. $3 + 5$ or $4 + 3$

POWER PRACTICE/TEST

1. Ring double facts. Then add all.

$$
\begin{array}{cc}
3 \\
+7 \\
\hline
\end{array}
\qquad
\begin{array}{cc}
6 \\
+6 \\
\hline
\end{array}
\qquad
\begin{array}{cc}
7 \\
+4 \\
\hline
\end{array}
\qquad
\begin{array}{cc}
1 \\
+9 \\
\hline
\end{array}
\qquad
\begin{array}{cc}
4 \\
+4 \\
\hline
\end{array}
\qquad
\begin{array}{cc}
5 \\
+5 \\
\hline
\end{array}
$$

2. Add. Ring sums of 10.

$$
\begin{array}{cc}
5 \\
+6 \\
\hline
\end{array}
\qquad
\begin{array}{cc}
5 \\
+5 \\
\hline
\end{array}
\qquad
\begin{array}{cc}
2 \\
+8 \\
\hline
\end{array}
\qquad
\begin{array}{cc}
7 \\
+3 \\
\hline
\end{array}
\qquad
\begin{array}{cc}
5 \\
+7 \\
\hline
\end{array}
\qquad
\begin{array}{cc}
4 \\
+7 \\
\hline
\end{array}
$$

3. Ring double-plus-one facts.
Then add all.

$$
\begin{array}{cc}
4 \\
+5 \\
\hline
\end{array}
\qquad
\begin{array}{cc}
5 \\
+6 \\
\hline
\end{array}
\qquad
\begin{array}{cc}
4 \\
+6 \\
\hline
\end{array}
\qquad
\begin{array}{cc}
8 \\
+4 \\
\hline
\end{array}
\qquad
\begin{array}{cc}
9 \\
+1 \\
\hline
\end{array}
\qquad
\begin{array}{cc}
6 \\
+5 \\
\hline
\end{array}
$$

4. Add.

$$
\begin{array}{cc}
5 \\
2 \\
+4 \\
\hline
\end{array}
\qquad
\begin{array}{cc}
4 \\
1 \\
+5 \\
\hline
\end{array}
\qquad
\begin{array}{cc}
2 \\
4 \\
+5 \\
\hline
\end{array}
\qquad
\begin{array}{cc}
5 \\
1 \\
+6 \\
\hline
\end{array}
\qquad
\begin{array}{cc}
3 \\
4 \\
+5 \\
\hline
\end{array}
\qquad
\begin{array}{cc}
4 \\
3 \\
+4 \\
\hline
\end{array}
$$

5. Draw more or cross out to show the story.

Sally has 4 .

Tony has 3 .

ENRICHMENT
Comparing Quantity

Work with a partner. Use counters.
Compare the number in each group.
Tell and write how many more or fewer.
Ring the one with more or fewer.

| 1 more peach | 2 fewer apples |

1.

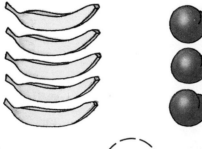

__2__ more 🍌 ⚫

2.

____ more

3.

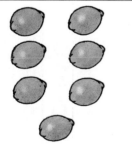

____ more

4.

____ fewer

5.

____ fewer

6.

____ fewer

CUMULATIVE REVIEW

Subtract.

1.

   $5 - 2 =$ ___
   - ○ 4
   - ○ 1
   - ○ 3

2.

   $6 - 2 =$ ___
   - ○ 1
   - ○ 4
   - ○ 5

3.

   $6 - 4 =$ ___
   - ○ 1
   - ○ 2
   - ○ 3

4.
   $$\begin{array}{r} 4 \\ -\,0 \\ \hline \end{array}$$
   - ○ 4
   - ○ 3
   - ○ 0

Count on to add.

5. $4 + 2 =$ ___
   - ○ 7
   - ○ 6
   - ○ 5

6. $4¢ + 3¢ =$ ___
   - ○ 8¢
   - ○ 7¢
   - ○ 9¢

7.
   $$\begin{array}{r} 3 \\ +\,0 \\ \hline \end{array}$$
   - ○ 4
   - ○ 0
   - ○ 3

8. Which is the turnaround fact for $2 + 6 = 8$?
   - ○ $6 + 3 = 9$
   - ○ $2 + 4 = 6$
   - ○ $6 + 2 = 8$

9. Choose the correct number sentence.

   - ○ $3 - 1 = 2$
   - ○ $4 + 1 = 3$
   - ○ $4 - 3 = 1$

Chapter 6   Cumulative Review

7
Measurement

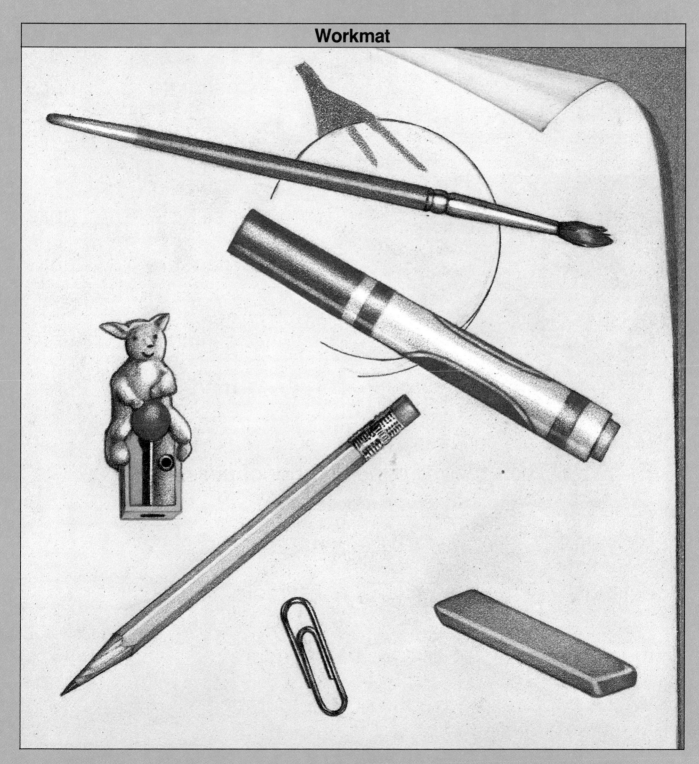

Theme: Making Things

Name _____

Estimating and Measuring Length
Nonstandard Units

Estimate how many units long.
Use  to measure.

1.
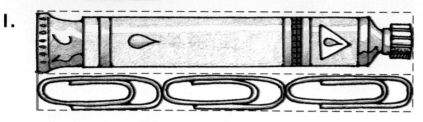

estimate _____ units

measure _____ units

2.
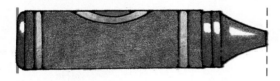

estimate _____ units

measure _____ units

3.

estimate _____ units

measure _____ units

TALK ABOUT IT

4. Estimate. Then measure the number of units.

estimate _____ 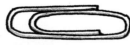   estimate _____

measure _____    measure _____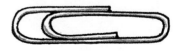

5. Which paper clip gave the greater number
of units? Tell why.

Using a Ruler
Feet

A foot (ft) ruler is 12 inches long.
Work in a group. Use a foot ruler.
Cut pieces of yarn as long as those
shown. Compare the yarn with the
part of your body. Ring **longer**
or **shorter**.

1.

The yarn is

longer.

shorter.

your
height

2.

The yarn is

longer.

shorter.

elbow to fingertips

3.

The yarn is

longer.

shorter.

arm
length

4.

The yarn is

longer.   shorter.

arm
span

Work in a group. Use your foot ruler.
Measure. Ring the best answer.

1. your desk top

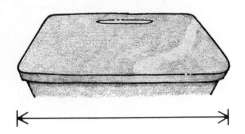

longer than 2 ⊏▭▭▭⊐
same as 2 ⊏▭▭▭⊐
shorter than 2 ⊏▭▭▭⊐

2. your teacher's desk top

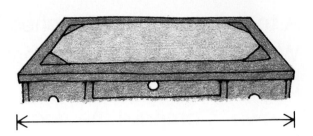

longer than 4 ⊏▭▭▭⊐
same as 4 ⊏▭▭▭⊐
shorter than 4 ⊏▭▭▭⊐

3. Draw something in your classroom. How many foot rulers long is it?

____

POWER PRACTICE/QUIZ

1. Estimate how many 🖇 long.
Use 🖇 to measure.

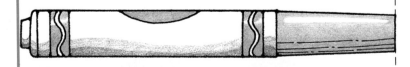

estimate ____ units

measure ____ units

2. Estimate how many inches.
Then measure.

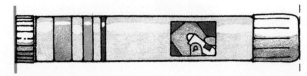

estimate ____ | inch |

measure ____ | inch |

Name _____

Ordering by Length and Height

Order from shortest to longest, too.

1. Order the ribbons from longest to shortest. Mark where each ends.

Place ribbon here. Mark.	Place ribbon here. Mark.	Place ribbon here. Mark.	Place ribbon here. Mark.

A

C

B

D

2. Which is longest? _____   3. Which is shortest? _____

4. Which two are in between? _____

1. Order the clothespin dolls from tallest to shortest. Then paste.

| Paste here. | Paste here. | Paste here. | Paste here. |

2. Which is tallest? _____

3. Which is shortest? _____

4. Which two are in between? _____

More Practice, page 418, set A

Estimating and Measuring Length
Centimeters

Estimate in centimeters (cm).
Ring your estimate.
Use your punchout centimeter ruler to check.

I centimeter

1   2   3   4   5   6   7   8   9   10   11   12   13   14   15

centimeter ruler

1. your pencil

more than 10 centimeters
10 centimeters
less than 10 centimeters

2. your eraser

more than 5 centimeters
5 centimeters
less than 5 centimeters

3. your shoe length

more than 20 centimeters
20 centimeters
less than 20 centimeters

4. the width of your hand

more than 10 centimeters
10 centimeters
less than 10 centimeters

5. Choose something to measure. Draw it here.

about _____ centimeters

Use your punchout
centimeter ruler.
Estimate. Then measure.

centimeter ruler

estimate __6__ cm   measure __5__ cm

1.   estimate ____ cm

measure ____ cm

2.   estimate ____ cm

measure ____ cm

3.   estimate ____ cm

measure ____ cm

4.

estimate ____ cm

measure ____ cm

PROBLEM SOLVING

5. Megan's bow is 6 centimeters long.
Joan's bow is double the length.
How long is Joan's bow?

It is ____ centimeters long.

Estimating and Measuring Length
Decimeters

Make a decimeter (dm) paper strip unit.
Ring your estimate. Then use your
decimeter unit strip to check.

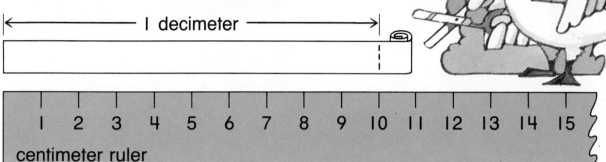

|← ———————— I decimeter ———————— →|

centimeter ruler

I. your crayon length

more than I decimeter
I decimeter
less than I decimeter

2. your paintbrush length

more than I decimeter
I decimeter
less than I decimeter

3. your paste
jar height

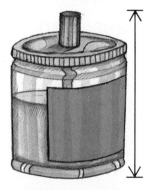

more than I decimeter
I decimeter
less than I decimeter

4. your shoe width

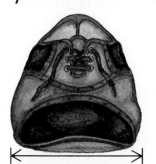

more than I decimeter
I decimeter
less than I decimeter

Tape 3 decimeter paper strip units
together. Ring your estimate.
Then use your decimeter unit train
to check.

1. your book length

more than 3 decimeters
3 decimeters
less than 3 decimeters

2. your book width

more than 2 decimeters
2 decimeters
less than 2 decimeters

3. your shoe length

more than 2 decimeters
2 decimeters
less than 2 decimeters

4. height of a
paper cup

more than 1 decimeter
1 decimeter
less than 1 decimeter

MAKE AN ESTIMATE

5. Find something that
is about 1 decimeter
long. Use your ruler
to check. Then draw it.

Estimating and Measuring Capacity

Work in a group. How many paper cups will each container fill? Estimate. Then pour to measure. Color to show your measure.

1.  I estimate it will fill _____ paper cups.

2.  I estimate it will fill _____ paper cups.

3.  I estimate it will fill _____ paper cups.

4.  Choose something to measure. Draw it.

I estimate it will fill _____ paper cups.

Estimating and Measuring Weight

Work in a group. Use 12 cubes.
Estimate how many cubes will balance
each object. Then measure.
Color cubes to show your measure.

1. my pencil    I estimate that ____ cubes will balance it.

 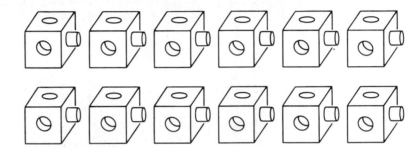

2. a comb   I estimate that ____ cubes will balance it.

 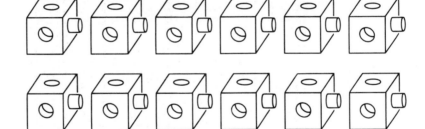

3. 3 nickels   I estimate that ____ cubes will balance them.

 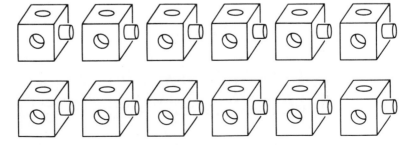

4. Order the objects above from
heaviest to lightest.   ____ , ____ , ____

Name _____

Problem Solving
Determining Reasonable Answers

UNDERSTAND
FIND DATA
PLAN
ESTIMATE
SOLVE
CHECK

Listen to the story. Ring the answer if it makes sense. Cross out if it does not make sense. Make an estimate that does make sense.

1. Bobby is about 3 feet tall.

About how many feet tall is Jill?

_2_ feet

___ feet

2. This red pitcher fills 4 glasses.

How many glasses does this blue pitcher fill?

_8_ glasses

___ glasses

3. This hamster and cage weigh 2 pounds.

How many pounds do these hamsters and cages weigh?

_3_ pounds   ___ pounds

Problem Solving Strategy
Draw a Picture

UNDERSTAND
FIND DATA
PLAN
ESTIMATE
SOLVE
CHECK

Listen to the story. Draw pictures to help answer the question.

1.

_____ houses in all

2.

_____ flowers in all

Name _____

POWER PRACTICE/TEST

Estimate how many inches.
Then use your inch ruler to measure.

1.

estimate _____ inches

measure _____ inches

2. Use your foot ruler. Measure.
Ring the best answer.

longer than 3

same as 3

shorter than 3

3. Order from longest to shortest.

A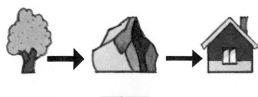

B

C

____ , ____ , ____

4. Measure.

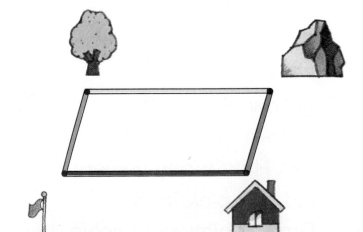

☐ + ☐ = ____

____ inches

Name _____

POWER PRACTICE/TEST

Estimate how many centimeters.
Then use your centimeter ruler to measure.

1.    estimate _____ cm

    measure _____ cm

2. **Ring your estimate.**

    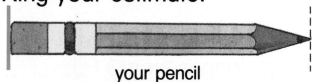
    your pencil

    more than 1 decimeter

    1 decimeter

    less than 1 decimeter

3. How many paper cups will the
   container fill? Estimate. Then pour to
   measure. Ring the number of cups to show
   your measure.

      I estimate it will fill _____ paper cups.

4. Erin picked 3 yellow
   flowers. She picked
   1 fewer red than
   yellow. She picked
   1 more orange than
   red. How many flowers
   did she pick in all?
   Draw a picture to solve.   _____ flowers in all

8
Subtraction Facts
Count Backs, Zeros, and Doubles

Workmat

Theme: In the Air

Counting Back 1 or 2

Work with a partner. Use counters.
Lay out the number shown.
Take away 1 or 2 as you count
back. Finish the number sentence.

1. 9 ----- ___ ===== ___

2. 7 ----- ___ ===== ___

3. 6 ----- ___ ===== ___

4. 8 ----- ___ ===== ___

Subtract.

5. $\begin{array}{r} 7 \\ -2 \\ \hline \end{array}$ $\begin{array}{r} 10 \\ -1 \\ \hline \end{array}$ $\begin{array}{r} 9 \\ -1 \\ \hline \end{array}$ $\begin{array}{r} 11 \\ -2 \\ \hline \end{array}$ $\begin{array}{r} 4 \\ -1 \\ \hline \end{array}$ $\begin{array}{r} 5 \\ -2 \\ \hline \end{array}$

6. $\begin{array}{r} 8 \\ -2 \\ \hline \end{array}$ $\begin{array}{r} 6 \\ -1 \\ \hline \end{array}$ $\begin{array}{r} 3 \\ -1 \\ \hline \end{array}$ $\begin{array}{r} 4 \\ -2 \\ \hline \end{array}$ $\begin{array}{r} 6 \\ -2 \\ \hline \end{array}$ $\begin{array}{r} 7 \\ -1 \\ \hline \end{array}$

SHOW WITH COUNTERS

7. Count back to subtract.

8. Use counters to check one fact.

Counting Back 3

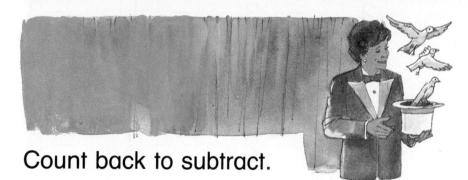

$$9 - 3 = 6$$

Count back to subtract.

1.

7   ⟨6, 5, 4⟩

$$7 - 3 = \underline{\hphantom{0}}$$

2.

5

$$5 - 3 = \underline{\hphantom{0}}$$

3.

11

$$11 - 3 = \underline{\hphantom{0}}$$

4.

4

$$4 - 3 = \underline{\hphantom{0}}$$

5.

9

$$9 - 3 = \underline{\hphantom{0}}$$

6.

12

$$12 - 3 = \underline{\hphantom{0}}$$

7.

10

$$10 - 3 = \underline{\hphantom{0}}$$

8.

8

$$8 - 3 = \underline{\hphantom{0}}$$

9.

6

$$6 - 3 = \underline{\hphantom{0}}$$

Subtract.

(7, 6, **5**)

1.

$$\begin{array}{r} 8 \\ -3 \\ \hline 5 \end{array}$$
$$\begin{array}{r} 10 \\ -3 \\ \hline \end{array}$$
$$\begin{array}{r} 7 \\ -2 \\ \hline \end{array}$$
$$\begin{array}{r} 11 \\ -3 \\ \hline \end{array}$$
$$\begin{array}{r} 10 \\ -1 \\ \hline \end{array}$$
$$\begin{array}{r} 6 \\ -3 \\ \hline \end{array}$$

2.

$$\begin{array}{r} 9 \\ -3 \\ \hline \end{array}$$
$$\begin{array}{r} 5 \\ -3 \\ \hline \end{array}$$
$$\begin{array}{r} 12 \\ -3 \\ \hline \end{array}$$
$$\begin{array}{r} 11 \\ -2 \\ \hline \end{array}$$
$$\begin{array}{r} 7 \\ -3 \\ \hline \end{array}$$
$$\begin{array}{r} 4 \\ -3 \\ \hline \end{array}$$

3.

$$\begin{array}{r} 11 \\ -1 \\ \hline \end{array}$$
$$\begin{array}{r} 10 \\ -2 \\ \hline \end{array}$$
$$\begin{array}{r} 12 \\ -3 \\ \hline \end{array}$$
$$\begin{array}{r} 6 \\ -3 \\ \hline \end{array}$$
$$\begin{array}{r} 9 \\ -2 \\ \hline \end{array}$$
$$\begin{array}{r} 8 \\ -3 \\ \hline \end{array}$$

4.

$$\begin{array}{r} 8 \\ -1 \\ \hline \end{array}$$
$$\begin{array}{r} 7 \\ -3 \\ \hline \end{array}$$
$$\begin{array}{r} 11 \\ -3 \\ \hline \end{array}$$
$$\begin{array}{r} 8 \\ -2 \\ \hline \end{array}$$
$$\begin{array}{r} 4 \\ -3 \\ \hline \end{array}$$
$$\begin{array}{r} 9 \\ -3 \\ \hline \end{array}$$

5.

$$\begin{array}{r} 7 \\ -1 \\ \hline \end{array}$$
$$\begin{array}{r} 6 \\ -2 \\ \hline \end{array}$$
$$\begin{array}{r} 5 \\ -3 \\ \hline \end{array}$$
$$\begin{array}{r} 10 \\ -3 \\ \hline \end{array}$$
$$\begin{array}{r} 7 \\ -2 \\ \hline \end{array}$$
$$\begin{array}{r} 5 \\ -2 \\ \hline \end{array}$$

USE CRITICAL THINKING

6. Write + or − in ◯.

$$\begin{array}{r} \bigcirc\ 5 \\ 2 \\ \hline 7 \end{array}$$
$$\begin{array}{r} \bigcirc\ 5 \\ 2 \\ \hline 3 \end{array}$$
$$\begin{array}{r} \bigcirc\ 9 \\ 1 \\ \hline 8 \end{array}$$
$$\begin{array}{r} \bigcirc\ 9 \\ 1 \\ \hline 10 \end{array}$$
$$\begin{array}{r} \bigcirc\ 8 \\ 2 \\ \hline 6 \end{array}$$
$$\begin{array}{r} \bigcirc\ 8 \\ 2 \\ \hline 10 \end{array}$$

Name _____

Counting Back 1, 2, or 3

Work with a partner.

Use punchouts ☐1 , ☐2 , and ☐3 .

Take turns. Pick a card.

Write the number below.

Count back to subtract.

$$\begin{array}{r} 5 \\ -\,2 \\ \hline 3 \end{array}$$

1.

$$\begin{array}{r} 4 \\ - \\ \hline \end{array}$$
$$\begin{array}{r} 7 \\ - \\ \hline \end{array}$$
$$\begin{array}{r} 9 \\ - \\ \hline \end{array}$$
$$\begin{array}{r} 3 \\ - \\ \hline \end{array}$$
$$\begin{array}{r} 10 \\ - \\ \hline \end{array}$$

2.

$$\begin{array}{r} 5 \\ - \\ \hline \end{array}$$
$$\begin{array}{r} 10 \\ - \\ \hline \end{array}$$
$$\begin{array}{r} 3 \\ - \\ \hline \end{array}$$
$$\begin{array}{r} 6 \\ - \\ \hline \end{array}$$
$$\begin{array}{r} 7 \\ - \\ \hline \end{array}$$

3. Match each fact to its answer.

9 − 1		7		12 − 3
11 − 2		8		9 − 2
10 − 3		9		10 − 2

Count back 1, 2, or 3 to subtract.

Are you subtracting 1, 2, or 3? Count back.

1. $7 - 3 = \underline{4}$ $9 - 2 = \underline{}$

2. $7 - 1 = \underline{}$ $12 - 3 = \underline{}$ $8 - 3 = \underline{}$

3. $11 - 2 = \underline{}$ $10 - 1 = \underline{}$ $10 - 3 = \underline{}$

4. $9 - 2 = \underline{}$ $4 - 3 = \underline{}$ $5 - 2 = \underline{}$

5. $6 - 2 = \underline{}$ $4 - 2 = \underline{}$ $4 - 3 = \underline{}$

POWER PRACTICE/QUIZ

Subtract.

1.
$\begin{array}{r} 9 \\ -2 \\ \hline \end{array}$
$\begin{array}{r} 9 \\ -3 \\ \hline \end{array}$
$\begin{array}{r} 8 \\ -3 \\ \hline \end{array}$
$\begin{array}{r} 10 \\ -3 \\ \hline \end{array}$
$\begin{array}{r} 8 \\ -2 \\ \hline \end{array}$
$\begin{array}{r} 7 \\ -1 \\ \hline \end{array}$

2.
$\begin{array}{r} 11 \\ -2 \\ \hline \end{array}$
$\begin{array}{r} 9 \\ -1 \\ \hline \end{array}$
$\begin{array}{r} 12 \\ -3 \\ \hline \end{array}$
$\begin{array}{r} 11 \\ -3 \\ \hline \end{array}$
$\begin{array}{r} 10 \\ -1 \\ \hline \end{array}$
$\begin{array}{r} 6 \\ -2 \\ \hline \end{array}$

Problem Solving
Understanding the Operations

UNDERSTAND
FIND DATA
PLAN
ESTIMATE
SOLVE
CHECK

Listen to the story. Use counters to show it. Write the number sentence.

1. the  story

____ ◯ ____ = ____

____ butterflies

2. the  story

____ ◯ ____ = ____

____ bluebirds

3. the story

____ ◯ ____ = ____

____ dragonflies

Calculator

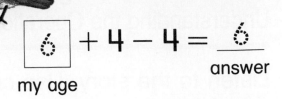

Write your age in each ☐.
Will the answer be your age?
Guess. Ring **yes** or **no**.
Calculate the answer.
Write it.

$\boxed{6} + 4 - 4 = \underline{6}$
my age   answer

My Guess

    yes   no

Press. $\boxed{6}$ $\boxed{+}$ $\boxed{4}$ $\boxed{-}$ $\boxed{4}$ $\boxed{=}$

My Guess

1. $\boxed{} + 6 - 6 = \underline{}$ yes   no
   my age   answer

2. $\boxed{} + 8 - 8 = \underline{}$ yes   no
   my age   answer

3. $\boxed{} + 12 - 12 = \underline{}$ yes   no
   my age   answer

4. $\boxed{} + 8 - 7 = \underline{}$ yes   no
   my age   answer

5. $\boxed{} + 18 - 17 = \underline{}$ yes   no
   my age   answer

6. $\boxed{} + 19 - 19 = \underline{}$ yes   no
   my age   answer

Zero Subtraction Facts

Nigerian Calabashes

$$\begin{array}{r} 4 \\ -0 \\ \hline 4 \end{array}$$

All are left.

$$\begin{array}{r} 4 \\ -4 \\ \hline 0 \end{array}$$

0 is left.

Subtract. Ring all zero facts.

1.
$$\begin{array}{r} 7 \\ -7 \\ \hline 0 \end{array}$$
$$\begin{array}{r} 8 \\ -3 \\ \hline \end{array}$$
$$\begin{array}{r} 7 \\ -2 \\ \hline \end{array}$$
$$\begin{array}{r} 5 \\ -0 \\ \hline 5 \end{array}$$
$$\begin{array}{r} 9 \\ -2 \\ \hline \end{array}$$
$$\begin{array}{r} 4 \\ -4 \\ \hline \end{array}$$

2.
$$\begin{array}{r} 11 \\ -2 \\ \hline \end{array}$$
$$\begin{array}{r} 9 \\ -9 \\ \hline \end{array}$$
$$\begin{array}{r} 3 \\ -3 \\ \hline \end{array}$$
$$\begin{array}{r} 0 \\ -0 \\ \hline \end{array}$$
$$\begin{array}{r} 10 \\ -3 \\ \hline \end{array}$$
$$\begin{array}{r} 2 \\ -2 \\ \hline \end{array}$$

3.
$$\begin{array}{r} 8 \\ -0 \\ \hline \end{array}$$
$$\begin{array}{r} 9 \\ -3 \\ \hline \end{array}$$
$$\begin{array}{r} 11 \\ -3 \\ \hline \end{array}$$
$$\begin{array}{r} 6 \\ -0 \\ \hline \end{array}$$
$$\begin{array}{r} 10 \\ -2 \\ \hline \end{array}$$
$$\begin{array}{r} 7 \\ -1 \\ \hline \end{array}$$

4. Write and continue the number pattern in .

_____, _____, _____, _____, _____, _____, _____, _____, _____

Subtract.

1.

$\begin{array}{r} 1 \\ -1 \\ \hline \end{array}$
$\begin{array}{r} 9 \\ -3 \\ \hline \end{array}$
$\begin{array}{r} 8 \\ -2 \\ \hline \end{array}$
$\begin{array}{r} 3 \\ -0 \\ \hline \end{array}$
$\begin{array}{r} 11 \\ -2 \\ \hline \end{array}$
$\begin{array}{r} 7 \\ -1 \\ \hline \end{array}$

2.

$\begin{array}{r} 6 \\ -2 \\ \hline \end{array}$
$\begin{array}{r} 7 \\ -0 \\ \hline \end{array}$
$\begin{array}{r} 8 \\ -1 \\ \hline \end{array}$
$\begin{array}{r} 10 \\ -2 \\ \hline \end{array}$
$\begin{array}{r} 4 \\ -4 \\ \hline \end{array}$
$\begin{array}{r} 10 \\ -3 \\ \hline \end{array}$

Be fast!

5. $9 - 2 = \underline{\quad}$

$7 - 3 = \underline{\quad}$

4. $5 - 2 = \underline{\quad}$

$4 - 2 = \underline{\quad}$

$3 - 3 = \underline{\quad}$

$5 - 5 = \underline{\quad}$

3. $4 - 3 = \underline{\quad}$

$11 - 3 = \underline{\quad}$

$6 - 0 = \underline{\quad}$

$6 - 3 = \underline{\quad}$

$3 - 2 = \underline{\quad}$

$12 - 3 = \underline{\quad}$

PROBLEM SOLVING

□ owls

□ parrots

6. Count the owls and parrots.
How many more owls than parrots are
there? Ring and finish the number
sentence that answers the question.

$4 + 2 = \underline{\quad}$

$4 - 2 = \underline{\quad}$

Adding to Check Subtraction

Addition checks the subtraction answer.

7
5 · in all · 2

$$\begin{array}{r} 7 \\ -2 \\ \hline 5 \end{array}$$ add-to-check fact ⟶ $$\begin{array}{r} 2 \\ +5 \\ \hline 7 \end{array}$$

Add-to-Check Facts

Add.

1.
$$\begin{array}{r} 9 \\ +3 \\ \hline \end{array}$$
$$\begin{array}{r} 3 \\ +8 \\ \hline \end{array}$$
$$\begin{array}{r} 7 \\ +3 \\ \hline \end{array}$$
$$\begin{array}{r} 9 \\ +2 \\ \hline \end{array}$$
$$\begin{array}{r} 2 \\ +8 \\ \hline \end{array}$$
$$\begin{array}{r} 7 \\ +2 \\ \hline \end{array}$$

Subtract. Finish the add-to-check fact.

2.

12 − 3	3 +
10 − 3	3 +
11 − 2	2 +

3.

10 − 2	2 +
11 − 3	3 +
9 − 2	2 +

Subtract. Finish the add-to-check fact.
Cross out the other fact.

1. $7 - 2 = \underline{5}$ $2 + 5 = \underline{7}$ ~~$7 + 2 =$~~

2. $6 - 3 = \underline{}$ $3 + 4 = \underline{}$ $3 + 3 = \underline{}$

3. $9 - 2 = \underline{}$ $2 + 9 = \underline{}$ $2 + 7 = \underline{}$

4. $11 - 2 = \underline{}$ $2 + 8 = \underline{}$ $2 + 9 = \underline{}$

5. $4 - 0 = \underline{}$ $0 + 4 = \underline{}$ $4 + 4 = \underline{}$

SHOW WITH COUNTERS

6. Subtract. Write the add-to-check fact.
   Use counters to check.

8	
− 2	+

7	
− 3	+

5	
− 3	+

Subtraction Doubles

The add-to-check double fact helps you find the answer.

8	4
− 4	+ 4
4	8

10	5
− 5	+ 5
5	10

12	6
− 6	+ 6
6	12

Subtract. Finish the add-to-check fact.

1.

8	4
− 4	+ 4
4	8

12	6
− 6	+

6	3
− 3	+

2.

12	6
− 6	+

10	5
− 5	+

2	1
− 1	+

3.

6	3
− 3	+

8	4
− 4	+

4	2
− 2	+

Ring the subtraction double facts.
Then subtract all.

1.
$$10 - 5 = 5$$ $$9 - 3$$ $$6 - 2$$ $$9 - 2$$ $$12 - 6$$

2.
$$10 - 2$$ $$5 - 0$$ $$8 - 4$$ $$11 - 2$$ $$9 - 1$$ $$10 - 3$$

3.
$$3 - 2$$ $$8 - 2$$ $$12 - 3$$ $$8 - 2$$ $$10 - 5$$ $$7 - 3$$

4.
$$8 - 4$$ $$5 - 3$$ $$9 - 0$$ $$12 - 6$$ $$8 - 3$$ $$4 - 3$$

5. Do these as fast as you can.

$$7 - 2 = \underline{\quad}$$ $$8 - 8 = \underline{\quad}$$ $$5 - 2 = \underline{\quad}$$

$$11 - 3 = \underline{\quad}$$ $$4 - 2 = \underline{\quad}$$ $$6 - 3 = \underline{\quad}$$

USE MENTAL MATH

6. Think about these facts.
   Ring the one that has
   the greater answer.

$$12 - 3 = ?$$

$$12 - 6 = ?$$

Name _____

Fact Practice

What did the bee say
to the flower?

To find out, first subtract.
Then write the letter code for
each answer in the box below.
Read the message.

Secret Code

1 = u	4 = s	7 = h
2 = t	5 = y	8 = e
3 = w	6 = n	9 = o

$$\begin{array}{r} 9 \\ -2 \\ \hline 7 \\ h \end{array}$$

$$\begin{array}{r} 12 \\ -3 \\ \hline \end{array}$$

$$\begin{array}{r} 8 \\ -2 \\ \hline \end{array}$$

$$\begin{array}{r} 11 \\ -3 \\ \hline \end{array}$$

$$\begin{array}{r} 10 \\ -5 \\ \hline \end{array}$$
_____ , I'm

$$\begin{array}{r} 8 \\ -4 \\ \hline \end{array}$$

$$\begin{array}{r} 4 \\ -1 \\ \hline \end{array}$$

$$\begin{array}{r} 8 \\ -0 \\ \hline \end{array}$$

$$\begin{array}{r} 10 \\ -2 \\ \hline \end{array}$$

$$\begin{array}{r} 5 \\ -3 \\ \hline \end{array}$$

$$\begin{array}{r} 11 \\ -2 \\ \hline \end{array}$$

$$\begin{array}{r} 12 \\ -6 \\ \hline \end{array}$$

$$\begin{array}{r} 8 \\ -3 \\ \hline \end{array}$$

$$\begin{array}{r} 10 \\ -1 \\ \hline \end{array}$$

$$\begin{array}{r} 4 \\ -3 \\ \hline \end{array}$$
.

Subtract. When each row is correct,
draw and color the bee's face.

1.
$$5¢ - 2¢ = 3¢$$ $$10¢ - 5¢$$ $$12¢ - 3¢$$ $$4¢ - 2¢$$ $$5¢ - 1¢$$

2.
$$8¢ - 4¢$$ $$5¢ - 3¢$$ $$8¢ - 8¢$$ $$11¢ - 2¢$$ $$9¢ - 3¢$$

3.
$$7¢ - 3¢$$ $$11¢ - 3¢$$ $$12¢ - 6¢$$ $$7¢ - 2¢$$ $$4¢ - 0¢$$

MIXED REVIEW

4. Use your punchout centimeter
ruler. Estimate. Then measure.

estimate _____ cm

measure _____ cm

5. A

B

C

Which paintbrush is longest? _____

Which paintbrush is shortest? _____

Problem Solving
Asking the Question

UNDERSTAND
FIND DATA
PLAN
ESTIMATE
SOLVE
CHECK

Listen to the story.
Use counters to show it.
Ring the question you would ask.

1. the 🐦 story

   Ring one.
   How many birds are there?

   How many birds are left?

2. the 🧑 story

   Ring one.
   How many in all are going to the movie?

   How many boys are left?

Problem Solving Strategy
Choose the Operation

UNDERSTAND
FIND DATA
PLAN
ESTIMATE
SOLVE
CHECK

Listen to the stories. Think about
the action. Paste the pictures
where they belong.

Addition	Subtraction
Put Together	Take Away Compare

WRAP UP

MATH WORDS

Ring examples of each.

1. counting back to subtract	8 −1	10 −5	9 −9	10 −2
2. zero facts	7 −2	5 −0	6 −3	4 −4
3. subtraction doubles	7 −3	8 −4	12 −6	5 −5

MATH REASONING

Ring the fact that has the smaller difference. Tell how you know.

4.
9 −3   or   9 −1

5.
7 −1   or   7 −2

6.
 10 −2   or    8 −2

7.
7 −3   or    10 −3

8.
 12 −6   or   8 −4

9.
6 −3   or   10 −5

Name _____

POWER PRACTICE/TEST

Subtract.

1.

$$3 - 1 = \underline{}$$

2.

$$4 - 2 = \underline{}$$

3.

| $\begin{array}{r} 9 \\ -3 \\ \hline \end{array}$ | $\begin{array}{r} 4 \\ -2 \\ \hline \end{array}$ | $\begin{array}{r} 10 \\ -1 \\ \hline \end{array}$ | $\begin{array}{r} 12 \\ -6 \\ \hline \end{array}$ | $\begin{array}{r} 7 \\ -0 \\ \hline \end{array}$ | $\begin{array}{r} 11 \\ -5 \\ \hline \end{array}$ |

4.

| $\begin{array}{r} 8 \\ -4 \\ \hline \end{array}$ | $\begin{array}{r} 6 \\ -0 \\ \hline \end{array}$ | $\begin{array}{r} 8 \\ -3 \\ \hline \end{array}$ | $\begin{array}{r} 10¢ \\ -5¢ \\ \hline \end{array}$ | $\begin{array}{r} 5¢ \\ -5¢ \\ \hline \end{array}$ | $\begin{array}{r} 6¢ \\ -3¢ \\ \hline \end{array}$ |

5. Subtract. Write the add-to-check fact.

| $\begin{array}{r} 12 \\ -\ 3 \\ \hline \end{array}$ | $+\ \underline{}$ |

| $\begin{array}{r} 8 \\ -\ 3 \\ \hline \end{array}$ | $+\ \underline{}$ |

| $\begin{array}{r} 10 \\ -\ 4 \\ \hline \end{array}$ | $+\ \underline{}$ |

6. Ring the question to finish the story.

3 and 4 are by the pond.

How many are left?

How many are there in all?

ENRICHMENT
Finding 1-Foot Units

Work with a partner. Find objects in
your classroom that are about I foot
long. Draw them. Then check the
length with your foot ruler.

	Draw your object.	Is it I foot long? Ring one.
I.		yes no
2.		yes no
3.		yes no

CUMULATIVE REVIEW

Add.

1.

○ 12
○ 10
○ 11

$5 + 5 =$ ___

2. $8 + 2 =$ ___

○ 11
○ 10
○ 9

3.
```
   6
 + 5
```

○ 11
○ 12
○ 9

4.
```
   5
   4
 + 3
```

○ 11
○ 12
○ 10

Use your inch ruler to measure each length.

5.

○ 1 inch
○ 2 inches
○ 3 inches

6.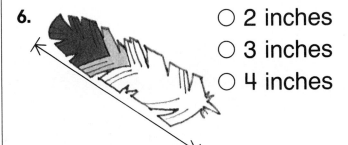

○ 2 inches
○ 3 inches
○ 4 inches

7. Which is longest?

A
B
C

○ A
○ B
○ C

8. Which pencil above is shortest?

○ A
○ B
○ C

9. How much do 3 🦕 cost?

dinosaurs	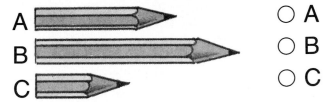		
cost	2¢	4¢	___ ¢

○ 6¢
○ 5¢
○ 3¢

9
Geometry

Theme: At the Store

Sorting Solids

Ring objects with the same shape.

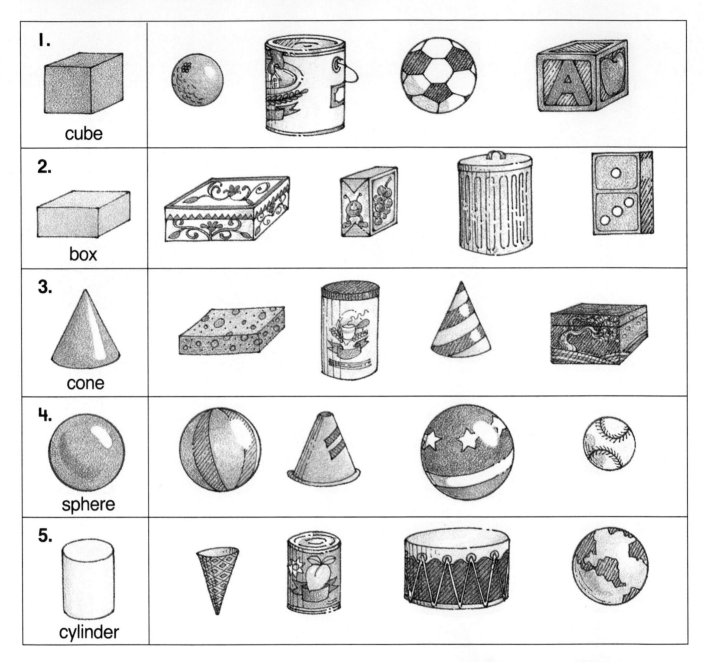

1. cube	
2. box	
3. cone	
4. sphere	
5. cylinder	

TALK ABOUT IT

6. Cross out the one that is not a cube. Tell why not.

Name _____

Graphing Solids

Look for  ◯ , ▱ , △ , and ⬭ in the picture. Put an X on the graph for each solid you find. Cross out as you graph.

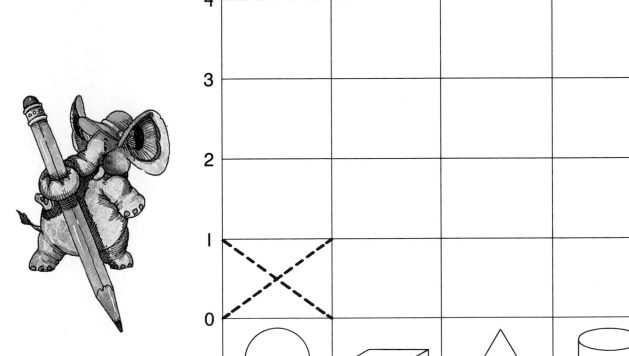

	sphere	box	cone	cylinder

1. Put an X on the graph for each solid you find. Cross out as you graph.

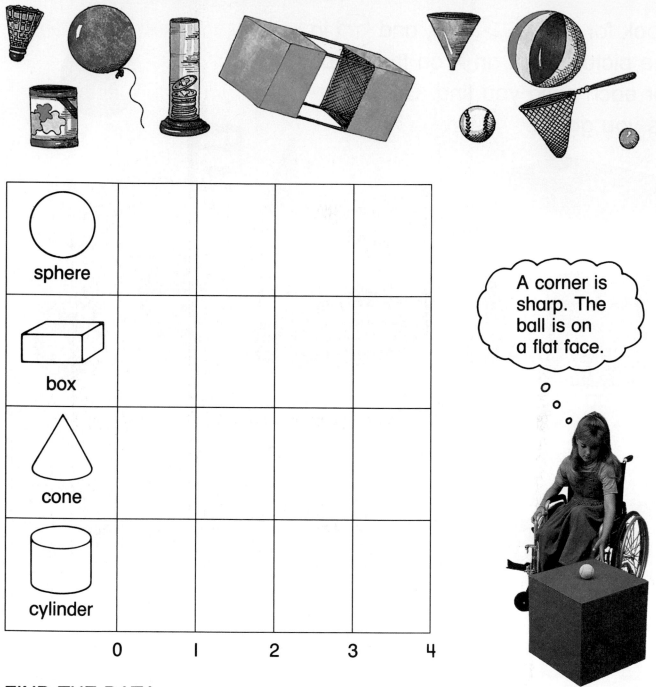

sphere				
box				
cone				
cylinder				
	0	1	2	3	4

A corner is sharp. The ball is on a flat face.

FIND THE DATA

Data Hunt Get a cube.

2. How many flat faces does it have? _____ flat faces

3. How many corners does it have? _____ corners

Plane Figures and Solids

Use a solid. Draw around the flat
face shown. Match to the plane figure.

solid	flat face	plane figure

1.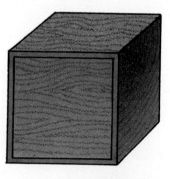

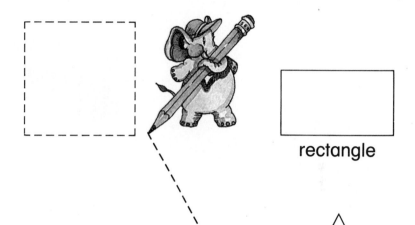

rectangle

2.

triangle

3.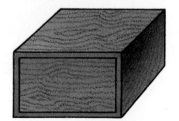

square

4.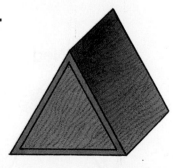

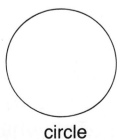

circle

1. Match the plane figures to the solids.

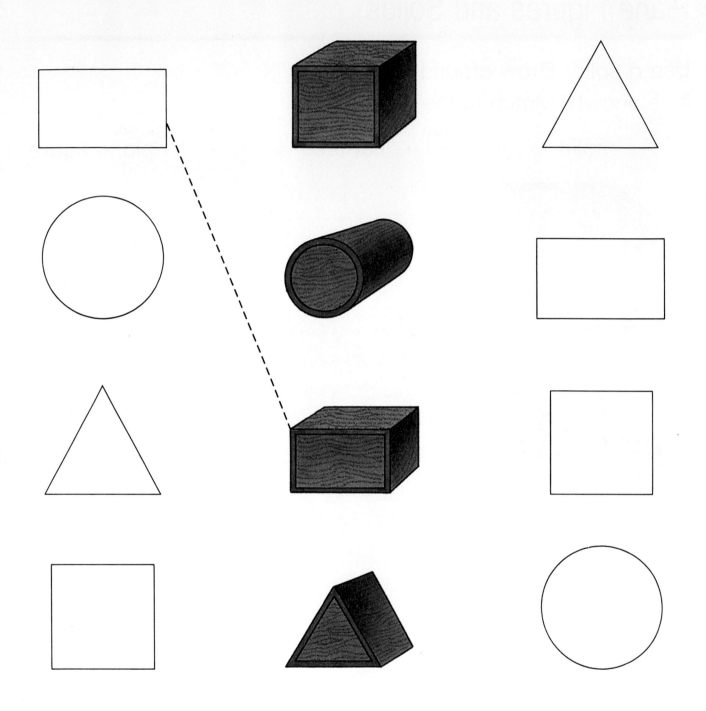

MAKE AN ESTIMATE

2. Who walks farther?
   Ring one.
   Tell why.

Ted

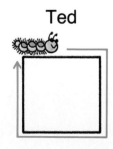

Ned

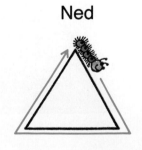

Name _____

Sides and Corners

Color  the straws. Color  the clay.
Count the sides and corners. Write how many.

1.

sides __3__

corners __3__

2.

sides _____

corners _____

3.

sides _____

corners _____

4.

sides _____

corners _____

5.

sides _____

corners _____

6.

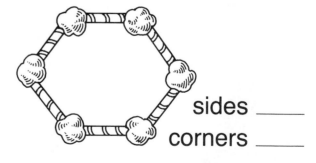

sides _____

corners _____

7. Which figure has the most sides? Ring
with ![crayon].

8. Which two figures have the fewest sides? Ring
with ![crayon].

Draw the figure. Color sides 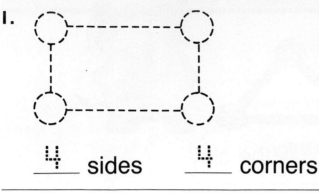.
Color corners 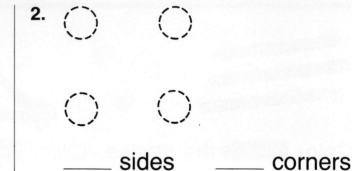. Write how many.

1.

___4___ sides   ___4___ corners

2.

_____ sides   _____ corners

3.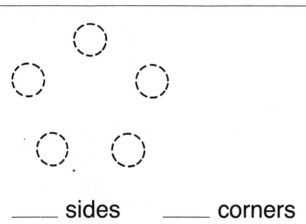

_____ sides   _____ corners

4. your choice

_____ sides   _____ corners

POWER PRACTICE/QUIZ

1. Match.

2. Match the plane figures to the solids.

Name _____

My Geometry Book

Use your punchouts. Paste each picture next to the shape it matches. Write how many sides and corners the shape has.

rectangle

| Paste here. | | Paste here. |
| Paste here. | | Paste here. |

_____ sides   _____ corners

square

| Paste here. | | Paste here. |
| Paste here. | | Paste here. |

_____ sides

_____ corners

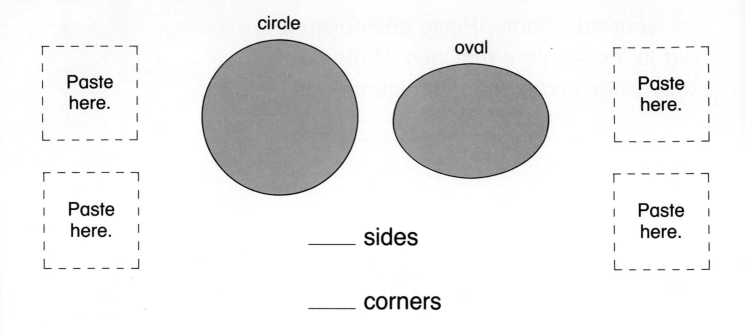

circle

oval

_____ sides

_____ corners

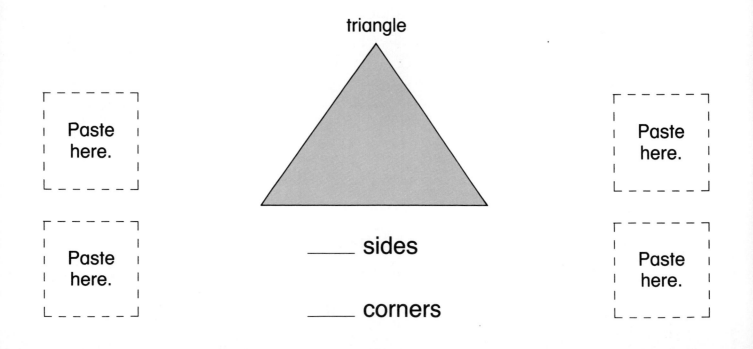

triangle

_____ sides

_____ corners

Name _____

Problem Solving
Understanding the Operations

UNDERSTAND
FIND DATA
PLAN
ESTIMATE
SOLVE
CHECK

Listen to the story. Use and draw coins to answer the question.

---

1. I have 4¢. How much more do I need?

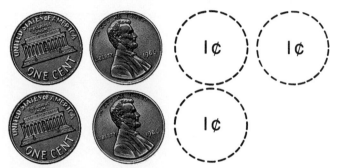

_____ ¢

7¢

ORK

---

2. I have 5¢. How much more do I need?

_____ ¢

9¢

BIP

---

3. I have 6¢. How much more do I need?

_____ ¢

10¢

YOP

---

4. I have 6¢. How much more do I need?

_____ ¢

11¢

Draw KIP.

Using Critical Thinking

Draw a face on each figure.
Write its letter in the correct box.

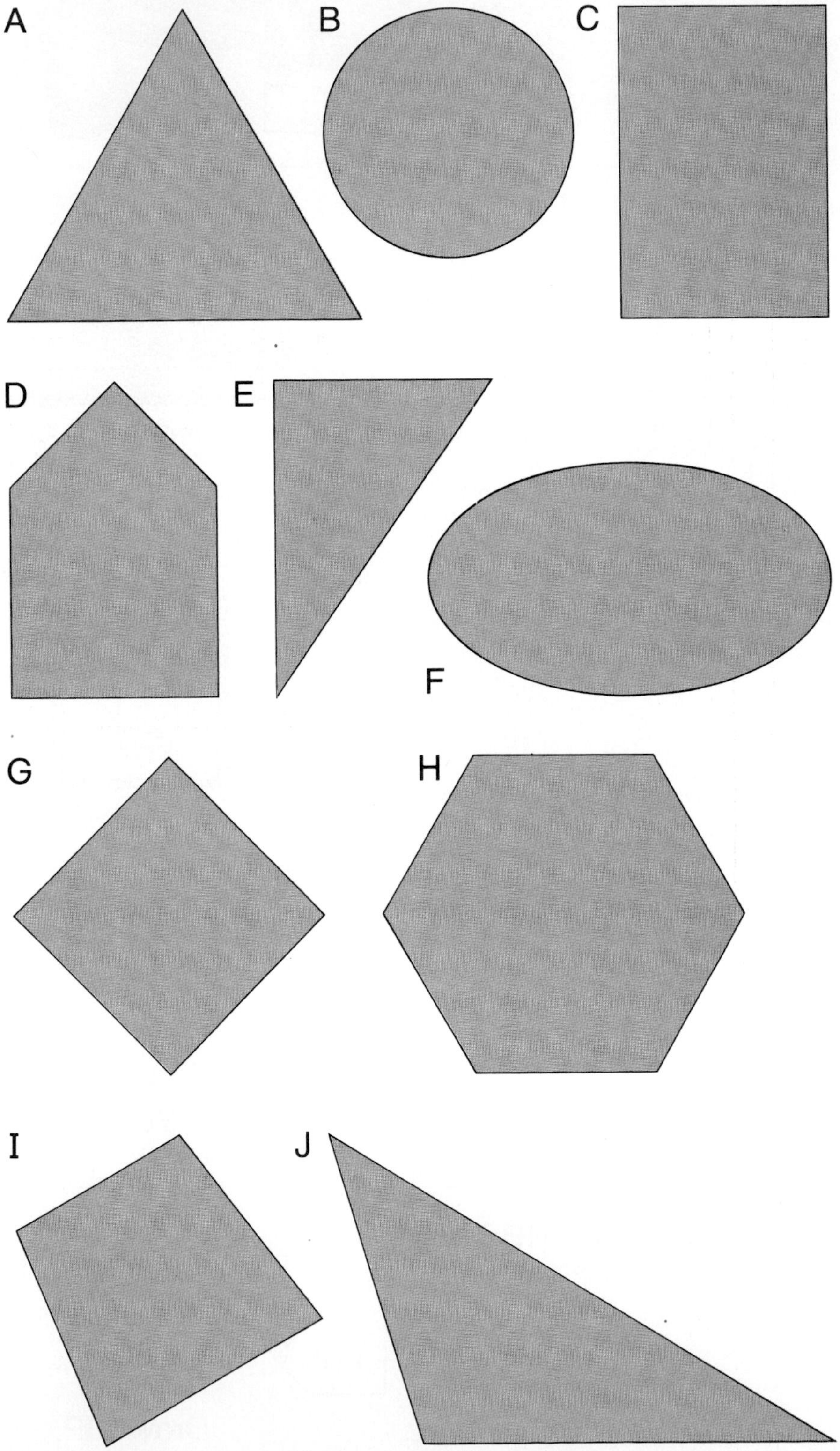

A

B

C

D

E

F

G

H

I

J

A

3 corners

4 sides

0 corners

more than 4 sides

Inside, Outside, and On

Work in a group. Make the figure on your geoboard. Write how many pegs inside, outside, and on.

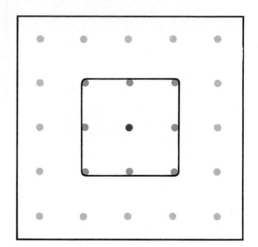

__1__ inside   • inside

__16__ outside   • outside

__8__ on   • on

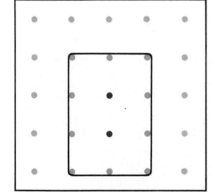

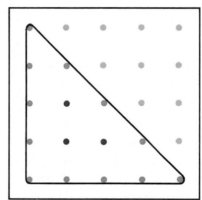

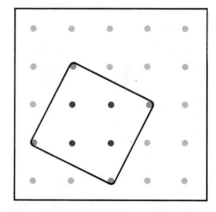

1. rectangle

____ inside

____ outside

____ on

2. triangle

____ inside

____ outside

____ on

3. square

____ inside

____ outside

____ on

4. Draw your own figure.

____ inside

____ outside

____ on

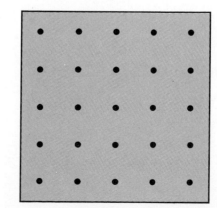

Work in a group. Make the shape on your geoboard.
Draw it here.

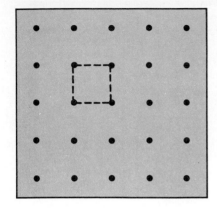

1. square
   0 inside

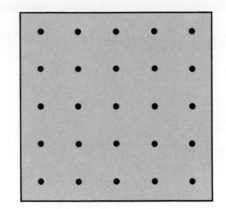

2. triangle
   0 inside

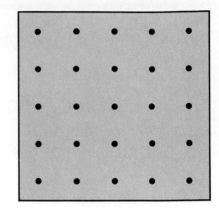

3. rectangle
   0 inside

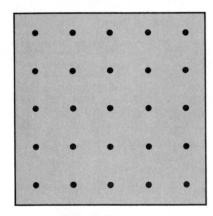

4. triangle
   1 inside

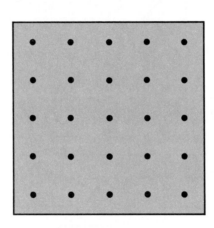

5. rectangle
   2 inside

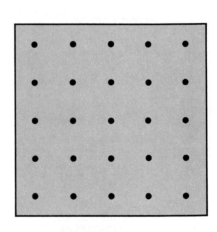

6. square
   4 inside

PROBLEM SOLVING

7. The inside pegs are covered.
   How many pegs are inside?

   _____ pegs

More Practice, page 420, set A Chapter 9

Symmetric Figures

Cut out the squares.
Paste to make
figures that match.

Both parts match.

1.

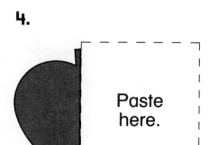

Paste here.

2.

Paste here.

3.

Paste here.

4.

Paste here.

5.

Paste here.

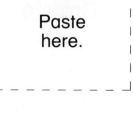

6.

Paste here.

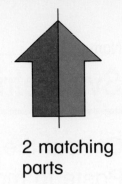

2 matching parts

Draw a line to make two matching parts. Color one part and the other .

1.

2.

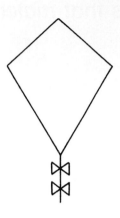

3.

4.

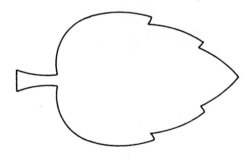

USE CRITICAL THINKING

5. Fold a piece of paper in half. Draw a figure. Start and end it at the fold. Say what it will look like when you unfold. Cut and unfold to check.

Congruent Figures

Work in a group. Take turns working in pairs. Make a figure on your geoboard. Draw it. Your partner makes one the same size and shape and draws it. Ring **yes** or **no** to answer the question.

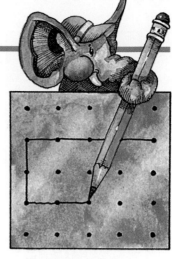

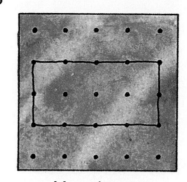

You draw.   Partner draws.

Same size and shape?   (yes)   no

1.

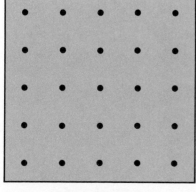

You draw.   Partner draws.

Same size and shape?

yes   no

2.

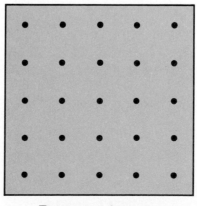

You draw.   Partner draws.

Same size and shape?

yes   no

Draw one the same size and shape.

1. 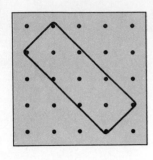 You draw.

2. 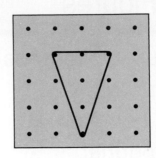 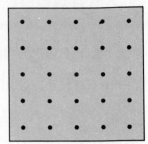 You draw.

Look at the first one. Ring ones
that are the same size and shape.

3.

4.

MIXED REVIEW

5. Subtract. Write the add-to-check fact.

$$11 - 3 \quad +$$

$$12 - 6 \quad +$$

$$9 - 2 \quad +$$

6. Add.

$6 + 3 =$ _____ $4 + 4 =$ _____ $5 + 6 =$ _____

Problem Solving
Finding Data from a Map

UNDERSTAND
FIND DATA
PLAN
ESTIMATE
SOLVE
CHECK

Listen to the story. Use your inch ruler.
Write how many inches.

1. How far is it from home
to the store?

___ inches

2. How far is it from home
past the pond to school?

___ inches

3. How far is the shortest way
from school to home?

___ inches

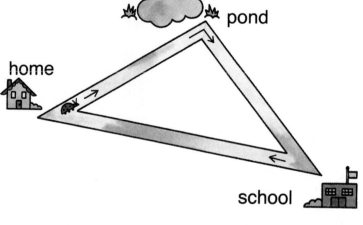

4. Start at home.
Go all the way around
the park. How far is it?

___ inches

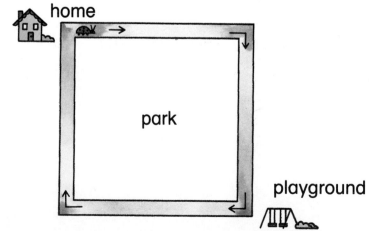

Problem Solving Strategy
Look for a Pattern

Listen to the story. Color the one that comes next. Talk about the patterns you see.

Things for school

1.

2.

3.

4.

5. Draw your own pattern.

More Practice, page 421, set B   Chapter 9

WRAP UP

MATH WORDS

Cross out words that do not name the pictures.

1. triangle	2. cylinder	3. rectangle	4. circle 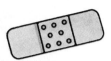
5. cube	6. square	7. circle	8. cone
9. sphere	10. cone	11. cylinder	12. triangle

MATH REASONING

Look at the cutout lines. How many sides and corners will the figure have?

13.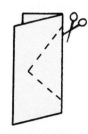

_____ sides

_____ corners

14.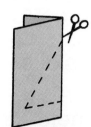

_____ sides

_____ corners

15.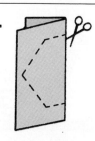

_____ sides

_____ corners

16.

_____ sides

_____ corners

Name _____

POWER PRACTICE/TEST

1. Match.

2. Match.

3. Write how many.

corners _____

sides _____

4. Write how many pegs.

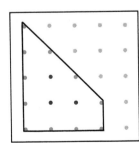

inside _____

outside _____

on _____

5. Use your centimeter ruler. How far is it from home past the store to school? Write how many centimeters.

_____ centimeters

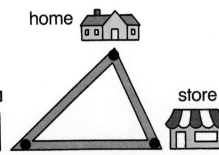

200   (two hundred)

Chapter 9   Power Practice/Test

ENRICHMENT
Making Shapes

Use pattern blocks to make the shapes. Draw what you did.

1. Try a different way for each ⬡.

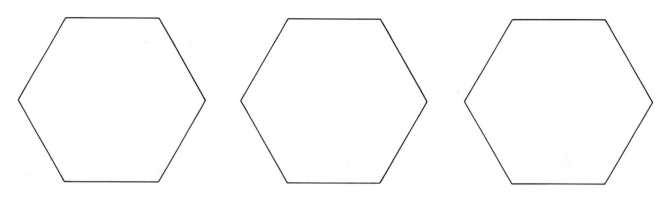

2. Use all ⬭.

3. Use some △ and some ◇.

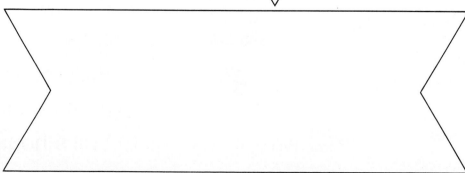

Name _____

CUMULATIVE REVIEW

Use your centimeter ruler to measure the length or height.

1.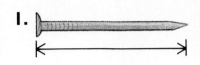
   - ○ 2 cm
   - ○ 3 cm
   - ○ 4 cm

2.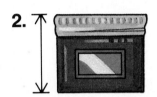
   - ○ 2 cm
   - ○ 3 cm
   - ○ 4 cm

3. Which is longest?

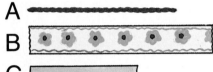

A
B
C

   - ○ A
   - ○ B
   - ○ C

4. Which is tallest?

A B C

   - ○ A
   - ○ B
   - ○ C

Subtract.

5.

   $9 - 3 = $ _____

   - ○ 6
   - ○ 8
   - ○ 7

6. $12 - 6 = $ _____

   - ○ 5
   - ○ 6
   - ○ 7

7. $\begin{array}{r} 9 \\ -\ 0 \\ \hline \end{array}$

   - ○ 8
   - ○ 0
   - ○ 9

8. Which is the add-to-check fact for $9 - 4 = 5$?

   - ○ $5 + 4 = 9$
   - ○ $9 - 5 = 4$
   - ○ $5 + 5 = 10$

9. Whose house is closest to Sal?

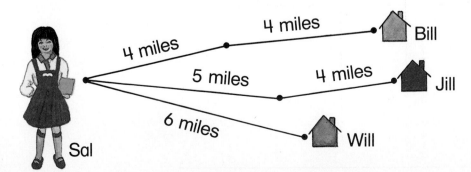

4 miles
4 miles
5 miles
4 miles
6 miles

Bill
Jill
Will
Sal

   - ○ Bill's house
   - ○ Jill's house
   - ○ Will's house

10
Subtraction Facts
to 12

Workmat

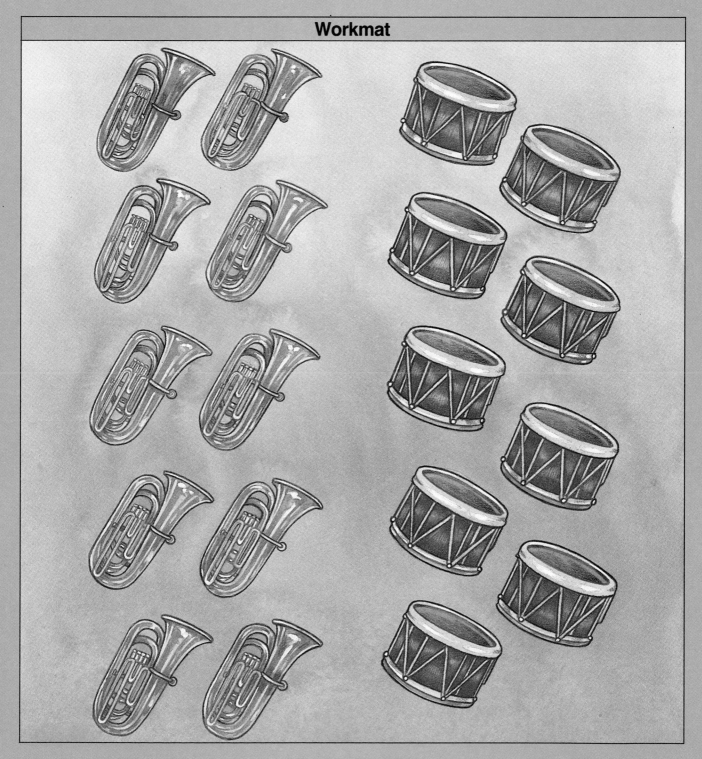

Theme: Music

Name _____

Subtracting from 9 and 10

Work with a partner.
Use 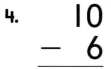 and counters
to subtract.

Take away
1 of the 9.
That leaves 8.

1. $10 - 8 =$ ___

2. $9 - 2 =$ ___

3. $10 - 4 =$ ___

4. $\begin{array}{r} 10 \\ -\ 6 \\ \hline \end{array}$ $\begin{array}{r} 10 \\ -\ 9 \\ \hline \end{array}$ $\begin{array}{r} 9 \\ -\ 3 \\ \hline \end{array}$

5. $\begin{array}{r} 10 \\ -\ 3 \\ \hline \end{array}$ $\begin{array}{r} 9 \\ -\ 5 \\ \hline \end{array}$ $\begin{array}{r} 9 \\ -\ 6 \\ \hline \end{array}$

USE CRITICAL THINKING

6. Draw and color what is missing.

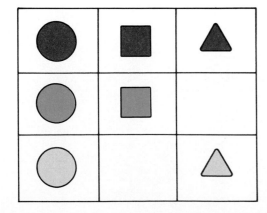

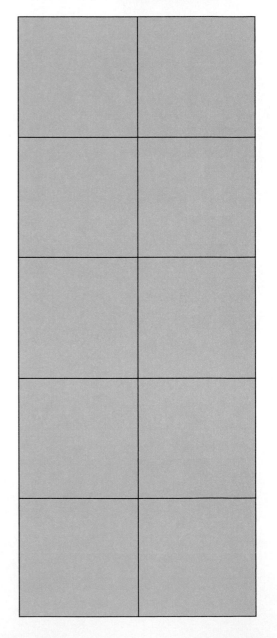

Fact Practice

Why are fish so smart?
To find out, first subtract. Then
write the letter code for each answer
below. Read the message.

Secret Code	
0 = w	7 = i
1 = h	8 = m
2 = t	9 = s
3 = l	10 = y
4 = e	11 = n
5 = c	12 = a
6 = o	

1.

$$10 - 8 = 2$$ T

$$1 - 0 = $$ _____

$$10 - 6 = $$ _____

$$10 - 0 = $$ _____

2.

$$12 - 3 = $$ _____

$$6 - 6 = $$ _____

$$10 - 3 = $$ _____

$$11 - 3 = $$ _____

3.

$$9 - 2 = $$ _____

$$11 - 0 = $$ _____

$$12 - 0 = $$ _____

4.

$$11 - 2 = $$ _____

$$9 - 4 = $$ _____

$$4 - 3 = $$ _____

$$12 - 6 = $$ _____

$$10 - 4 = $$ _____

$$6 - 3 = $$ _____

Subtract.

1.

7	10	12	8	10	9
− 2	− 6	− 6	− 0	− 3	− 6
5					

2.

8¢	10¢	9¢	10¢	12¢	9¢
− 4¢	− 1¢	− 5¢	− 2¢	− 3¢	− 2¢

3.

$3 - 1 =$ ___

$7 - 0 =$ ___

$5 - 5 =$ ___

$10 - 6 =$ ___

$9 - 5 =$ ___

$9 - 3 =$ ___

$10 - 2 =$ ___

$9 - 4 =$ ___

$10 - 7 =$ ___

4. Do these as fast as you can.

$8 - 3 =$ ___ $10 - 9 =$ ___ $11 - 2 =$ ___

$10 - 7 =$ ___ $9 - 4 =$ ___ $7 - 3 =$ ___

USE MENTAL MATH

5. Finish the number sentences.

$9 - 5 + 1 =$ ___

$9 - 4 + 2 =$ ___

Problem Solving
Understanding the Operations

UNDERSTAND
FIND DATA
PLAN
ESTIMATE
SOLVE
CHECK

Write the addition or subtraction
sentence for the story. Answer the question.

1. Taj saw 4 trumpet players in the
parade. I trumpet player left. How
many trumpet players are there now?

____ trumpet
players

2. 4 harps were big. 5 harps were
small. How many harps were there
in all?

____ harps

3. Fumiko saw 4 red drums. Caitlin saw
2 blue drums. How many more drums
did Fumiko see than Caitlin?

____ drums

Data Analysis

Take a survey. Find out what musical instruments your classmates like best.

1. Write **Music Survey** to name your graph.

2. Mark an x for each vote.

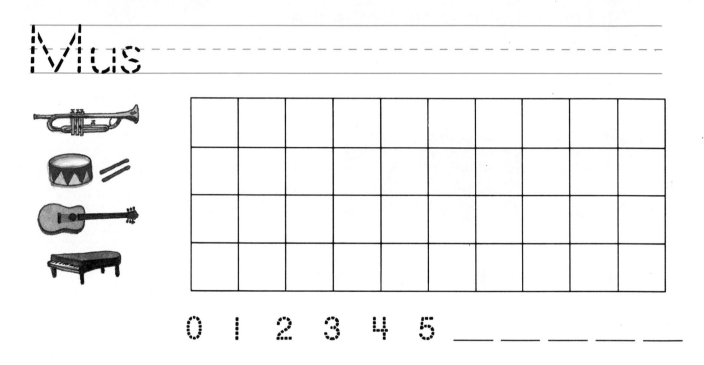

Mus

0 1 2 3 4 5 _____

3. Write the numbers across the bottom of your graph.

4. Ring what your classmates liked best.

Name _____

Counting Up to Subtract

That is a count-up fact. The numbers are close to each other.

6

8

7, 8

$$\begin{array}{r} 8 \\ -\,6 \\ \hline 2 \end{array}$$

6, 7, 8

Subtract. Look for count-up facts.

1.   5, 6, 7, 8
$$\begin{array}{r} 8 \\ -\,5 \\ \hline 3 \end{array}$$

8, 9
$$\begin{array}{r} 9 \\ -\,8 \\ \hline \end{array}$$

9, 10, 11
$$\begin{array}{r} 11 \\ -\,9 \\ \hline \end{array}$$

6, 7, 8, 9
$$\begin{array}{r} 9 \\ -\,6 \\ \hline \end{array}$$

2.
$$\begin{array}{r} 6 \\ -\,1 \\ \hline \end{array}$$
$$\begin{array}{r} 12 \\ -\,9 \\ \hline \end{array}$$
$$\begin{array}{r} 7 \\ -\,7 \\ \hline \end{array}$$
$$\begin{array}{r} 11 \\ -\,2 \\ \hline \end{array}$$
$$\begin{array}{r} 8 \\ -\,6 \\ \hline \end{array}$$

3.
$$\begin{array}{r} 8 \\ -\,4 \\ \hline \end{array}$$
$$\begin{array}{r} 9 \\ -\,7 \\ \hline \end{array}$$
$$\begin{array}{r} 7 \\ -\,5 \\ \hline \end{array}$$
$$\begin{array}{r} 6 \\ -\,0 \\ \hline \end{array}$$
$$\begin{array}{r} 11 \\ -\,8 \\ \hline \end{array}$$

4. Write one count-up fact and its add-to-check fact.

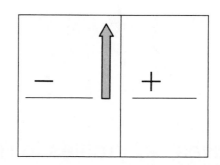

Ring the count-up facts.
Then subtract all.

$$\begin{array}{r} 9 \\ -7 \\ \hline 2 \end{array} \uparrow \; 7, 8, 9$$

1.
$$\begin{array}{r} 10 \\ -\ 2 \\ \hline \end{array} \qquad \begin{array}{r} 9 \\ -7 \\ \hline \end{array} \qquad \begin{array}{r} 12 \\ -\ 6 \\ \hline \end{array} \qquad \begin{array}{r} 7 \\ -5 \\ \hline \end{array}$$

2.
$$\begin{array}{r} 8 \\ -3 \\ \hline \end{array} \quad \begin{array}{r} 8 \\ -6 \\ \hline \end{array} \quad \begin{array}{r} 10 \\ -\ 5 \\ \hline \end{array} \quad \begin{array}{r} 11 \\ -\ 9 \\ \hline \end{array} \quad \begin{array}{r} 9 \\ -2 \\ \hline \end{array} \quad \begin{array}{r} 9 \\ -6 \\ \hline \end{array}$$

3.
$$\begin{array}{r} 9 \\ -8 \\ \hline \end{array} \quad \begin{array}{r} 11 \\ -\ 2 \\ \hline \end{array} \quad \begin{array}{r} 8 \\ -2 \\ \hline \end{array} \quad \begin{array}{r} 9 \\ -7 \\ \hline \end{array} \quad \begin{array}{r} 12 \\ -\ 3 \\ \hline \end{array} \quad \begin{array}{r} 8 \\ -7 \\ \hline \end{array}$$

4.
$$\begin{array}{r} 8 \\ -4 \\ \hline \end{array} \quad \begin{array}{r} 11 \\ -\ 8 \\ \hline \end{array} \quad \begin{array}{r} 10 \\ -\ 4 \\ \hline \end{array} \quad \begin{array}{r} 6 \\ -4 \\ \hline \end{array} \quad \begin{array}{r} 10 \\ -\ 3 \\ \hline \end{array} \quad \begin{array}{r} 12 \\ -\ 9 \\ \hline \end{array}$$

PROBLEM SOLVING

5. Tell one way to make the numbers
the same. Use counters to help.

Ty has 6 rattles.　　　　　Rashunda has 2 rattles.

Ty gives _____ rattles to Rashunda.

Fact Practice

Subtract. Then color.

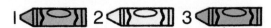

1 ◁⦿▷ 2 ◁⦿▷ 3 ◁⦿▷

4 ◀⦿▶

5 ◁⦿▶

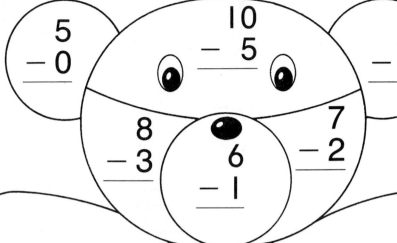

$5 - 0$

$\begin{array}{r} 10 \\ -\ 5 \\ \hline \end{array}$

$\begin{array}{r} 9 \\ -\ 4 \\ \hline \end{array}$

$\begin{array}{r} 8 \\ -\ 3 \\ \hline \end{array}$

$\begin{array}{r} 6 \\ -\ 1 \\ \hline \end{array}$

$\begin{array}{r} 7 \\ -\ 2 \\ \hline \end{array}$

$9 - 7 = \underline{\hspace{1cm}}$ $5 - 3 = \underline{\hspace{1cm}}$ $8 - 6 = \underline{\hspace{1cm}}$

$9 - 8 = \underline{\hspace{1cm}}$

$12 - 9 = \underline{\hspace{1cm}}$

$\begin{array}{r} 8 \\ -\ 5 \\ \hline \end{array}$

$\begin{array}{r} 10 \\ -\ 6 \\ \hline \end{array}$

$\begin{array}{r} 11 \\ -\ 8 \\ \hline \end{array}$

$\begin{array}{r} 8 \\ -\ 4 \\ \hline \end{array}$

$\begin{array}{r} 9 \\ -\ 6 \\ \hline \end{array}$

$3 - 2 = \underline{\hspace{1cm}}$ $6 - 5 = \underline{\hspace{1cm}}$

$6 - 1 = \underline{\hspace{1cm}}$ $5 - 0 = \underline{\hspace{1cm}}$

Ring the ways that make the answer.

1. **3**

(11 − 8)
(9 − 6)
8 − 5
9 − 5
12 − 9

2. **4**

8 − 4
9 − 5
7 − 3
10 − 6
6 − 3

3. **9**

11 − 2
12 − 6
10 − 2
12 − 3
10 − 1

POWER PRACTICE/QUIZ

Subtract. Cross out to show
what you take away.

1.

$$\begin{array}{r} 9 \\ -\ 4 \\ \hline \end{array}$$
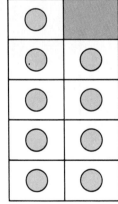

$$\begin{array}{r} 10 \\ -\ 8 \\ \hline \end{array}$$
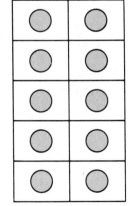

$$\begin{array}{r} 9 \\ -\ 5 \\ \hline \end{array}$$

Ring the count-up facts.
Then subtract all.

2.

$$\begin{array}{r} 11 \\ -\ 9 \\ \hline \end{array}$$
$$\begin{array}{r} 10 \\ -\ 4 \\ \hline \end{array}$$
$$\begin{array}{r} 8 \\ -\ 6 \\ \hline \end{array}$$
$$\begin{array}{r} 9 \\ -\ 2 \\ \hline \end{array}$$
$$\begin{array}{r} 7 \\ -\ 5 \\ \hline \end{array}$$
$$\begin{array}{r} 10 \\ -\ 3 \\ \hline \end{array}$$

Adding to Check Subtraction

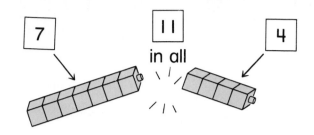

7   11 in all   4

add-to-check fact

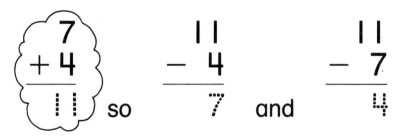

$$\begin{array}{r} 7 \\ + 4 \\ \hline 11 \end{array}$$ so $$\begin{array}{r} 11 \\ - 4 \\ \hline 7 \end{array}$$ and $$\begin{array}{r} 11 \\ - 7 \\ \hline 4 \end{array}$$

Finish the add-to-check fact.
Use cubes to help. Then subtract.

1. $$\begin{array}{r} 5 \\ + 7 \\ \hline \end{array}$$ $$\begin{array}{r} 12 \\ - 7 \\ \hline \end{array}$$ and $$\begin{array}{r} 12 \\ - 5 \\ \hline \end{array}$$

2. $$\begin{array}{r} 6 \\ + 5 \\ \hline \end{array}$$ $$\begin{array}{r} 11 \\ - 5 \\ \hline \end{array}$$ and $$\begin{array}{r} 11 \\ - 6 \\ \hline \end{array}$$

3. $$\begin{array}{r} 4 \\ + 7 \\ \hline \end{array}$$ $$\begin{array}{r} 11 \\ - 4 \\ \hline \end{array}$$ and $$\begin{array}{r} 11 \\ - 7 \\ \hline \end{array}$$

4. $$\begin{array}{r} 9 \\ + 3 \\ \hline \end{array}$$ $$\begin{array}{r} 12 \\ - 3 \\ \hline \end{array}$$ and $$\begin{array}{r} 12 \\ - 9 \\ \hline \end{array}$$

5. $$\begin{array}{r} 4 \\ + 5 \\ \hline \end{array}$$ $$\begin{array}{r} 9 \\ - 5 \\ \hline \end{array}$$ and $$\begin{array}{r} 9 \\ - 4 \\ \hline \end{array}$$

6. $$\begin{array}{r} 8 \\ + 4 \\ \hline \end{array}$$ $$\begin{array}{r} 12 \\ - 4 \\ \hline \end{array}$$ and $$\begin{array}{r} 12 \\ - 8 \\ \hline \end{array}$$

Subtract. Finish the add-to-check fact.

1.

12	4
− 4	+ 8
8	12

9	5
− 5	+

10	6
− 6	+

2.

11	5
− 5	+

12	9
− 9	+

11	7
− 7	+

3.

12	5
− 5	+

12	8
− 8	+

11	6
− 6	+

SHOW WITH CUBES

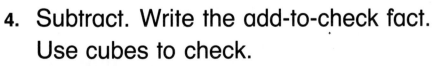

4. Subtract. Write the add-to-check fact.
Use cubes to check.

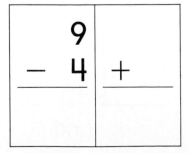

9	
− 4	+

11	
− 8	+

12	
− 4	+

Name

Fact Families

Work in a group. Use 12 cubes of one color and 12 cubes of another color. Show fact families. Make a train. Snap it.

Finish the number sentences.

1. Make a fact family with 12.

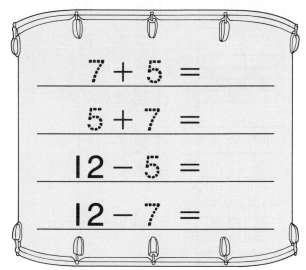

$$7 + 5 =$$
$$5 + 7 =$$
$$12 - 5 =$$
$$12 - 7 =$$

2. Make a fact family with 11.

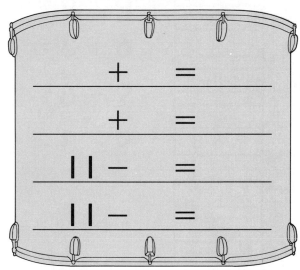

$$+ \quad =$$
$$+ \quad =$$
$$11 - \quad =$$
$$11 - \quad =$$

3. Make a different fact family with 12.

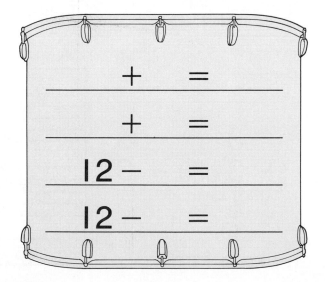

$$+ \quad =$$
$$+ \quad =$$
$$12 - \quad =$$
$$12 - \quad =$$

4. Make a different fact family with 11.

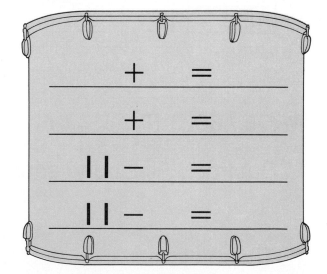

$$+ \quad =$$
$$+ \quad =$$
$$11 - \quad =$$
$$11 - \quad =$$

Make a fact family. Add or subtract.

1.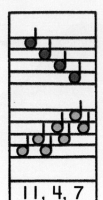
11, 4, 7

$4 + 7 = \underline{\quad}$

$7 + 4 = \underline{\quad}$

$11 - 7 = \underline{\quad}$

$11 - 4 = \underline{\quad}$

2.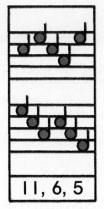
11, 6, 5

$5 + 6 = \underline{\quad}$

$6 + 5 = \underline{\quad}$

$11 - 6 = \underline{\quad}$

$11 - 5 = \underline{\quad}$

3.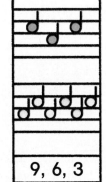
9, 6, 3

$3 + 6 = \underline{\quad}$

$6 + 3 = \underline{\quad}$

$9 - 6 = \underline{\quad}$

$9 - 3 = \underline{\quad}$

4.
12, 7, 5

$5 + 7 = \underline{\quad}$

$7 + 5 = \underline{\quad}$

$12 - 7 = \underline{\quad}$

$12 - 5 = \underline{\quad}$

5.
12, 8, 4

$4 + 8 = \underline{\quad}$

$8 + 4 = \underline{\quad}$

$12 - \underline{\quad} = \underline{\quad}$

$12 - \underline{\quad} = \underline{\quad}$

6.
9, 5, 4

$4 + 5 = \underline{\quad}$

$5 + 4 = \underline{\quad}$

$9 - \underline{\quad} = \underline{\quad}$

$9 - \underline{\quad} = \underline{\quad}$

WRITE ABOUT IT

7. Subtract. Finish the sentence.

$$\begin{array}{r} 3 \\ + 3 \\ \hline \end{array} \text{ and } \begin{array}{r} 6 \\ - 3 \\ \hline 6 \end{array}$$

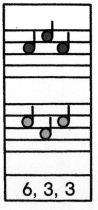
6, 3, 3

These two _____ make a family.

Name _____

Fact Practice

Check Percy Penguin's work.
If correct, write **C**. If not, cross out
and write the answer.

Start.
↓

1. $3 - 3 =$ ~~6~~   [O]

2. $8 - 4 = 4$ [C]

3. $11 - 9 = 2$ [ ]

4. $8 - 3 = 6$ [ ]

5. $9 - 6 = 3$ [ ]

6. $12 - 9 = 3$ [ ]

7. $9 - 7 = 4$ [ ]

8. $11 - 8 = 3$ [ ]

9. $9 - 5 = 4$ [ ]

10. $10 - 8 = 3$ [ ]

11. $8 - 6 = 2$ [ ]

12. $10 - 3 = 7$ [ ]

13.

$$\begin{array}{r} 9 \\ -4 \\ \hline 5 \end{array}$$
[C]

$$\begin{array}{r} 8 \\ -5 \\ \hline \not2 \end{array}$$
[3]

$$\begin{array}{r} 9 \\ -2 \\ \hline 6 \end{array}$$
[ ]

$$\begin{array}{r} 2 \\ -2 \\ \hline 0 \end{array}$$
[ ]

$$\begin{array}{r} 9 \\ -3 \\ \hline 6 \end{array}$$
[ ]

$$\begin{array}{r} 6 \\ -1 \\ \hline 4 \end{array}$$
[ ]

14. The smallest difference on the page is _____ .

Subtract. Finish the add-to-check fact.

1.

10 − 4 6	4 + 6 10

11 − 8	8 +

9 − 6	6 +

2.

12 − 9	9 +

9 − 5	5 +

10 − 7	7 +

3.

8 − 6	6 +

10 − 2	2 +

7 − 4	4 +

MIXED REVIEW

Add.

4.

$$\begin{array}{r} 4 \\ 0 \\ +3 \\ \hline \end{array} \qquad \begin{array}{r} 5 \\ 1 \\ +5 \\ \hline \end{array} \qquad \begin{array}{r} 2 \\ 2 \\ +3 \\ \hline \end{array} \qquad \begin{array}{r} 6 \\ 6 \\ +0 \\ \hline \end{array} \qquad \begin{array}{r} 3 \\ 1 \\ +3 \\ \hline \end{array} \qquad \begin{array}{r} 4 \\ 4 \\ +1 \\ \hline \end{array}$$

5. $6 + 4 = \underline{}$ $3 + 8 = \underline{}$ $7 + 1 = \underline{}$

6. $0 + 8 = \underline{}$ $5 + 5 = \underline{}$ $9 + 2 = \underline{}$

Name ________________________________

Problem Solving

Telling a Story

UNDERSTAND
FIND DATA
PLAN
ESTIMATE
SOLVE
CHECK

Work with a partner. Tell an addition or subtraction story. Write the number sentence.

1. 

____ ◯ ____ = ____

____ boys ____ went away. ____ boys are left.

2. 

____ ◯ ____ = ____

____ violins ____ banjos There are ____ in all.

3. 

____ ◯ ____ = ____

____ girls ____ stopped playing. ____ girls are left.

4. 

____ ◯ ____ = ____

____ bells ____ broke. ____ bells are left.

Problem Solving Strategy
Use Logical Reasoning

UNDERSTAND
FIND DATA
PLAN
ESTIMATE
SOLVE
CHECK

Find Melia.

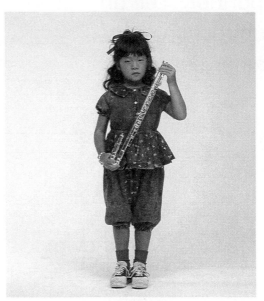

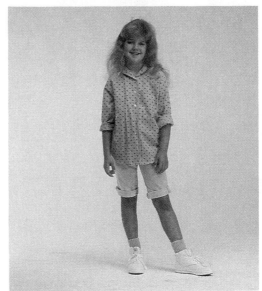

She has a .

She does not have 👓.

She has a 😊.

Ring Melia.

Name _____

WRAP UP

MATH WORDS

1. Match.

count-up fact

add-to-check fact

fact family

$$3 + 6 = 9 \qquad 9 - 3 = 6$$
$$6 + 3 = 9 \qquad 9 - 6 = 3$$

$$12 - 9 = 3$$

$$11 - 6 = 5 \qquad 5 + 6 = 11$$

MATH REASONING

Fill in the blanks. Use the numbers and the ⊞ and ⊟. Use each as many times as you need to.

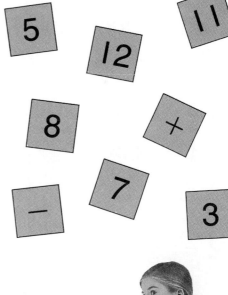

2.
$$\begin{array}{r} 7 \\ \underline{} \\ 12 \end{array} \qquad \begin{array}{r} 3 \\ \underline{} \\ 11 \end{array} \qquad \begin{array}{r} 5 \\ 8 \\ \underline{} \\ 12 \end{array} \qquad \begin{array}{r} 8 \\ \underline{} \\ 11 \end{array}$$

3.
$$\begin{array}{r} 8 \\ \underline{} \\ 3 \end{array} \qquad \begin{array}{r} 11 \\ \underline{} \\ 8 \end{array} \qquad \begin{array}{r} 5 \\ \underline{} \\ 7 \end{array} \qquad \begin{array}{r} 12 \\ \underline{} \\ 5 \end{array}$$

POWER PRACTICE/TEST

Subtract. Cross out to show
what you take away.

1.
  10
  − 7
  ‾‾‾‾

  9
  − 5
  ‾‾‾‾

  9
  − 4
  ‾‾‾‾

2. Ring the count-up facts.
    Then subtract all.

  7   10   9   7   11   8
  − 3   − 8   − 7   − 0   − 9   − 3
  ‾‾‾   ‾‾‾   ‾‾‾   ‾‾‾   ‾‾‾   ‾‾‾

Finish the fact family.
Add or subtract.

3. 4 + 8 = ____
    8 + 4 = ____
    12 − ___ = ___
    12 − ___ = ___

4. 6 + 5 = ____
    5 + 6 = ____
    11 − ___ = ___
    11 − ___ = ___

5. 7 + 4 = ____
    4 + 7 = ____
    11 − ___ = ___
    11 − ___ = ___

6. Suki saw 7 clowns. 3 clowns
    ran away. How many clowns
    are there now?

    ____ clowns

Finish the number
sentence.

____ ◯ ____ = ____

Name _____

ENRICHMENT
Finding All Ways

Mrs. Chen used blue, yellow, and red paint
for art class. She asked Alex to put the paint
back on the shelf after class. Color to show
all the different ways Alex could put the
paint back. Use cubes to help.

1.
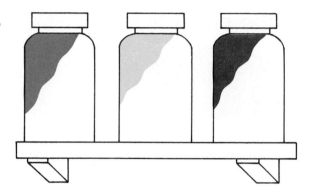

2.
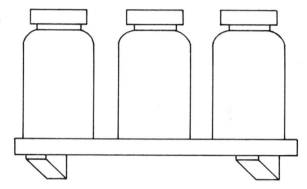

3.
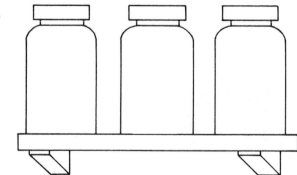

4.
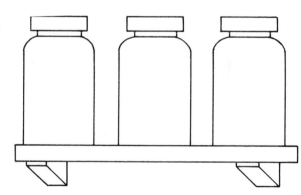

5.
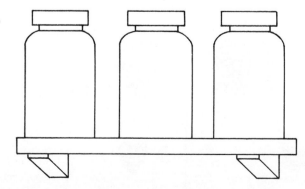

6.
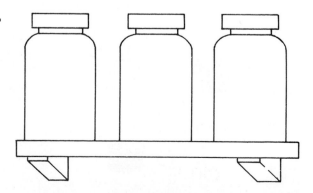

CUMULATIVE REVIEW

Subtract.

1.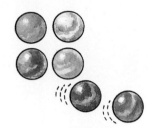

$$\begin{array}{r} 6 \\ -2 \\ \hline \end{array}$$

○ 4
○ 5
○ 3

2.

$$\begin{array}{r} 10 \\ -\ 5 \\ \hline \end{array}$$

○ 6
○ 4
○ 5

3. $$\begin{array}{r} 9 \\ -0 \\ \hline \end{array}$$

○ 8
○ 9
○ 0

4. Find the add-to-check fact for $7 - 3 = 4$.

○ $4 + 3 = 7$
○ $4 - 3 = 1$
○ $4 + 4 = 8$

5. Match the shape.

○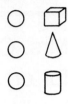
○ △
○ ⬭

6. Match the flat face to the plane figure.

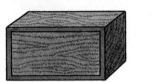

○ □
○ △
○ ▭

7. Find how many corners.

○ 5
○ 7
○ 6

8. Match the shape.

○
○ ◯
○ ◺
○ ⬭

9. Choose the toy that comes next in Meg's pattern.

○   ○   ○

11

Place Value

Workmat

Theme: Toy Factory

Grouping by Tens

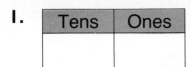

Take a pile of cubes.
Make trains of 10 cubes.
Write how many tens and extra ones.

1.

Tens	Ones

2.

Tens	Ones

3.

Tens	Ones

4.

Tens	Ones

5.

Tens	Ones

Ring groups of tens.
Write how many tens and ones.

6.

Tens	Ones
4	3

7.

Tens	Ones

USE MENTAL MATH

8. How many fingers do you have?

_____ fingers

9. How many fingers do 3 friends have?

_____ fingers

10. How many fingers do 6 people have?

_____ fingers

Showing Tens and Ones

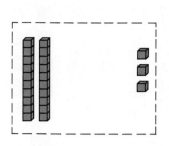

Paste.

I see 2 ▮ and 3 ▱.

Tens	Ones
2	3

Use the tens and ones punchouts.
Place them to show the tens and ones.
☑ if correct. Then paste.

1.

Tens	Ones	
2	6	

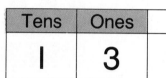

Paste here.

2.

Tens	Ones	
1	3	

Paste here.

3.

Tens	Ones	
6	1	

Paste here.

4.

Tens	Ones	
3	2	

Paste here.

5.

Tens	Ones	
4	5	

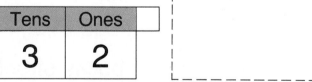

Paste here.

6.

Tens	Ones	
5	4	

Paste here.

Ring to show the tens and ones.
Count. Then ☑ if correct.

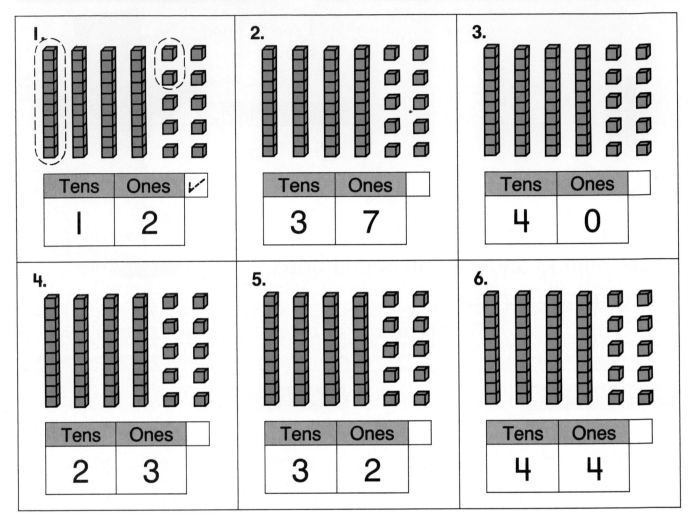

1.	Tens	Ones	✓
	1	2	

2.	Tens	Ones	
	3	7	

3.	Tens	Ones	
	4	0	

4.	Tens	Ones	
	2	3	

5.	Tens	Ones	
	3	2	

6.	Tens	Ones	
	4	4	

FIND THE DATA

Data Bank (See page 398.)

7. How many ten-packs of soldiers are there? How many extras are there? Write the numbers in the box.

Tens	Ones

8. How many ten-packs of bowling pins are there? How many extras are there? Write the numbers in the box.

Tens	Ones

Decade Numbers and Names

1. Cut out the number cards.
Put a card in the box. Use
blocks to show the number.

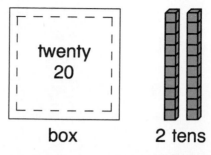

box   2 tens

First Card	Second Card	Third Card

2. Put all the cards in order on the
train. Count. Then paste.

| ten 10 |
| twenty 20 |
| thirty 30 |
| forty 40 |
| fifty 50 |
| sixty 6C |
| seventy 70 |
| eighty 80 |
| ninety 90 |

ten	10
twenty	20
thirty	30
forty	40
fifty	50
sixty	60
seventy	70
eighty	80
ninety	90

1. Write the tens.

Write the number that tells how many.

2. 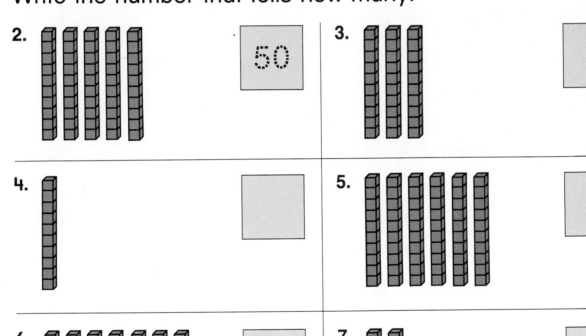 50

3.

4.

5.

6.

7.

8.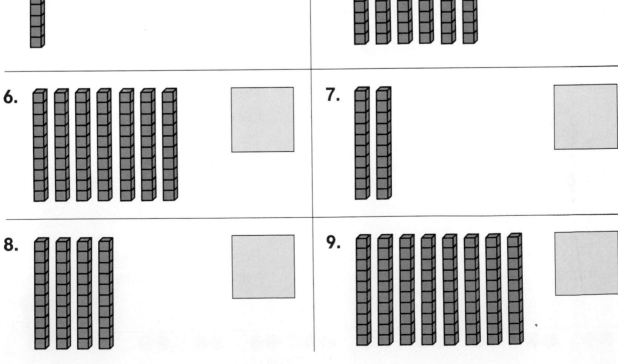

9.

Showing and Writing 2-Digit Numbers

Write 43.

43

Count the tens and ones.
Use blocks to help. Write the number.

1.

2.

3.

4.

5.

6.

7.
100

Ring the tens and ones
to show how many. Count.
Then ✔ if correct.

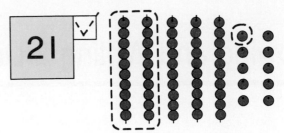

1. 49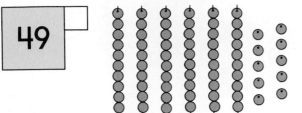

2. 31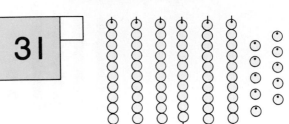

3. 26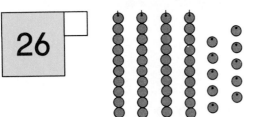

4. 65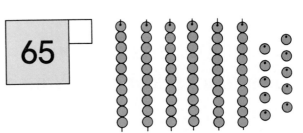

POWER PRACTICE/QUIZ

1. Ring the tens and ones
to show how many.

Tens	Ones
3	4

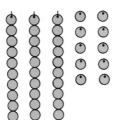

2. Ring groups of ten. Write
how many tens and ones.

Tens	Ones

Write the number that tells how many.

3.  ▢

4.  ▢

Chapter 11

Tens and Ones

Work in a group. Use blocks.
Spin and show a number of tens.
Write it. Spin and show a number
of ones. Write it. Then ring
and write how many.

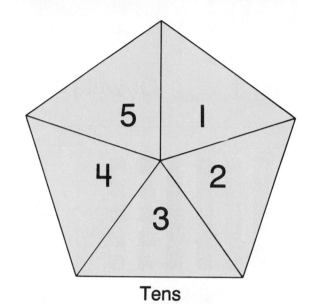

Tens

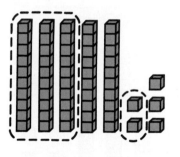 Ring it.

Tens	Ones
3	2

Write it.

Write how many.

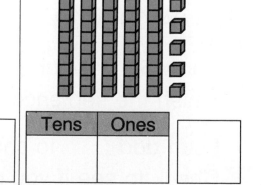

Ones

1.

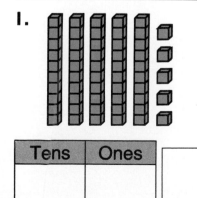

Tens	Ones	

2.

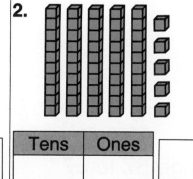

Tens	Ones	

3.

Tens	Ones	

Fill in what is missing.

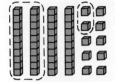

Ring it.

Tens	Ones
2	2

Or write it.

Or write how many.

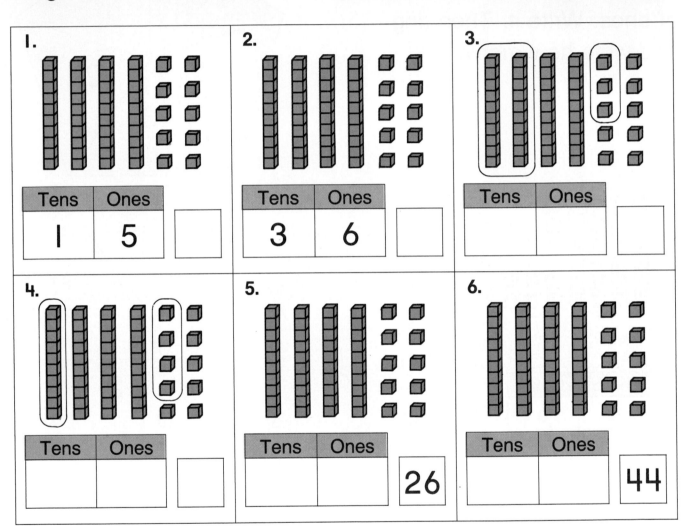

1.

Tens	Ones	
1	5	

2.

Tens	Ones	
3	6	

3.

Tens	Ones	

4.

Tens	Ones	

5.

Tens	Ones	
		26

6.

Tens	Ones	
		44

TRY A CALCULATOR

7. Show 57 on your 🖩 .
Finish the sentence.

I can add _____ to change 57 to 67.
Check to see if you are right.

Name _____

Problem Solving
Understanding the Operations

UNDERSTAND
FIND DATA
PLAN
ESTIMATE
SOLVE
CHECK

Listen to the story. Color the tens.
Finish the number sentence.
Then write the answer.

1. How many blue and
black pens are there?

4 tens 2 tens = ____ tens   ____ pens

2. How many more blue than
black pens are there?

       ▢ ▢

5 tens 4 tens = ____ ten   ____ pens

3. How many blue and
black pens are there?

       ▢ ▢

7 tens 2 tens = ____ tens   ____ pens

Informal Algebra

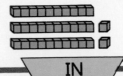

Think about the
packing machine.
Write how many
in each box.

Put in 3 tens and 2 ones.
Out comes a box of 32.

IN

Packing Machine

OUT

32 blocks

1.

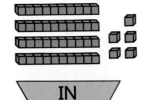

IN

Packing Machine

OUT

blocks

2.

IN

Packing Machine

OUT

blocks

3.

IN

Packing Machine

OUT

blocks

Think about the unpacking machine.
Draw the tens and ones.

4.

13 blocks

IN

Unpacking Machine

OUT

5.

24 blocks

IN

Unpacking Machine

OUT

6.

43 blocks

IN

Unpacking Machine

OUT

Name _____

Trading Dimes and Pennies

Show 13 pennies.	Trade for a dime.	Write it.

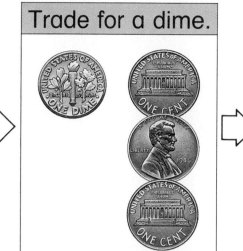

Dimes	Pennies
1	3

Trade 10 pennies for 1 dime.

Work in a group. Use your penny
and dime punchouts. Show the pennies.
Trade for dimes. Write it.

1. Show.   Write it.

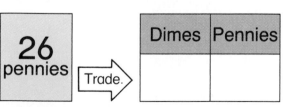

26 pennies   Trade.

Dimes	Pennies

2. Show.   Write it.

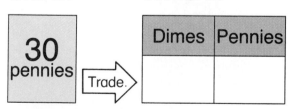

30 pennies   Trade.

Dimes	Pennies

3. Show.   Write it.

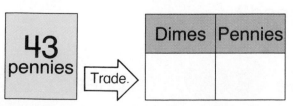

43 pennies   Trade.

Dimes	Pennies

4. Show.   Write it.

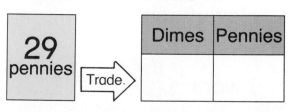

29 pennies   Trade.

Dimes	Pennies

Trade pennies for dimes.
Color enough dimes.
Color enough pennies.
Write how many.

I traded 70 pennies for 7 dimes. I had 3 pennies left over.

1.

73 pennies

Dimes	Pennies
7	3

2.

52 pennies

Dimes	Pennies

3.

25 pennies

Dimes	Pennies

4.

40 pennies

Dimes	Pennies

PROBLEM SOLVING

5. How much more money do I need?

I want 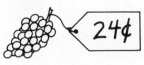 24¢.   I have .   I need ___ ¢.

Dimes and Pennies

Work in a group. Use your coin punchouts. Spin and show a number of dimes. Write it. Spin and show a number of pennies. Write it. Then write how much money.

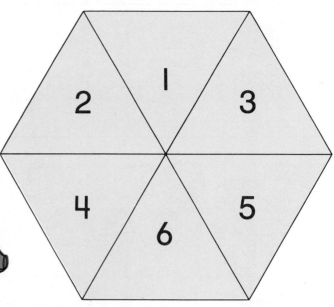

Dimes	Pennies
6	3

Write it.   Write how much money.

1.

Dimes	Pennies

2.

Dimes	Pennies

3.

Dimes	Pennies

4.

Dimes	Pennies

What did you spin?

5. Write the largest amount.

6. Write the smallest amount.

Show how much money.
Color  enough dimes.
Color  enough pennies.

21¢

1.

29¢

2.

12¢

3.

53¢

MIXED REVIEW

4. Add.

4	2	0	6	6	3
+5	+8	+5	+3	+6	+7

5. Subtract.

9	11	7	8	12	10
−5	−9	−5	−4	−3	−6

240   (two hundred forty)   More Practice, page 423, set B   Chapter 11

Problem Solving
Making Estimates

Listen to the story.
Without counting, tell about how many.
Ring your estimate.
Ring tens to check.

1.

About how many
strawberries are there?

10   30   70   100

2.

About how many pears
are there?

10   20   80   100

3.

About how many oranges
are there?

10   30   70   100

4.

About how many grapes
are there?

10   30   50   100

5.

About how many pieces of fruit are there?

10   50   100   200

UNDERSTAND
FIND DATA
PLAN
ESTIMATE
SOLVE
CHECK

Problem Solving Strategy
Make a List

UNDERSTAND
FIND DATA
PLAN
ESTIMATE
SOLVE
CHECK

Use 2 tens and 3 ones blocks.
Draw and write to show the
2-digit numbers you can make.

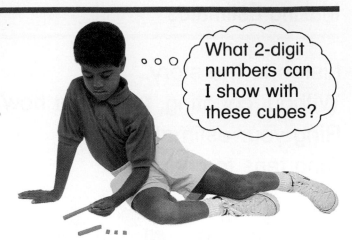

What 2-digit numbers can I show with these cubes?

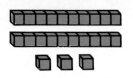

Draw.	Write.
	11

Draw.	Write.

Draw.	Write.

Draw.	Write.

Draw.	Write.

Draw.	Write.

Draw.	Write.

Draw.	Write.

Wrap Up

MATH WORDS

Ring what belongs. Tell why.

1.   seventeen   17

Tens	Ones
1	8

2. forty

Tens	Ones
4	0

3. 35

Tens	Ones
5	3

thirty-five

4. 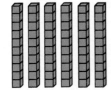   6 tens   61   sixty

MATH REASONING

5. Use three dime and three penny punchouts. Take three coins at a time. Find different sums each time. Fill in the chart.

Number of Dimes	Number of Pennies	Money in All
0	3	
1		

Name _____

POWER PRACTICE/TEST

Ring groups of ten. Write
how many tens and ones.

1.

Tens	Ones

2.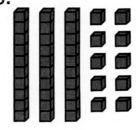

Tens	Ones

3. Ring to show the
tens and ones.

Tens	Ones
2	7

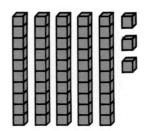

4. Write the number.

5. Trade pennies for dimes.
Write how much money.

Dimes	Pennies

6. Color enough dimes and
pennies to buy the toy.

7. Finish the number sentence.
How many more than are there?

5 tens $\bigcirc$ 3 tens = _____ tens   _____

ENRICHMENT
Temperature

Cold Day

Warm Day

Hot Day

Match each picture to its temperature.

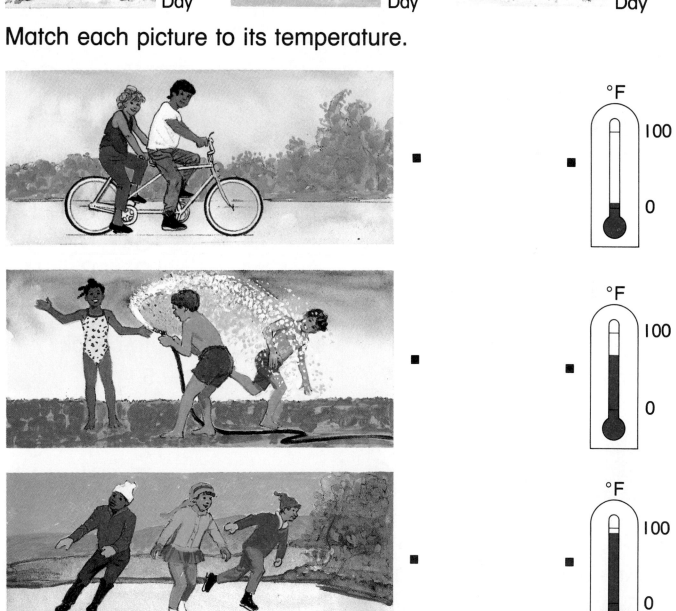

Name _____

CUMULATIVE REVIEW

1. Match the shape.

○ ○
○ △
○ □

2. Find how many sides.

○ 5
○ 6
○ 4

3. Find how many pegs are inside.

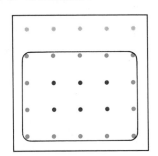

○ 5
○ 6
○ 14

4. Which shape is divided into two matching parts?

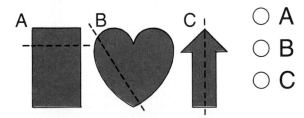

○ A
○ B
○ C

Subtract.

5. $9 - 3 = $ _____

○ 5
○ 6
○ 7

6. $\begin{array}{r} 11 \\ -8 \\ \hline \end{array}$

○ 2
○ 4
○ 3

7. Find a fact in the same family as $8 + 4 = 12$.

○ $7 + 5 = 12$
○ $8 - 4 = 4$
○ $12 - 8 = 4$

8. Find the add-to-check fact for $12 - 5 = 7$.

○ $7 + 5 = 12$
○ $12 - 7 = 5$
○ $7 + 4 = 11$

9. Choose the correct number sentence. Kris had 9 pens. She gave 5 away. How many pens are left?

○ $9 - 5 = 4$

○ $9 - 4 = 5$

○ $4 + 5 = 9$

Chapter 11   Cumulative Review

12
Number Relationships and Counting Patterns

Workmat

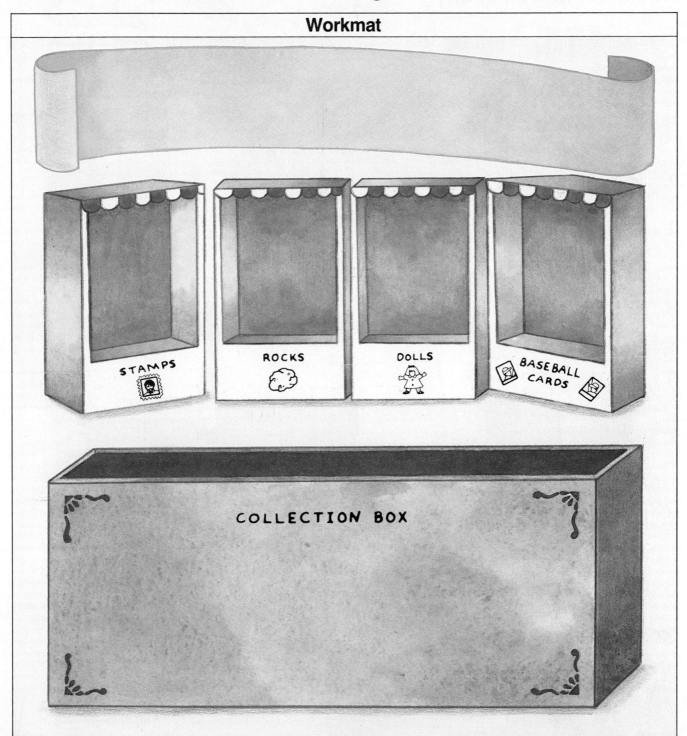

STAMPS

ROCKS

DOLLS

BASEBALL CARDS

COLLECTION BOX

Theme: Collections

Name

Counting to 50

One more than 19 makes another ten. That's 2 tens or 20.

Work in a group. Use blocks to show the number. Put in 1 more block. Write how many.

1.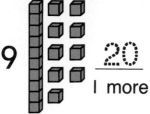

19   *20*   _____   _____   _____   _____   _____

1 more   1 more   1 more   1 more   1 more   1 more

2. 27   _____ _____ _____ _____ _____ _____

3. 34   _____ _____ _____ _____ _____ _____

Count. Write how many.

4. 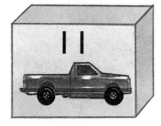 11   

12   _____   _____

5.  27   

_____   _____   _____

USE MENTAL MATH

Count on 2 more.

30, 2 more is 31, 32.

6. | Start 30 | →2 more | |

7. | Start 42 | →2 more | |

Name _____

Counting On and Back

Work in a group. Spin a tens number. Write it.
Spin a ones number. Write it.
Count on and back. Write the numbers.

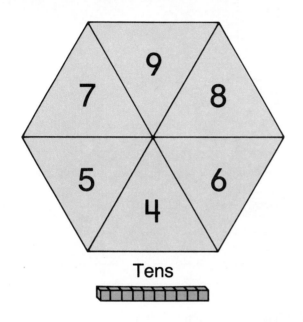

Tens

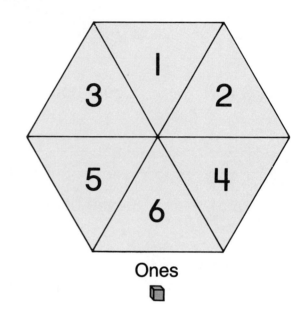

Ones

1. ⬅ Count back.

Tens	Ones
6	4

Count on. ➡

_61_ , _62_ , _63_ , _65_ , _66_ , _67_

2. ⬅ Count back.

Tens	Ones

Count on. ➡

_____ , _____ , _____ , _____ , _____ , _____

3. ⬅ Count back.

Tens	Ones

Count on. ➡

_____ , _____ , _____ , _____ , _____ , _____

4. ⬅ Count back.

Tens	Ones

Count on. ➡

_____ , _____ , _____ , _____ , _____ , _____

Count on and back. Write the numbers.

1. ← Count back. | Tens | Ones | Count on. →

_____ , _____ , *67* ,

Tens	Ones
6	8

, *69* , _____ , _____

---

2. ← Count back. | Tens | Ones | Count on. →

_____ , _____ , _____ ,

Tens	Ones
5	1

, _____ , _____ , _____

---

3. ← Count back. | Tens | Ones | Count on. →

_____ , _____ , _____ ,

Tens	Ones
8	2

, _____ , _____ , _____

---

4. ← Count back. | Tens | Ones | Count on. →

_____ , _____ , _____ ,

Tens	Ones
2	4

, _____ , _____ , _____

---

5. Check by counting. Start with the smallest number in each row.

PROBLEM SOLVING

How many do I have in all?

6. I had

26

I bought

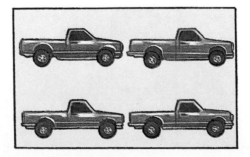

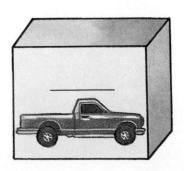

_____

Numbers Before, After, Between

Work in a group. Use blocks. Show the red number. Put in 1 more ones block. Write the number. Show the blue number. Take away 1 ones block. Write the number. Then write the number between.

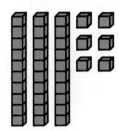   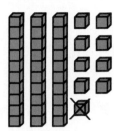

Between

1. 35 Put in 1 more. → 36 ☐ 3̶8̶ Take away 1. ← 39

2. 21 Put in 1 more. → ☐ ☐ ☐ Take away 1. ← 25

3. 38 Put in 1 more. → ☐ ☐ ☐ Take away 1. ← 42

4. 24 Put in 1 more. → ☐ ☐ ☐ Take away 1. ← 28

Write the number that comes after.

6 ones,
I more is 7.

Think
I more 🔲.

1. | 46 | 47 |

2. | 39 | |

3. | 96 | |

4. | 14 | |

5. | 59 | |

Write the number that comes before.

6 ones,
I less is 5.

Think
I less 🔲.

6. | 35 | 36 |

7. | | 58 |

8. | | 88 |

9. | | 63 |

10. | | 70 |

Write the number that comes between.

Think I more
or I less.

11. | 25 | | 27 |

12. | 96 | | 98 |

13. | 13 | | 15 |

14. | 78 | | 80 |

Comparing Numbers

The one with more tens has more.

The tens are the same. Look at the ones.

Work with a partner. Use blocks to show the tens. ✔ if the tens are the same. Use blocks to show the ones. Color the box that has more. Take turns saying which has more.

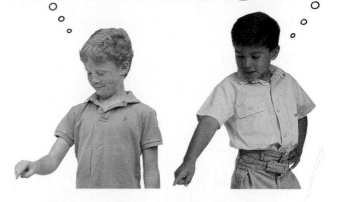

1. 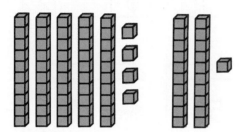 54   21 ☐

2. 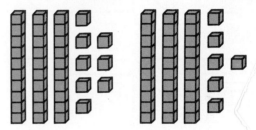 38   36 ✔

3. 51   50 ☐

4. 50   40 ☐

5. 33   53 ☐

6. 41   42 ☐

7. 31   35 ☐

8. 84   91 ☐

Work with a partner.
☑ if the tens are the same.
Color the box that has fewer.
Take turns saying which
has fewer.

The tens are the same. Look at the ones. 2 ones is less than 4 ones.

1.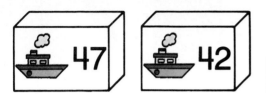

2.

3. 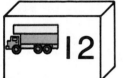  ☐

4.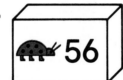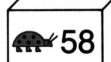

POWER PRACTICE/QUIZ

1. Write the missing numbers.

| 41 | | 43 | 44 | | 46 | | 48 | 49 | |

2. Count on and back. Write the numbers.

⬅ Count back. | Tens | Ones | Count on. ➡
                | 2 | 2 |

___ , ___ , ___ ,   , ___ , ___ , ___

3. Write the number that comes before.

___ , 60

4. Write the number that comes between.

39, ___ , 41

Name _____

Problem Solving
Understanding the Operations

Ten cards
in each pack.

UNDERSTAND
FIND DATA
PLAN
ESTIMATE
SOLVE
CHECK

Listen to the story.
Color the plant cards green.
Color the animal cards brown.
Finish the number sentence.

1. How many more animal
   than plant cards are there?

   5 tens $\bigcirc$ I ten = _____ tens

   _____ more animal cards

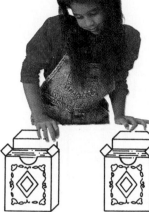

2. How many more animal than
   plant cards are there?

   4 tens $\bigcirc$ 2 tens = _____ tens

   _____ more animal cards

3. How many more plant than
   animal cards are there?

   5 tens $\bigcirc$ 2 tens = _____ tens

   _____ more plant cards

Calculator

Count with your calculator. Then write the number. Press ON/C to start each time.

1. Start with [1]. Press [+] [1] [=].

   Then press [=] [=] [=] [Keep on going.]

   I counted to

2. Start with [10]. Press [+] [10] [=].

   Then press [=] [=] [=] [Keep on going.]

   I counted to

3. Start with [3]. Press [+] [10] [=].

   Then press [=] [=] [=] [Keep on going.]

   I counted to

4. Pick a number. [ ] Press [+] [10] [=].

   Then press [=] [=] [=] [Keep on going.]

   I counted to

Name _____

Counting Patterns for 10s

1. Write the missing numbers.

2. Use blocks. Start with 10. Count by 10s.
   Color as you count aloud.

1	2	3	4		6	7		9	10
11	12		14	15	16		18	19	20
21		23	24	25		27	28	29	
31	32		34	35	36	37		39	40
41	42	43		45	46	47	48		50
	52	53	54		56	57	58	59	60
61		63	64	65	66		68	69	70
71	72	73		75	76	77	78	79	
81	82	83	84	85		87	88		90
91	92		94		96	97		99	100

3. Work with a partner.
   Use your ladder punchout.
   Put the ladder on some numbers in the chart.
   Count the numbers you see. Try again.

Start at the top of the ladder. Write as you count aloud ten more.

Add I more ten. The ones stay the same.

1.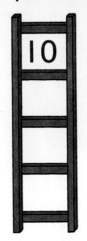
10

2.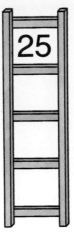
25

3.
36

4.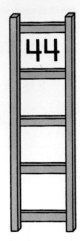
44

5.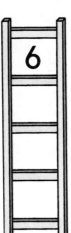
6

6.
43

7.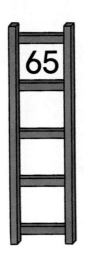
65

8.
59

MIXED REVIEW

9. Write how much.

 _____ ¢

 _____ ¢

 _____ ¢

10. Add. Ring sums of 10¢.

5¢	4¢	3¢	4¢	5¢	8¢
+ 5¢	+ 3¢	+ 9¢	+ 6¢	+ 6¢	+ 2¢

Name _____

Ordinal Numbers

1. Cut out the number cards.
   Put them in order on the train.
   Check by counting. Then paste.

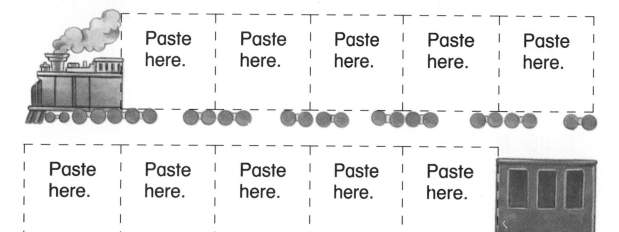

2. Count and color the trucks.

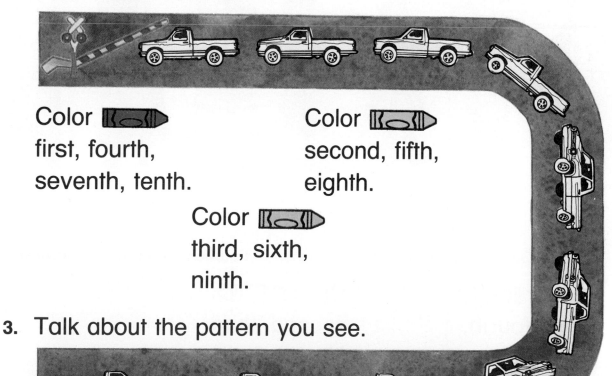

Color 🖍 first, fourth, seventh, tenth.

Color 🖍 second, fifth, eighth.

Color 🖍 third, sixth, ninth.

3. Talk about the pattern you see.

first	1st
second	2nd
third	3rd
fourth	4th
fifth	5th
sixth	6th
seventh	7th
eighth	8th
ninth	9th
tenth	10th

1. Count and color the race cars.

Color 🖍
first, third,
fifth, seventh.

Color 🖍
second, fourth,
sixth.

2. Count the dolls. Color the card for each doll.

Tlingit   Guatemalan   South African   Filipino   Peruvian   Uruguayan   Japanese

Color 🖍
...st, fourth,
...venth.

Color 🖍
second, third,
fifth, sixth.

3. Talk about the patterns you see.

Problem Solving
Finding Extra Data

UNDERSTAND
FIND DATA
PLAN
ESTIMATE
SOLVE
CHECK

Write the number sentence.
Underline the extra data.

1. Lisa has 4 butterflies.
   2 are blue. 3 fly away.
   How many butterflies does she have now?

   ___ ◯ ___ = ___   She has ___ butterfly.

2. Peter won 8 marbles on Monday.
   He is 7 years old. He won 10 marbles on Friday.
   How many more did he win on Friday?

   ___ ◯ ___ = ___   He won ___ more.

3. Megan has 7 acorns.
   She gives 3 to a squirrel. The squirrel eats 1.
   How many acorns does Megan have now?

   ___ ◯ ___ = ___   She has ___ acorns.

4. Eric found 6 shells.
   He found 4 rocks. He found 3 more shells.
   He gave away 2 rocks.
   How many shells does he have now?

   ___ ◯ ___ = ___   He has ___ shells.

Problem Solving Strategy
Make a Table

UNDERSTAND
FIND DATA
PLAN
ESTIMATE
SOLVE
CHECK

Finish the tables. Use the tables
to tell how much money.

My Nickel Table

Number of Nickels	1	2	3	4	5	6	7	8	9
Amount	5¢	10¢	15¢	20¢	25¢				

1.

_____

2.

_____

My Dime Table

Number of Dimes	1	2	3	4	5	6	7	8	9
Amount	10¢				50¢				

3.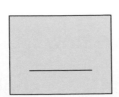

_____

4.

_____

WRAP UP

MATH WORDS

1. Match. Then write the missing numbers.

Count by 5s.   ▪

Count by 10s.   ▪

Count by 2s.   ▪

Count back.   ▪

Count on.   ▪

| ▪ | 17 | 18 | 19 | 20 | |

| ▪ | 66 | 65 | 64 | | 62 |

| ▪ | 25 | 30 | | 40 | 45 |

| ▪ | 42 | 44 | 46 | | 50 |

| ▪ | 20 | | 40 | 50 | 60 |

MATH REASONING

Read the clues. Answer the riddle.

2. I am a number between 50 and 75.
   You say me when you count by 5s.
   My tens digit is 1 more than
   my ones digit. What am I?   _____

3.

I am after the second car.
I am not the fifth car.
I am not blue. Ring me.

POWER PRACTICE/TEST

1. Write the numbers.

64		66			56	57		27	28

between   before   after

Ring the number that is less.

2. 67   76 | 3. 85   93 | 4. 33   83

5. Count by 10s.

20						

6. Count by 5s.

10						

7. Color 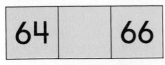 first, fifth, ninth.
Color 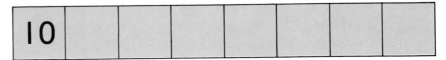 second, sixth, tenth.

8. Finish the number sentence.
Underline the extra data.

11 frogs sat on a rock.

3 ducks swam on the pond.

5 frogs hopped away.

How many frogs are left?

____ ◯ ____ = ____

____ frogs are left.

13
Money

Workmat

Theme: At the Farm

Counting Dimes and Pennies

Use coin punchouts.
Cover each coin as you count.
Write the total amount.

Count dimes first,
then pennies.

1.

_____

2.

_____

3.

_____

4.

_____

PROBLEM SOLVING

5. Sid has 4 pennies. He has just as many dimes. How much money does he have? _____

Counting Dimes, Nickels, and Pennies

Work in a group. Use your
spinner and punchout coins.
Put coins in the coin box as you
count. Spin for dimes. Count.
Spin for nickels. Count on.
Spin for pennies. Count on.

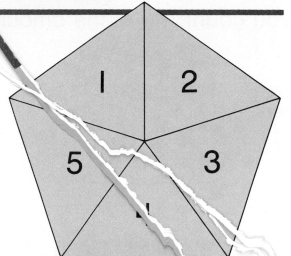

Coin Box		
Dimes	Nickels	Pennies

Write how much in all.

1. first try   _____ ¢   2. second try   _____ ¢

3. third try   _____ ¢   4. fourth try   _____ ¢

5. fifth try   _____ ¢   6. sixth try   _____ ¢

Use 4 , and 4 , and 4 punchouts. Cover each coin as you count. Write the amount.

Count dimes first, then nickels, then pennies.

1.

Start here.

17¢

2.

_____

3.

_____

4.

_____

5.

_____

6.

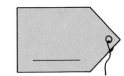

_____

FIND THE DATA

DATA BANK

7. Data Bank

Mat has

He wants a toy .

Ring the answer. (See page 399.)

He can buy it.

He cannot buy it.

Name _____

Counting and Comparing Money

Count dimes first, then nickels, then pennies.

Write the prices.
Ring the toy that costs less.

1.

10,   20,   25,   26,   27

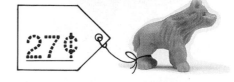
27¢

10,   20,   30,   31

_____

2.

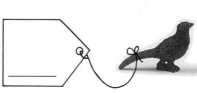

_____

_____

3.

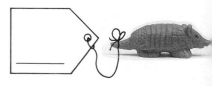

_____

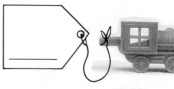

_____

Write the amounts.
Ring the one that is less.

Count dimes
first, then nickels,
then pennies.

1.

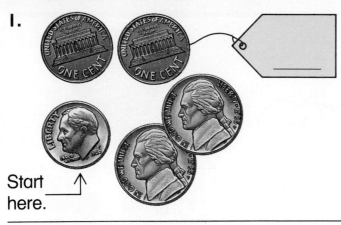

Start here. ↑

_____

_____

2.

_____

_____

POWER PRACTICE/QUIZ

Count how much.

1.

2.

_____

_____

3. Count the money. Write the amount.

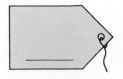

_____

_____ , _____ , _____ , _____ , _____ ,

Problem Solving
Understanding the Operations

UNDERSTAND
FIND DATA
PLAN
ESTIMATE
SOLVE
CHECK

Draw more or cross out some. Add or subtract. Then write the answers.

1. Tim had 4 nickels.
He spent 1 nickel.
How many does he have now?

   Tim has ____ nickels.

   4
   - 1

2. Shonie has 3 dimes. Flora has 2 dimes. How many dimes are there in all?

   There are ____ dimes in all.

3. Ali has 4 nickels. Jan has 2 nickels. How many more does Ali have?

   Ali has ____ more nickels.

4. Megan had 5 dimes. She gave 1 dime away. How many does she have now?

   Megan has ____ dimes.

Calculator

Work with a
partner.
Use a 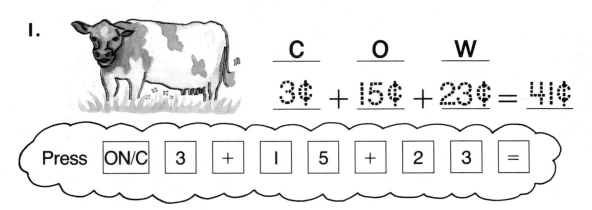. Look
at the chart. Write
the price of each
letter. Add.

Letter Prices

A	B	C	D	E	F	G	H	I	J	K	L	M
1¢	2¢	3¢	4¢	5¢	6¢	7¢	8¢	9¢	10¢	11¢	12¢	13¢

N	O	P	Q	R	S	T	U	V	W	X	Y	Z
14¢	15¢	16¢	17¢	18¢	19¢	20¢	21¢	22¢	23¢	24¢	25¢	26¢

1.

__c__ __o__ __w__

$3¢ + 15¢ + 23¢ = 41¢$

Press | ON/C | 3 | + | 1 | 5 | + | 2 | 3 | = |

2.

__p__ __i__ __g__

___ + ___ + ___ = ___

3.

__c__ __a__ __t__

___ + ___ + ___ = ___

4. Write your name. _____

Find the total price. _____

Name _____

Counting Quarters and Other Coins

I can trade for a quarter.

I can trade this way, too.

Use 1 , 2 , 3 , and
3 punchouts. Cover each coin
as you count. Write the price.

I quarter

or

25¢
25 cents

1.

__25__, __35__, _____, _____

41¢

2.

_____, _____, _____, _____

_____

3.

_____, _____, _____,

_____

Write how much is in each bank.

Count quarters first, then dimes, then nickels, then pennies.

1. _____

2. _____

3. _____

4. _____

Mixed Review

5. Count on and back.

Tens	Ones
4	2

_____ , _____ , _____ , _____ , 4 2 , _____ , _____

6. Write the number between.

79, _____ , 81

7. Ring the number that is less.

82   36

Name _____

Problem Solving
Using Data from a Newspaper Ad

| UNDERSTAND |
| FIND DATA |
| PLAN |
| ESTIMATE |
| SOLVE |
| CHECK |

PRODUCE SALE

45¢ 30¢ 41¢ 32¢ 28¢ 35¢

Count and write how much money each
person has. Is there enough to buy
what is wanted? Ring the answer.

1. Jake has ____.

He wants .

Jake can buy it.

Jake cannot buy it.

---

2. Kate has ____.

She wants .

Kate can buy it.

Kate cannot buy it.

---

3. Tom has ____.

He wants .

Tom can buy it.

Tom cannot buy it.

10¢

10¢

10¢

15¢

15¢

15¢

20¢

20¢

25¢

15¢

Problem Solving Strategy
Guess and Check

UNDERSTAND
FIND DATA
PLAN
ESTIMATE
SOLVE
CHECK

Work with a partner. Cut out the pictures. Listen to the story. Guess what each person bought. Use a [calculator] to check. Then paste.

I.

Mayumi

Mayumi spent ____.

| Paste here. | and | Paste here. | cost ____. |

2.

Kay

Kay spent ____.

| Paste here. | and | Paste here. | cost ____. |

3.

Max

Max spent ____.

| Paste here. | and | Paste here. | cost ____. |

WRAP UP

MATH WORDS

Ring what belongs. Tell why.

I.

dime  20¢ 10 pennies

2.
25 pennies 35¢ quarter

3.

5¢  nickel

MATH REASONING

4. How many of each coin do you need
to buy the object? Use the fewest
coins you can. Fill in the chart.

	Number of 🪙	Number of 🪙	Number of 🪙	Number of 🪙
🔨 41¢				
⚽ 33¢				
🚢 45¢				

Name _____

POWER PRACTICE/TEST

Count how much.

1.  _____

2.  _____

3.  _____

4.  _____

Write the prices. Ring the toy that costs less.

5.

6.

Write how much is in each bank.

7.  _____

8.  _____

9. Count and write how much money.

Emi has _____ ¢. She wants a

Ring one.

Emi can buy it.

Emi cannot buy it.

ENRICHMENT
Dollar Bill

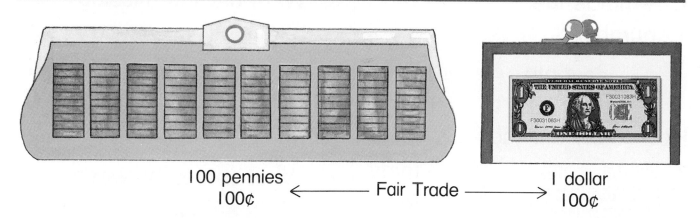

100 pennies
100¢ ←——— Fair Trade ———→ 1 dollar
100¢

Write how much money.
Is it a fair trade? Ring **yes** or **no.**

1.

_____      yes   no

2.

_____      yes   no

3.

_____      yes   no

CUMULATIVE REVIEW

1. What is the number?

seventy

- ○ 17
- ○ 70
- ○ 7

How many are there?

2.

- ○ thirty
- ○ forty
- ○ fifty

3.

- ○ 34
- ○ 23
- ○ 45

4. Count how much.

- ○ 70¢
- ○ 25¢
- ○ 52¢

5. What are the missing numbers?

46, ___, 48,
49, ___, 51

- ○ 47, 50
- ○ 49, 51
- ○ 46, 49

6. What comes between?

| 32 | | 34 |

- ○ 35
- ○ 33
- ○ 31

7. Which is greater?

- ○ 35
- ○ 55
- ○ 50

8. Count by 5s.

20, 25, 30, ___

- ○ 40
- ○ 33
- ○ 35

9. Choose the correct number sentence. How many more bird cards than cat cards are there?

- ○ 2 tens + 3 tens = 5 tens
- ○ 3 tens − 2 tens = 1 ten
- ○ 4 tens − 1 ten = 3 tens

14

Time

Theme: Clocks

Name _____

Clock Parts

Work with a partner. Use your punchout clock. Write a number for the time. Your partner shows the time on the clock. Take turns.

1. __2__ o'clock   2. _____ o'clock   3. _____ o'clock

4. _____ o'clock   5. _____ o'clock   6. _____ o'clock

Where are the hands? Write the numbers.

7.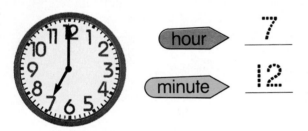

hour ▷ __7__

minute ▷ __12__

It is __7__ o'clock.

8.

hour ▷ _____

minute ▷ _____

It is _____ o'clock.

9.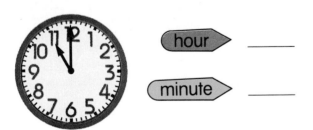

hour ▷ _____

minute ▷ _____

It is _____ o'clock.

10.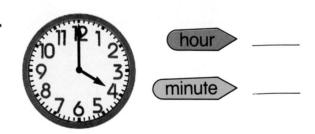

hour ▷ _____

minute ▷ _____

It is _____ o'clock.

PROBLEM SOLVING

11. Ned went to school at ➡  Ned woke up at
He woke up 2 hours earlier.
What time did he wake up?   _____ o'clock.

Name _____

Problem Solving
Understanding the Operations

UNDERSTAND
FIND DATA
PLAN
ESTIMATE
SOLVE
CHECK

Add or subtract to answer the question.

1. Sue's family went to Grandma's house.
   Mom drove 3 hours.
   Dad drove 2 hours.
   How long was the trip?

   _5_ hours

2. Sue played with Grandma's dog for
   5 minutes. She played with the
   cat for 7 minutes. How much
   longer did she play with the cat?

   _____ minutes

3. At Grandma's, Sue played ball for
   2 hours. She played in the park
   for 1 hour. How long did
   Sue play?

   _____ hours

4. Sue and Grandma dug up carrots from
   the garden in 9 minutes. They
   picked beans in 5 minutes. How much
   longer did it take to dig up carrots?

   _____ minutes

Estimation

About how long would it take?
Ring the better answer.

1. to make toast

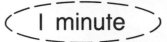(**1 minute**) 1 hour

2. to sleep at night

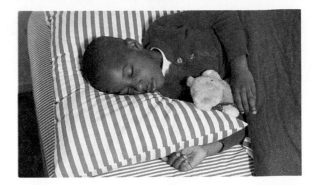

9 hours   9 days

3. to get over a cold

1 hour   1 week

4. to eat a sandwich

10 minutes   10 hours

5. to wash your hands

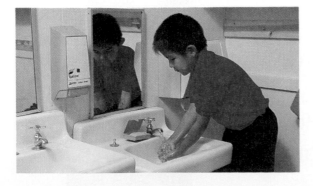

1 minute   1 hour

6. for your new tooth to come in all the way

2 days   2 months

Time on the Half Hour

7:00

7:30

Work with a partner. Use your punchout
clocks. Make them show one half
hour later than the blue clock. Then
show the time on the red clocks below.

1.

5:30

2.

:

3.

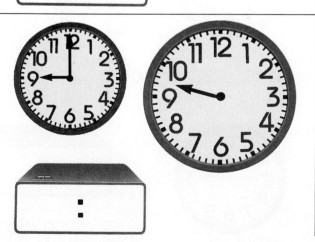

:

4.

:

Use the chart. Write each name
under the clock that shows
the bedtime.

1.

Cat Family Bedtimes			
Mimi	10:30	Meg	8:30
Cam	7:30	Cal	11:30

_____

_____

2.

_____

_____

3.

_____

4.

_____

POWER PRACTICE/QUIZ

1. Draw hands on the clock
to show the time.

6 o'clock

2. Where are the hands?
Write the numbers.

 _____

 _____

It is _____ o'clock.

Write each time two ways.

3.

_____ o'clock

4.

_____ o'clock

The Mouse Family's Time Book

Show the times.

A Day
with the
Mouse Family

Max and Mort
get home at

3:30

At night, Mama
comes home at

5:00

The family
eats dinner at

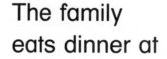

:

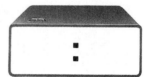

Mama and
Papa leave for
work at

:

The sitter and
Baby go to
the park at

10:00

Max and Mort play ball at  `4:00`

Baby wakes up at  `:`

Max and Mort go to bed at  `7:30`

The family watches the news at 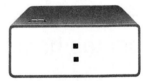 `:`

Sitter and Baby have lunch at 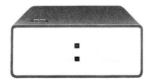 `:`

 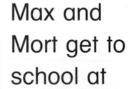

Max and Mort get to school at  `8:30`

Calendar

Make a calendar for this month.
Write the name and the dates.

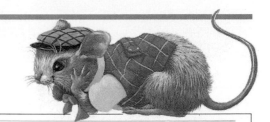

Sunday	Monday	Tuesday	Wednesday	Thursday	Friday	Saturday

Use the calendar to answer
the questions.

1. What day is the first
   of this month?

2. How many days are in this month? _____ days

3. What is today's date? _____

4. What date is one week from today? _____

5. What date is the third Sunday? _____

6. How many school days are in this month? _____ days

May						
Sunday	Monday	Tuesday	Wednesday	Thursday	Friday	Saturday
				1	2	3
4	5	6	7	8	9	10
11	12	13	14	15	16	17
18	19	20	21	22	23	24
25	26	27	28	29	30	31

Ring one.

1. Mother's Day is the second Sunday, May ____.

    1   4   (11)

2. May 5 is a ____.

    Sunday   Monday

3. May 15 is a ____.

    Thursday   Friday

4. Memorial Day is the last Friday of this month, May ____.

    23   30   31

5. The last day of this month is Saturday, May ____.

    25   30   31

6. There will be a full moon on the fourth Saturday of this month, May ____.

    10   18   24

FIND THE DATA **DATA BANK**

7. **Data Bank** The last day of March in the year 2000 is ____. Ring your answer. (See page 399.)

    Thursday   Friday

Name _____

Problem Solving
Using Data from a Chart

UNDERSTAND
FIND DATA
PLAN
ESTIMATE
SOLVE
CHECK

Use the chart. Write how long.
Then show the time.

Hours Spent

	Reading	Playing	Painting	Cleaning	Sleeping
Al	1	3	2	1	9
Sal	2	2	1	half hour	10

1. Sal read for __2__ hours.

   Sal began to read at

   She stopped at

2. Al painted for ____ hours.

   Al went to paint class at

   He stopped at

3. Sal cleaned _____ for a _____ hour.

   Sal began to clean at

   She stopped at

4. Al played for ____ hours.

   Al began to play at

   He stopped at

Problem Solving Strategy
Make a List

UNDERSTAND
FIND DATA
PLAN
ESTIMATE
SOLVE
CHECK

Answer the question.
Make a list to help.

Tim's grandmother has a cuckoo clock. The cuckoo comes out

   I time at I o'clock,

   2 times at 2 o'clock,

   3 times at 3 o'clock,

and so on.

The bird also comes out I time each half hour.

How many times does the bird come out?

1. from 1:00 to 3:00

Clock Time	Number of times bird comes out
1:00	I
1:30	I
2:00	I I
2:30	
3:00	

The bird comes out

_____ times.

2. from 2:30 to 5:00

Clock Time	Number of times bird comes out
2:30	I
3:00	III
3:30	
4:00	
4:30	
5:00	

The bird comes out

_____ times.

                                       Chapter 14

WRAP UP

MATH WORDS

1. Show the times on the clocks.
   Use  to draw the minute hand.
   Use  to draw the hour hand.

3 o'clock	10:00	7:30	5 o'clock

2. Look at the calendar. Ring

    the first Monday

    the second Sunday

    the last week

APRIL						
Sunday	Monday	Tuesday	Wednesday	Thursday	Friday	Saturday
					1	2
3	4	5	6	7	8	9
10	11	12	13	14	15	16
17	18	19	20	21	22	23
24	25	26	27	28	29	30

MATH REASONING

3. Use the calendar above.
   The baseball game is today, April 9.

   What day of the week is it? _____

4. The game starts at 2:00.
   It takes us 1 hour to get
   there. It is now 1:30.
   We have not left yet.

   Will we be
   on time?
   Ring one.
   yes   no

POWER PRACTICE/TEST

Write each time two ways.

1.  _____ o'clock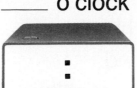

2.  _____ o'clock

Show the time on each clock.

3.

3:30

4.

5.

12:30

Ring one.

6. The first day of May is _____.

Friday   Tuesday   Sunday

May						
Sunday	Monday	Tuesday	Wednesday	Thursday	Friday	Saturday
		1	2	3	4	5
6	7	8	9	10	11	12

7. The second Friday of this month is May _____.

4   18   11

Show or write the time.

8. Sam wakes up at .

9. Jo goes to bed at _____ o'clock.

	Sam	Jen	Jo
Bedtime	9:30	8:30	9:00
Wake-up Time	7:30	6:30	7:30

10. Who goes to bed first? Ring one.   Sam   Jen

15
Addition Facts
Sums to 18

Workmat

Theme: Australia

Name _____

Adding 9

Work with a partner.
Use your punchout  and
two-color counters to add.

Start with 9 counters in ⊞.
Put 5 counters outside.
Move 1 counter to fill ⊞.
There are 10 and
4 extra, or 14 in all.

1.
$$9 + 6$$ $$1 + 9$$ $$9 + 9$$

2.
$$9 + 5$$ $$2 + 9$$ $$8 + 9$$

3.
$$9 + 2$$ $$9 + 1$$ $$6 + 9$$ $$9 + 7$$ $$4 + 9$$ $$9 + 3$$

4. $9 + 4 =$ ___ $5 + 9 =$ ___ $9 + 3 =$ ___

5. $6 + 9 =$ ___ $9 + 8 =$ ___ $7 + 9 =$ ___

PROBLEM SOLVING

6. Bev has 9¢. Ben has 7¢.
   Together, can they buy the ball?
   Finish the number sentence.

   $9¢ \bigcirc 7¢ =$ ____

17¢

7. Ring one.

   They can buy.

   They cannot buy.

Doubles Through 9 + 9

See a double?
Think of the
picture to help.

Add.

1.
$$\begin{array}{r} 6 \\ +\,6 \\ \hline 12 \end{array}$$

$$\begin{array}{r} 7 \\ +\,7 \\ \hline \end{array}$$

	February					
Sun	Mon	Tue	Wed	Thu	Fri	Sat
1	2	3	4	5	6	7
8	9	10	11	12	13	14
15	16	17	18	19	20	21
22	23	24	25	26	27	28

2.
$$\begin{array}{r} 8 \\ +\,8 \\ \hline \end{array}$$

$$\begin{array}{r} 9 \\ +\,9 \\ \hline \end{array}$$

Ring doubles. Then add all.

3.
$$\begin{array}{r} 8 \\ +\,8 \\ \hline 16 \end{array}$$
$$\begin{array}{r} 5 \\ +\,4 \\ \hline \end{array}$$
$$\begin{array}{r} 6 \\ +\,6 \\ \hline \end{array}$$
$$\begin{array}{r} 9 \\ +\,5 \\ \hline \end{array}$$
$$\begin{array}{r} 7 \\ +\,7 \\ \hline \end{array}$$
$$\begin{array}{r} 9 \\ +\,3 \\ \hline \end{array}$$

4.
$$\begin{array}{r} 9 \\ +\,6 \\ \hline \end{array}$$
$$\begin{array}{r} 7 \\ +\,7 \\ \hline \end{array}$$
$$\begin{array}{r} 8 \\ +\,9 \\ \hline \end{array}$$
$$\begin{array}{r} 5 \\ +\,5 \\ \hline \end{array}$$
$$\begin{array}{r} 6 \\ +\,4 \\ \hline \end{array}$$
$$\begin{array}{r} 5 \\ +\,6 \\ \hline \end{array}$$

5.
$$\begin{array}{r} 9 \\ +\,9 \\ \hline \end{array}$$
$$\begin{array}{r} 9 \\ +\,7 \\ \hline \end{array}$$
$$\begin{array}{r} 3 \\ +\,7 \\ \hline \end{array}$$
$$\begin{array}{r} 8 \\ +\,8 \\ \hline \end{array}$$
$$\begin{array}{r} 4 \\ +\,9 \\ \hline \end{array}$$
$$\begin{array}{r} 2 \\ +\,8 \\ \hline \end{array}$$

Add.

Look for doubles.

1.
$$\begin{array}{r} 7 \\ +7 \\ \hline 14 \end{array}$$
$$\begin{array}{r} 2 \\ +6 \\ \hline \end{array}$$
$$\begin{array}{r} 8 \\ +8 \\ \hline \end{array}$$
$$\begin{array}{r} 4 \\ +6 \\ \hline \end{array}$$
$$\begin{array}{r} 1 \\ +7 \\ \hline \end{array}$$

2.
$$\begin{array}{r} 9 \\ +7 \\ \hline \end{array}$$
$$\begin{array}{r} 6 \\ +6 \\ \hline \end{array}$$
$$\begin{array}{r} 5 \\ +4 \\ \hline \end{array}$$
$$\begin{array}{r} 3 \\ +6 \\ \hline \end{array}$$
$$\begin{array}{r} 8 \\ +2 \\ \hline \end{array}$$

3.
$$\begin{array}{r} 9 \\ +9 \\ \hline \end{array}$$
$$\begin{array}{r} 9 \\ +4 \\ \hline \end{array}$$
$$\begin{array}{r} 2 \\ +7 \\ \hline \end{array}$$
$$\begin{array}{r} 6 \\ +9 \\ \hline \end{array}$$
$$\begin{array}{r} 7 \\ +7 \\ \hline \end{array}$$
$$\begin{array}{r} 9 \\ +8 \\ \hline \end{array}$$

4.
$$\begin{array}{r} 6 \\ +5 \\ \hline \end{array}$$
$$\begin{array}{r} 8 \\ +8 \\ \hline \end{array}$$
$$\begin{array}{r} 2 \\ +0 \\ \hline \end{array}$$
$$\begin{array}{r} 9 \\ +9 \\ \hline \end{array}$$
$$\begin{array}{r} 5 \\ +9 \\ \hline \end{array}$$
$$\begin{array}{r} 7 \\ +2 \\ \hline \end{array}$$

PROBLEM SOLVING

5. Use and draw coins to help.

Kendra has 5 dimes.

Adam has 3 dimes.

How many more dimes does Kendra have than Adam? Ring and finish the number sentence that helps.

$5 + 3 = \underline{\hspace{1cm}}$

Kendra has _____ more dimes.

$5 - 3 = \underline{\hspace{1cm}}$

Fact Practice

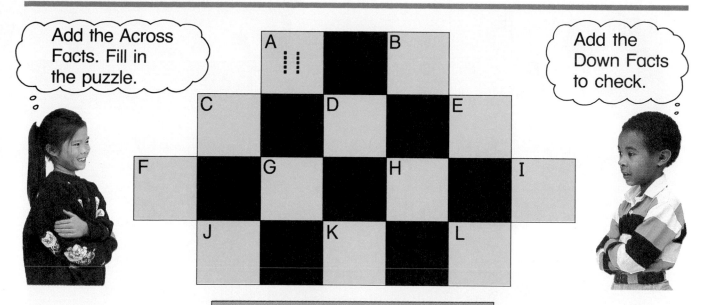

Add the Across Facts. Fill in the puzzle.

Add the Down Facts to check.

Across Facts

A
$$\begin{array}{r} 7 \\ +4 \\ \hline \end{array}$$

B
$$\begin{array}{r} 4 \\ +9 \\ \hline \end{array}$$

C
$$\begin{array}{r} 9 \\ +3 \\ \hline \end{array}$$

D
$$\begin{array}{r} 4 \\ +5 \\ \hline \end{array}$$

E
$$\begin{array}{r} 9 \\ +9 \\ \hline \end{array}$$

F
$$\begin{array}{r} 4 \\ +6 \\ \hline \end{array}$$

G
$$\begin{array}{r} 7 \\ +9 \\ \hline \end{array}$$

H
$$\begin{array}{r} 9 \\ +2 \\ \hline \end{array}$$

I
$$\begin{array}{r} 6 \\ +9 \\ \hline \end{array}$$

J
$$\begin{array}{r} 2 \\ +6 \\ \hline \end{array}$$

K
$$\begin{array}{r} 8 \\ +9 \\ \hline \end{array}$$

L
$$\begin{array}{r} 9 \\ +5 \\ \hline \end{array}$$

Down Facts

A
$$\begin{array}{r} 5 \\ +6 \\ \hline \end{array}$$

B
$$\begin{array}{r} 9 \\ +4 \\ \hline \end{array}$$

C
$$\begin{array}{r} 6 \\ +6 \\ \hline \end{array}$$

D
$$\begin{array}{r} 2 \\ +7 \\ \hline \end{array}$$

E
$$\begin{array}{r} 9 \\ +9 \\ \hline \end{array}$$

F
$$\begin{array}{r} 5 \\ +5 \\ \hline \end{array}$$

G
$$\begin{array}{r} 8 \\ +8 \\ \hline \end{array}$$

H
$$\begin{array}{r} 8 \\ +3 \\ \hline \end{array}$$

I
$$\begin{array}{r} 9 \\ +6 \\ \hline \end{array}$$

J
$$\begin{array}{r} 4 \\ +4 \\ \hline \end{array}$$

K
$$\begin{array}{r} 9 \\ +8 \\ \hline \end{array}$$

L
$$\begin{array}{r} 7 \\ +7 \\ \hline \end{array}$$

I. Add the Across Facts. Fill in the puzzle.
Add the Down Facts to check.

E

D F

C G

B H

A
12

Start.

I

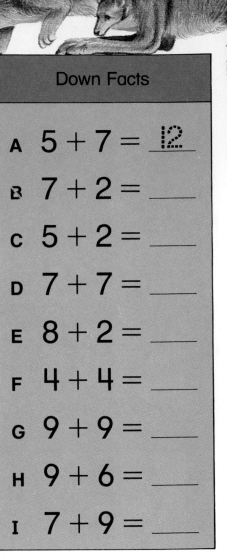

Down Facts

A $5 + 7 = $ **12**

B $7 + 2 = $ ___

C $5 + 2 = $ ___

D $7 + 7 = $ ___

E $8 + 2 = $ ___

F $4 + 4 = $ ___

G $9 + 9 = $ ___

H $9 + 6 = $ ___

I $7 + 9 = $ ___

Across Facts

A $6 + 6 = $ **12**   B $6 + 3 = $ ___

C $4 + 3 = $ ___   D $9 + 5 = $ ___

E $6 + 4 = $ ___   F $5 + 3 = $ ___

G $9 + 9 = $ ___   H $6 + 9 = $ ___

I $8 + 8 = $ ___

MAKE AN ESTIMATE

About how many will fit across the
chalk tray in your classroom?

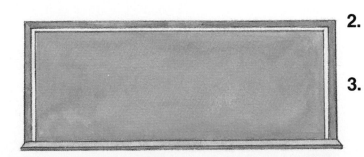

my guess   my count

2.

___   ___

3. Your Math Book

___   ___

Adding Three Numbers

Work with a partner. Each gets
punchouts ☐1 to ☐5. Take turns. Pick
three cards. Put them in an order that
is easy to add. Write them. Add.

Do it the
easy way.
$5 + 5 = 10$
$10 + 2 = 12$

5
5
+ 2
―――
12

I.

2.

       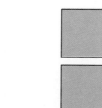   

Add the easy way. Ring the two
numbers to start. Look for sums
of 10 or doubles to help.

1.
  (4)
   1   8
  +(4)
  ───
   9

  (7)
   1   14
  +(7)
  ───

   2
  (3)   10
  +(7)
  ───

  (4)
  (6)   10
  + 3
  ───

  (3)
  (2)   6
  +(3)
  ───

2.
   8
   1
  + 8
  ───

   2
   8
  + 1
  ───

   2
   1
  + 9
  ───

   6
   4
  + 1
  ───

   5
   5
  + 3
  ───

   2
   4
  + 4
  ───

3.
   8
   2
  + 3
  ───

   1
   7
  + 3
  ───

   4
   6
  + 2
  ───

   1
   9
  + 5
  ───

   9
   9
  + 2
  ───

   5
   2
  + 5
  ───

FIND THE DATA   DATA BANK

4. **Data Bank** Sil, Wil, and Dil went to a toy sale.

   They bought a for 5¢,

   a 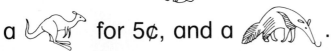 for 5¢, and a 🐜 .

   How much did the three toys cost?
   (See page 400.)

   ____ ¢

Name _____

Problem Solving
Understanding the Operations

UNDERSTAND
FIND DATA
PLAN
ESTIMATE
SOLVE
CHECK

Listen to the story. Use counters to
show it. Write how many more are needed.

1.

Need
5 to play.

_____ more must come.

2.

It takes 8
for the race.

_____ more must come.

3.

Need 4 to
sing the song.

_____ more must come.

Mental Math

Work with a partner.
Use punchouts $\boxed{9}$ to $\boxed{18}$.
Show each clue.
Write the number.

1. Count by 5s. You said the number.
   It is greater than 6 + 6.

   The number is __15__.

2. It is a doubles sum. It is less than a
   dozen.

   The number is ___.

3. It is less than 9 + 9. It is greater
   than 16.

   The number is ___.

4. Count by 2s. You said the number.
   It is greater than 12. It is less than 15.

   The number is ___.

5. It is a doubles sum. It is greater than
   8 + 8.

   The number is ___.

318 (three hundred eighteen)

Chapter 15

Doubles Plus One Through 8 + 9

Add.

13

1.

| I more |

$$\begin{array}{r} 6 \\ +6 \\ \hline 12 \end{array}$$ →
$$\begin{array}{r} 6 \\ +7 \\ \hline 13 \end{array}$$ or
$$\begin{array}{r} 7 \\ +6 \\ \hline 13 \end{array}$$

FEBRUARY

Sun	Mon	Tue	Wed	Thu	Fri	Sat
1	2	3	4	5	6	7
8	9	10	11	12	13	14
15	16	17	18	19	20	21
22	23	24	25	26	27	28

15

2.

| I more |

$$\begin{array}{r} 7 \\ +7 \\ \hline \end{array}$$ →
$$\begin{array}{r} 7 \\ +8 \\ \hline \end{array}$$ or
$$\begin{array}{r} 8 \\ +7 \\ \hline \end{array}$$

Ring the double-plus-one facts.
Then add all.

3. $(8 + 9) =$ __17__ $7 + 7 =$ ___ $3 + 6 =$ ___

4. $9 + 5 =$ ___ $7 + 8 =$ ___ $9 + 8 =$ ___

5. $8 + 7 =$ ___ $7 + 6 =$ ___ $4 + 4 =$ ___

6. $0 + 4 =$ ___ $2 + 6 =$ ___ $2 + 0 =$ ___

7. $8 + 9 =$ ___ $5 + 5 =$ ___ $6 + 4 =$ ___

8. $9 + 9 =$ ___ $6 + 7 =$ ___ $4 + 9 =$ ___

Write the double that helps. Add.

1.

$\begin{array}{r} 7 \\ +8 \\ \hline 15 \end{array}$ $\left(\begin{array}{r} 7 \\ +7 \\ \hline 14 \end{array}\right)$ $\begin{array}{r} 6 \\ +7 \\ \hline \end{array}$ $\left(\begin{array}{r} \\ + \\ \hline \end{array}\right)$ $\begin{array}{r} 8 \\ +7 \\ \hline \end{array}$ $\left(\begin{array}{r} \\ + \\ \hline \end{array}\right)$

Ring the double-plus-one facts.
Then add all.

2. $7 + 8 =$ _____ $8 + 2 =$ _____ $6 + 7 =$ _____

3. $3 + 7 =$ _____ $4 + 5 =$ _____ $8 + 7 =$ _____

4. $7 + 6 =$ _____ $2 + 9 =$ _____ $9 + 6 =$ _____

POWER PRACTICE/QUIZ

1. Write the addition fact for each picture.

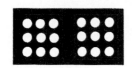

FEBRUARY						
Sun	Mon	Tue	Wed	Thu	Fri	Sat
1	2	3	4	5	6	7
8	9	10	11	12	13	14
15	16	17	18	19	20	21
22	23	24	25	26	27	28

___ + ___ = ___   ___ + ___ = ___   ___ + ___ = ___

Add.

2. $4 + 9 =$ _____ $9 + 3 =$ _____ $5 + 9 =$ _____

3.
$\begin{array}{r} 6 \\ 3 \\ +6 \\ \hline \end{array}$ $\begin{array}{r} 4 \\ 4 \\ +2 \\ \hline \end{array}$ $\begin{array}{r} 3 \\ 4 \\ +3 \\ \hline \end{array}$ $\begin{array}{r} 3 \\ 5 \\ +5 \\ \hline \end{array}$ $\begin{array}{r} 9 \\ 2 \\ +7 \\ \hline \end{array}$ $\begin{array}{r} 1 \\ 5 \\ +9 \\ \hline \end{array}$

Sums to 18

Put in 8. Then put in as many of the 5 as you can.

You have 10 and 3 extra.
8 + 5 = 13

$$\begin{array}{r} 8 \\ +5 \\ \hline 13 \end{array}$$

Work with a partner. Use counters and 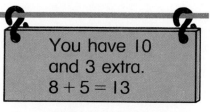. Put in counters for the greater number. Use the other number to make 10. Add the extras. Write the sum.

1. $\begin{array}{r} 8 \\ +6 \\ \hline \end{array}$

2. $\begin{array}{r} 4 \\ +7 \\ \hline \end{array}$

3. $\begin{array}{r} 7 \\ +5 \\ \hline \end{array}$

4. $\begin{array}{r} 8 \\ +4 \\ \hline \end{array}$

5. $\begin{array}{r} 5 \\ +8 \\ \hline \end{array}$

6. $\begin{array}{r} 6 \\ +8 \\ \hline \end{array}$

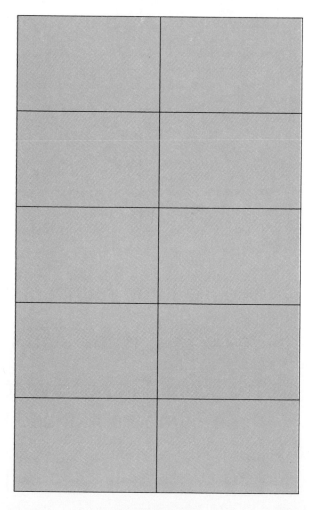

Add. Use counters and  to help.

1.
$$\begin{array}{r} 9 \\ +\ 1 \\ \hline \end{array}$$
$$\begin{array}{r} 8 \\ +\ 7 \\ \hline \end{array}$$
$$\begin{array}{r} 7 \\ +\ 4 \\ \hline \end{array}$$
$$\begin{array}{r} 6 \\ +\ 7 \\ \hline \end{array}$$
$$\begin{array}{r} 8 \\ +\ 4 \\ \hline \end{array}$$
$$\begin{array}{r} 5 \\ +\ 7 \\ \hline \end{array}$$

2.
$$\begin{array}{r} 5 \\ +\ 8 \\ \hline \end{array}$$
$$\begin{array}{r} 4 \\ +\ 9 \\ \hline \end{array}$$
$$\begin{array}{r} 4 \\ +\ 7 \\ \hline \end{array}$$
$$\begin{array}{r} 9 \\ +\ 3 \\ \hline \end{array}$$
$$\begin{array}{r} 6 \\ +\ 8 \\ \hline \end{array}$$
$$\begin{array}{r} 7 \\ +\ 7 \\ \hline \end{array}$$

3.
$$\begin{array}{r} 9 \\ +\ 7 \\ \hline \end{array}$$
$$\begin{array}{r} 4 \\ +\ 8 \\ \hline \end{array}$$
$$\begin{array}{r} 8 \\ +\ 8 \\ \hline \end{array}$$
$$\begin{array}{r} 8 \\ +\ 5 \\ \hline \end{array}$$
$$\begin{array}{r} 9 \\ +\ 5 \\ \hline \end{array}$$
$$\begin{array}{r} 8 \\ +\ 3 \\ \hline \end{array}$$

4.
$$\begin{array}{r} 9 \\ +\ 9 \\ \hline \end{array}$$
$$\begin{array}{r} 8 \\ +\ 6 \\ \hline \end{array}$$
$$\begin{array}{r} 6 \\ +\ 9 \\ \hline \end{array}$$
$$\begin{array}{r} 2 \\ +\ 9 \\ \hline \end{array}$$
$$\begin{array}{r} 7 \\ +\ 5 \\ \hline \end{array}$$
$$\begin{array}{r} 8 \\ +\ 9 \\ \hline \end{array}$$

TRY A CALCULATOR

5. Choose three numbers in a row.  I'll try 3, 4, and 5.

Use a . Is the sum 18?

Try again. Find and write the three numbers that add to 18.

$$\square + \triangle + \bigcirc = 18$$

| 2 | 3 | 4 | 5 | 6 | 7 | 8 | 9 |

Fact Practice

Kara Kangaroo, do you eat with your tail?

To find out, first add. Then write the code letters in the boxes below.

O | 5 + 4 = ___   F | 3 + 4 = ___

T | 8 + 9 = ___   R | 8 + 8 = ___

I | 8 + 5 = 13   V | 6 + 9 = ___   V | 7 + 8 = ___

A | 2 + 8 = ___   F | 2 + 5 = ___   N | 7 + 7 = ___

K | 3 + 5 = ___   I | 4 + 9 = ___   S | 6 + 6 = ___

O | 2 + 7 = ___   A | 5 + 5 = ___   Y | 9 + 9 = ___

V | 9 + 6 = ___   K | 6 + 2 = ___   E | 5 + 6 = ___

Read the message.

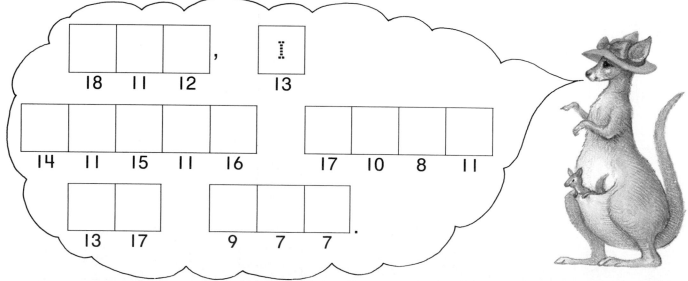

☐ ☐ ☐ , ☐
18 11 12   13

☐ ☐ ☐ ☐ ☐   ☐ ☐ ☐ ☐
14 11 15 11 16   17 10 8 11

☐ ☐   ☐ ☐ ☐ .
13 17   9   7   7

Add. Cross out each sum in the box to check.

1.
```
   6        9        5        8
 + 7      + 9      + 6      + 8
 ---      ---      ---      ---
  13
```

Check Box

7	~~13~~
8	14
9	15
10	16
11	17
12	18

2.
```
   9        6        5        6
 + 5      + 2      + 5      + 9
 ---      ---      ---      ---
```

3.
```
   8        3        8        5
 + 4      + 6      + 9      + 2
 ---      ---      ---      ---
```

MIXED REVIEW

4. Match.

| third | first | second | fifth | fourth |

5. Color the box that has more.

| 33 | 36 |

6. Color the box that has fewer.

| 53 | 41 |

Problem Solving
Determining Reasonable Answers

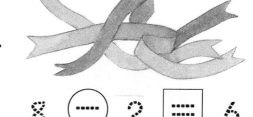

Ring if the number is correct.
Cross out if it is wrong.
Write the correct number sentence.

1. At the fiesta, 8 girls had ribbons
   in their hair. 2 did not have ribbons.
   How many more had ribbons?

   ~~10~~ more girls had ribbons.

   8 ⊖ 2 ▣ 6

2. 6 men were in the mariachi band.
   2 played trumpets.
   How many did not play trumpets?

   _8_ men did not play trumpets.

   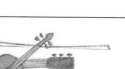

   ___ ◯ ___ ▢ ___

3. Luz made 5 tortillas.
   Then Luz made 2 more tortillas.
   How many did Luz make in all?

   Luz made _3_ tortillas in all.

   ___ ◯ ___ ▢ ___

4. 3 piñatas had prizes inside.
   I piñata did not. How many more
   had prizes than did not?

   _2_ more piñatas had prizes.

   ___ ◯ ___ ▢ ___

Problem Solving Strategy
Use Objects

Cut out the boats. Listen to the stories.
Use the boats to act them out.
Paste to match the second story.

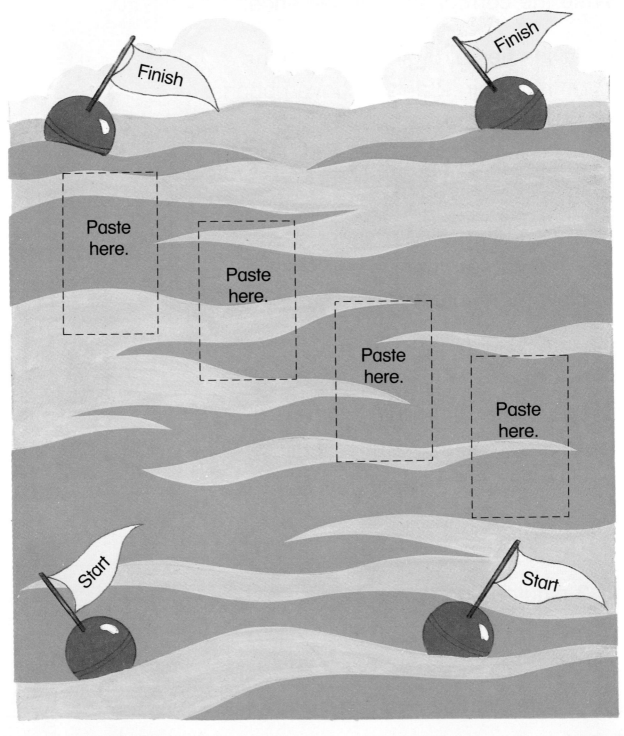

WRAP UP

MATH WORDS

Use  to ring the double facts.
Use  to ring the double-plus-one facts. Then add all.

1.

$$\begin{array}{r} 7 \\ +7 \\ \hline \end{array} \qquad \begin{array}{r} 7 \\ +6 \\ \hline \end{array} \qquad \begin{array}{r} 9 \\ +9 \\ \hline \end{array} \qquad \begin{array}{r} 6 \\ +7 \\ \hline \end{array} \qquad \begin{array}{r} 7 \\ +9 \\ \hline \end{array} \qquad \begin{array}{r} 8 \\ +3 \\ \hline \end{array}$$

2.

$$\begin{array}{r} 9 \\ +8 \\ \hline \end{array} \qquad \begin{array}{r} 8 \\ +8 \\ \hline \end{array} \qquad \begin{array}{r} 6 \\ +9 \\ \hline \end{array} \qquad \begin{array}{r} 8 \\ +7 \\ \hline \end{array} \qquad \begin{array}{r} 7 \\ +8 \\ \hline \end{array} \qquad \begin{array}{r} 6 \\ +6 \\ \hline \end{array}$$

MATH REASONING

Look at the figure.

3. How many triangles are there in all?   _____ triangles

4. Write a number in each circle so that each triangle has a sum of 18.

Try the numbers 5, 6, and 7.

POWER PRACTICE/TEST

1. Write the double fact for each picture.

      FEBRUARY

Sun	Mon	Tue	Wed	Thu	Fri	Sat
1	2	3	4	5	6	7
8	9	10	11	12	13	14
15	16	17	18	19	20	21
22	23	24	25	26	27	28

____ + ____ = ____   ____ + ____ = ____   ____ + ____ = ____

Add.

2.

$$\begin{array}{r} 8 \\ +8 \\ \hline \end{array} \qquad \begin{array}{r} 9 \\ +6 \\ \hline \end{array} \qquad \begin{array}{r} 9 \\ +9 \\ \hline \end{array} \qquad \begin{array}{r} 4 \\ +9 \\ \hline \end{array} \qquad \begin{array}{r} 7 \\ +7 \\ \hline \end{array} \qquad \begin{array}{r} 9 \\ +3 \\ \hline \end{array}$$

3. $4 + 5 =$ ____ $7 + 6 =$ ____ $7 + 8 =$ ____

4.

$$\begin{array}{r} 9 \\ 1 \\ +6 \\ \hline \end{array} \qquad \begin{array}{r} 5 \\ 5 \\ +4 \\ \hline \end{array} \qquad \begin{array}{r} 4 \\ 6 \\ +5 \\ \hline \end{array} \qquad \begin{array}{r} 2 \\ 3 \\ +7 \\ \hline \end{array} \qquad \begin{array}{r} 8 \\ 8 \\ +1 \\ \hline \end{array} \qquad \begin{array}{r} 8 \\ 2 \\ +3 \\ \hline \end{array}$$

5.

$$\begin{array}{r} 5 \\ +8 \\ \hline \end{array} \qquad \begin{array}{r} 7 \\ +4 \\ \hline \end{array} \qquad \begin{array}{r} 8 \\ +4 \\ \hline \end{array} \qquad \begin{array}{r} 6 \\ +8 \\ \hline \end{array} \qquad \begin{array}{r} 5 \\ +7 \\ \hline \end{array} \qquad \begin{array}{r} 8 \\ +6 \\ \hline \end{array}$$

6. Write how many more are needed. There are 3 children. It takes 6 children to play the game. How many more children must come to play the game?

____ more must come.

Name _____

ENRICHMENT
Exploring Addition

$3 + 4 + 5 = \underline{12}$ $3 + 4 + 5 = \underline{12}$

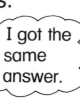

Work with a partner. Use cubes.
Add the red numbers to start.
Add the first way. Then add
the second way. Did you get
the same answer? Ring **yes** or **no**.

I got the same answer.

	First Way	Second Way	Same Answer?
1.	$2 + 4 + 3 = \underline{}$	$2 + 4 + 3 = \underline{}$	yes no
2.	$9 + 0 + 9 = \underline{}$	$9 + 0 + 9 = \underline{}$	yes no
3.	$8 + 1 + 3 = \underline{}$	$8 + 1 + 3 = \underline{}$	yes no
4.	$6 + 2 + 5 = \underline{}$	$6 + 2 + 5 = \underline{}$	yes no
5.	$7 + 2 + 7 = \underline{}$	$7 + 2 + 7 = \underline{}$	yes no

6. Write different ways you could
   add to find the sum of $4 + 2 + 5$.

   First Add   Then Add

   $\underline{} + \underline{}$ $+ \underline{} = \underline{}$

   $\underline{} + \underline{}$ $+ \underline{} = \underline{}$

   $\underline{} + \underline{}$ $+ \underline{} = \underline{}$

7. Does it matter in which
   order you add? Ring one.   yes   no

CUMULATIVE REVIEW

Count how much.

1.
   - ○ 11¢
   - ○ 12¢
   - ○ 21¢

2.
   - ○ 21¢
   - ○ 26¢
   - ○ 31¢

3.
   - ○ 39¢
   - ○ 42¢
   - ○ 47¢

4. Which is less?
   - ○ A
   - ○ B

   A

   B

What time is it?

5.
   - ○ 8 o'clock
   - ○ 7 o'clock
   - ○ 9 o'clock

6.
   - ○ 1:00
   - ○ 11:00
   - ○ 12:00

7. What is the time one half hour later?

   - ○ 10:30
   - ○ 10:00
   - ○ 9:30

8. How many days are in one week?
   - ○ 9 days
   - ○ 7 days
   - ○ 8 days

9. Raj had    He bought a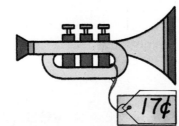

   How much money does he have now?
   - ○ 18¢
   - ○ 16¢
   - ○ 17¢

16
Addition and Subtraction Facts to 18

Workmat

Theme: Dinosaurs

Subtraction Doubles to 18

Work with a partner. Use counters.
Lay out your counters like the
picture. Write a doubles fact.
Take away the counters on one
side. Write a subtraction fact.

1. ●●● ○○○
   ●●● ○○○

   ___ + ___ = ___

   ___ − ___ = ___

2. ●●● ○○○
   ●●● ○○○
   ●●● ○○○

   ___ + ___ = ___

   ___ − ___ = ___

3. ●●●● ○○○○
   ●●●● ○○○○

   ___ + ___ = ___

   ___ − ___ = ___

4. ●●● ○○○
   ●●● ○○○
   ●●● ○○○

   ___ + ___ = ___

   ___ − ___ = ___

Ring the subtraction doubles.
Then subtract all.

5.
$$14 - 7 \qquad 10 - 4 \qquad 18 - 9 \qquad 12 - 9 \qquad 9 - 5 \qquad 16 - 8$$

TALK ABOUT IT

6. Write the answer. $+ 5 + 2 - 2 - 5 = $ ___

   Guess what the answer will be if you
   start with 6. Guess what the answer
   will be if you start with 8. Tell why.

Subtracting 9

Take out 9. Write what is left.

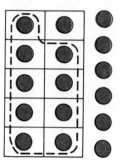

$$\begin{array}{r}16\\-\ 9\\\hline 7\end{array}$$

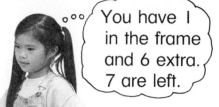

You have 1 in the frame and 6 extra. 7 are left.

Work with a partner.
Use counters and .
Show the first number
with ten and extras.
Take 9 from the.
Write what is left.

1. $\begin{array}{r}13\\-\ 9\\\hline\end{array}$ 2. $\begin{array}{r}17\\-\ 9\\\hline\end{array}$

3. $\begin{array}{r}16\\-\ 9\\\hline\end{array}$ 4. $\begin{array}{r}15\\-\ 9\\\hline\end{array}$

5. $\begin{array}{r}12\\-\ 9\\\hline\end{array}$ 6. $\begin{array}{r}14\\-\ 9\\\hline\end{array}$

Ring where you subtract 9.
Then subtract all.
Use counters and ▤ to help.

When I subtract 9, my answer is the extras and 1 more.

1.
$$\begin{array}{r} 13 \\ -\ 9 \\ \hline \end{array}$$
$$\begin{array}{r} 4 \\ -\ 3 \\ \hline \end{array}$$
$$\begin{array}{r} 16 \\ -\ 9 \\ \hline \end{array}$$
$$\begin{array}{r} 7 \\ -\ 3 \\ \hline \end{array}$$
$$\begin{array}{r} 8 \\ -\ 5 \\ \hline \end{array}$$
$$\begin{array}{r} 15 \\ -\ 9 \\ \hline \end{array}$$

2.
$$\begin{array}{r} 4 \\ -\ 2 \\ \hline \end{array}$$
$$\begin{array}{r} 9 \\ -\ 3 \\ \hline \end{array}$$
$$\begin{array}{r} 7 \\ -\ 0 \\ \hline \end{array}$$
$$\begin{array}{r} 14 \\ -\ 9 \\ \hline \end{array}$$
$$\begin{array}{r} 6 \\ -\ 2 \\ \hline \end{array}$$
$$\begin{array}{r} 8 \\ -\ 2 \\ \hline \end{array}$$

3.
$$\begin{array}{r} 7 \\ -\ 2 \\ \hline \end{array}$$
$$\begin{array}{r} 17 \\ -\ 9 \\ \hline \end{array}$$
$$\begin{array}{r} 6 \\ -\ 4 \\ \hline \end{array}$$
$$\begin{array}{r} 9 \\ -\ 4 \\ \hline \end{array}$$
$$\begin{array}{r} 18 \\ -\ 9 \\ \hline \end{array}$$
$$\begin{array}{r} 6 \\ -\ 5 \\ \hline \end{array}$$

4.
$$\begin{array}{r} 12 \\ -\ 9 \\ \hline \end{array}$$
$$\begin{array}{r} 9 \\ -\ 0 \\ \hline \end{array}$$
$$\begin{array}{r} 10 \\ -\ 7 \\ \hline \end{array}$$
$$\begin{array}{r} 15 \\ -\ 9 \\ \hline \end{array}$$
$$\begin{array}{r} 14 \\ -\ 7 \\ \hline \end{array}$$
$$\begin{array}{r} 11 \\ -\ 9 \\ \hline \end{array}$$

PROBLEM SOLVING

5. Use coins to solve.

I have 9¢.

How much more do I need to buy the ball?

I need ____ ¢.

13¢

Fact Practice

Subtract the Across Facts.
Fill in the puzzle. Subtract
the Down Facts to check.

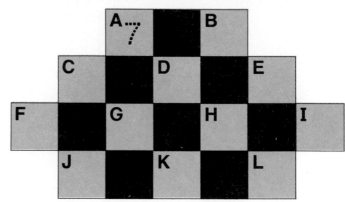

| Across Facts |

A 14
 − 7
 ‾‾7

B 17
 − 9

C 14
 − 9

D 12
 − 9

E 12
 − 6

F 10
 − 6

G 10
 − 8

H 16
 − 8

I 10
 − 3

J 10
 − 5

K 18
 − 9

L 13
 − 9

| Down Facts |

A 16
 − 9

B 11
 − 3

C 9
 − 4

D 11
 − 8

E 15
 − 9

F 8
 − 4

G 11
 − 9

H 10
 − 2

I 9
 − 2

J 8
 − 3

K 9
 − 0

L 7
 − 3

1. Subtract the Across Facts.
Fill in the puzzle. Subtract the
Down Facts to check.

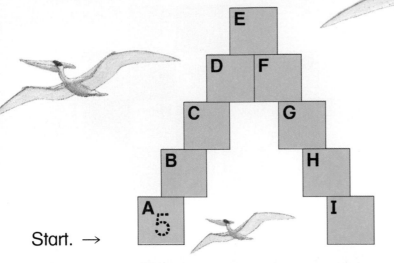

Start. →

Across Facts

A $10 - 5 = \underline{5}$ B $9 - 7 = \underline{}$

C $13 - 9 = \underline{}$ D $10 - 7 = \underline{}$

E $10 - 4 = \underline{}$ F $18 - 9 = \underline{}$

G $16 - 8 = \underline{}$ H $14 - 7 = \underline{}$

I $11 - 9 = \underline{}$

Down Facts

A $14 - 9 = \underline{}$

B $8 - 6 = \underline{}$

C $8 - 4 = \underline{}$

D $5 - 2 = \underline{}$

E $15 - 9 = \underline{}$

F $10 - 1 = \underline{}$

G $17 - 9 = \underline{}$

H $16 - 9 = \underline{}$

I $10 - 8 = \underline{}$

USE CRITICAL THINKING

2. Here are three square numbers.
Show the next square number with
dots. Then write the number.

1   4   9   _____

Problem Solving
Understanding the Operations

| UNDERSTAND |
| FIND DATA |
| PLAN |
| ESTIMATE |
| SOLVE |
| CHECK |

Use counters to show the story.
Finish the subtraction sentence.

1. There are 7 dinosaurs by the swamp.

3 are . The rest are .

How many  are by the
swamp?

____

2. There are 5 dinosaurs on
    the grass. 4 eat plants.
    The others eat meat.
    How many eat meat?

____ dinosaur

3. 8 dinosaurs wake up.

3 are . The rest are .

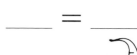

How many  wake up?

4. There are 6 dinosaurs by the tree.
    2 have plates on their back.
    The rest do not.
    How many do not have plates?

____ dinosaurs

Informal Algebra

Use these numbers.
Guess which number goes
in the ☐. Write it. Check.
Try again if you need to.

1.

$4 + \boxed{} = 12$

$4 + \boxed{} = 12$

$4 + \boxed{} = 12$

I needed _____ guesses.

2.

$6 + \boxed{} = 13$

$6 + \boxed{} = 13$

$6 + \boxed{} = 13$

I needed _____ guesses.

3.

$9 + \boxed{} = 12$

$9 + \boxed{} = 12$

$9 + \boxed{} = 12$

I needed _____ guesses.

4.

$7 + \boxed{} = 13$

$7 + \boxed{} = 13$

$7 + \boxed{} = 13$

I needed _____ guesses.

5.

$\boxed{} + 5 = 9$

$\boxed{} + 5 = 9$

$\boxed{} + 5 = 9$

I needed _____ guesses.

6.

$\boxed{} + 8 = 13$

$\boxed{} + 8 = 13$

$\boxed{} + 8 = 13$

I needed _____ guesses.

Using Addition to Subtract 4, 5, and 6

13 in all

5 → 8

add-to-check fact

| 8
+ 5
13 | → SO | 13
− 5
8 |

Work with a partner. Use the add-to-check fact to help subtract. Show with cubes.

1.

| 9
+ 5
14 | → SO | 14
− 5
9 |

2.

| 9
+ 4 | → SO | 13
− 4 |

3.

| 9
+ 6 | → SO | 15
− 6 |

4.

| 8
+ 6 | → SO | 14
− 6 |

5.

| 8
+ 4 | → SO | 12
− 4 |

6.

| 7
+ 6 | → SO | 13
− 6 |

Subtract. Use the add-to-check fact to help.

If it helps, use cubes to show.

1.

6 + 9 15	15 − 6

4 + 5	9 − 4

2.

2 + 5	7 − 2

6 + 7	13 − 6

2 + 2	4 − 2

3.

5 + 9	14 − 5

3 + 7	10 − 3

4 + 9	13 − 4

POWER PRACTICE/QUIZ

1. Ring the subtraction doubles.
Then subtract all.

14 − 7	11 − 2	12 − 6	18 − 9	12 − 3	16 − 8

2. Subtract.

10 − 9	10 − 5	13 − 9	15 − 9	18 − 9	12 − 6

Name _____

Using Addition to Subtract 7 and 8

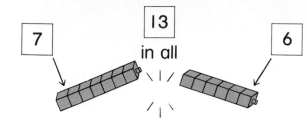

13
in all

7   6

Taking one part from the whole leaves the other part.

$7 + 6 = \underline{13}$

so → $13 - 7 = \underline{6}$

Work with a partner. Use the add-to-check fact to help subtract. Show with cubes.

1. $7 + 8 = \underline{15}$

   so → $15 - 8 = \underline{7}$

2. $5 + 8 = \underline{}$

   so → $13 - 8 = \underline{}$

3. $9 + 8 = \underline{}$

   so → $17 - 8 = \underline{}$

4. $8 + 7 = \underline{}$

   so → $15 - 7 = \underline{}$

5. $9 + 7 = \underline{}$

   so → $16 - 7 = \underline{}$

6. $6 + 8 = \underline{}$

   so → $14 - 8 = \underline{}$

Subtract. Use the add-to-check fact to help.

If it helps, use cubes to show.

1. 8 + 5 = 13

13 − 8 = 5

2. 7 + 8 = ___

15 − 8 = ___

3. 8 + 8 = ___

16 − 8 = ___

4. 8 + 9 = ___

17 − 8 = ___

5. 7 + 7 = ___

14 − 7 = ___

6. 8 + 7 = ___

15 − 8 = ___

7. 7 + 9 = ___

16 − 7 = ___

8. 6 + 6 = ___

12 − 6 = ___

MAKE AN ESTIMATE

9. Look at the picture. About how many of the first graders would it take to be as tall as the dinosaur?

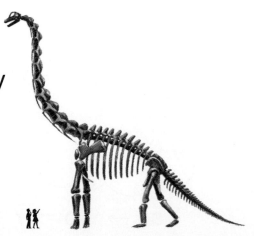

___ first graders

Talk about how to check.

Related Subtraction Facts

14
in all

8   6

$$\begin{array}{r} 14 \\ -\ 8 \\ \hline 6 \end{array}$$ ← and → $$\begin{array}{r} 14 \\ -\ 6 \\ \hline 8 \end{array}$$

Work with a partner. Use cubes. Start with the greater number. Take away one of the parts. Write the other part.

1. $$\begin{array}{r} 13 \\ -\ 6 \\ \hline \end{array}$$ and $$\begin{array}{r} 13 \\ -\ 7 \\ \hline \end{array}$$

2. $$\begin{array}{r} 15 \\ -\ 6 \\ \hline \end{array}$$ and $$\begin{array}{r} 15 \\ -\ 9 \\ \hline \end{array}$$

3. $$\begin{array}{r} 14 \\ -\ 5 \\ \hline \end{array}$$ and $$\begin{array}{r} 14 \\ -\ 9 \\ \hline \end{array}$$

4. $$\begin{array}{r} 15 \\ -\ 7 \\ \hline \end{array}$$ and $$\begin{array}{r} 15 \\ -\ 8 \\ \hline \end{array}$$

5. $$\begin{array}{r} 13 \\ -\ 5 \\ \hline \end{array}$$ and $$\begin{array}{r} 13 \\ -\ 8 \\ \hline \end{array}$$

6. $$\begin{array}{r} 13 \\ -\ 4 \\ \hline \end{array}$$ and $$\begin{array}{r} 13 \\ -\ 9 \\ \hline \end{array}$$

Finish the subtraction facts.

1.
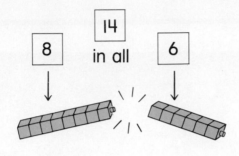

$14 - 8 =$ _____ and

$14 - 6 =$ _____

2.
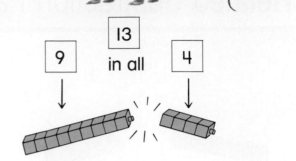

$13 - 9 =$ _____ and

$13 - 4 =$ _____

3.
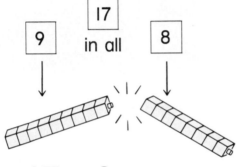

$17 - 9 =$ _____ and

$17 - 8 =$ _____

4.
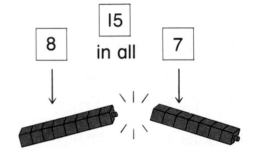

$15 - 8 =$ _____ and

$15 - 7 =$ _____

FIND THE DATA   DATA BANK

5. Data Bank How much longer is

 the  than the ?

(See page 400.) Ring the number sentence that helps. Count by tens. Write the answer.

$40 + 30 =$ _____

$40 - 30 =$ _____

_____ feet

Fact Families

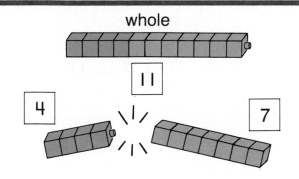

whole

| 11 |
| 4 | 7 |

4	7	11	11
+7	+4	−4	−7
11	11	7	4

Work in a group. Use cubes. Show each fact family. Write to finish.

I.

| 13 |
| 7 | 6 |

7	6	13	13
+6	+7	−7	−6
13			

2.

| 16 |
| 9 | 7 |

9	7	16	16
+7	+9	−9	−7

3.

| 12 |
| 7 | 5 |

7	5	12	12
+5	+7	−7	−5

4.

| 11 |
| 6 | 5 |

6	5	11	11
+5	+6	−6	−5

5.

| 15 |
| 7 | 8 |

7	8	15	15
+8	+7	−7	−8

6.

| 12 |
| 8 | 4 |

8	4	12	12
+4	+8	−8	−4

Cross out the one that is not in the
fact family. Finish the others.
Use counters and ▦ to help.

1. $8 + 9 = \underline{17}$　　　$9 + 8 = \underline{17}$　　　$17 - 9 = \underline{}$

~~$9 + 7 =$~~　　　$17 - 8 = \underline{}$

___

2. $9 + 4 = \underline{}$　　　$13 - 4 = \underline{}$

$4 + 9 = \underline{}$　　　$13 - 5 = \underline{}$　　　$13 - 9 = \underline{}$

___

3. $5 + 8 = \underline{}$　　　$13 - 5 = \underline{}$

$8 + 5 = \underline{}$　　　$13 - 9 = \underline{}$　　　$13 - 8 = \underline{}$

MIXED REVIEW

4. Count how many.
   Write the number.

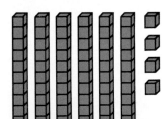

___

5. Color to show the tens
   and ones.

Tens	Ones
2	4

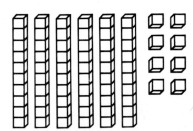

6. Add. Can you trade for a dime?　　　Ring **yes** or **no.**

yes

no

$4¢ + 5¢ = \underline{}¢$

Problem Solving
Using a Number Sentence

UNDERSTAND
FIND DATA
PLAN
ESTIMATE
SOLVE
CHECK

Write the number sentence for the story.
Write the answer. Ring to finish the story.

1. 5 dinosaurs were eating
   plants. 3 ran away.
   How many stayed?

   ____ dinosaurs ran away.
   ____ dinosaurs are still there.

2.

   3 ![stegosaurus] and 5 ![brontosaurus]
   are looking for food. How
   many are looking for food?

   ____ dinosaurs in all.
   ____ dinosaurs are left.

3. ![dinosaur]

   3 big ![dinosaur] are joined
   by 2 little ones.
   How many more big ones
   than little ones are there?

   ____ dinosaurs in all.
   ____ more big than little.

Problem Solving Strategy
Use Objects

UNDERSTAND
FIND DATA
PLAN
ESTIMATE
SOLVE
CHECK

Cut out the dinosaurs. Listen to the story. Find and write the ways the dinosaurs can line up.

___A___ then ___T___ then ___S___   _____ then _____ then _____

_____ then _____ then _____   _____ then _____ then _____

_____ then _____ then _____   _____ then _____ then _____

_____ ways in all

| A | for Apatosaurus | T | for Tyrannosaurus | S | for Stegosaurus |

WRAP UP

MATH WORDS

1. Use  to ring subtraction doubles.
   Use to ring where you subtract 9.
   Then subtract all.

$$
\begin{array}{cccccc}
14 & 13 & 16 & 16 & 17 & 15 \\
-7 & -9 & -8 & -9 & -9 & -7 \\
\hline
\end{array}
$$

2. Subtract. $13 - 7 = \underline{}$

   Write the add-to-check fact. $\underline{} + \underline{} = \underline{}$

   Finish the fact family.

   $\underline{} \bigcirc \underline{} = \underline{}$ $\underline{} \bigcirc \underline{} = \underline{}$

MATH REASONING

Write + or − in each $\bigcirc$.

3. $16 \bigcirc 7 = 18 \bigcirc 9$

4. $6 \bigcirc 2 = 14 \bigcirc 6$

5. $9 \bigcirc 4 = 8 \bigcirc 5$

6. $17 \bigcirc 9 = 4 \bigcirc 4$

7. $9 \bigcirc 9 = 6 \bigcirc 6$

POWER PRACTICE/TEST

Ring the subtraction doubles. Then subtract all.

1.
$$\begin{array}{r} 18 \\ -9 \\ \hline \end{array}\qquad \begin{array}{r} 15 \\ -7 \\ \hline \end{array}\qquad \begin{array}{r} 10 \\ -5 \\ \hline \end{array}\qquad \begin{array}{r} 13 \\ -9 \\ \hline \end{array}\qquad \begin{array}{r} 11 \\ -9 \\ \hline \end{array}\qquad \begin{array}{r} 10 \\ -7 \\ \hline \end{array}$$

2.
$$\begin{array}{r} 14 \\ -9 \\ \hline \end{array}\qquad \begin{array}{r} 12 \\ -6 \\ \hline \end{array}\qquad \begin{array}{r} 16 \\ -8 \\ \hline \end{array}\qquad \begin{array}{r} 13 \\ -4 \\ \hline \end{array}\qquad \begin{array}{r} 15 \\ -9 \\ \hline \end{array}\qquad \begin{array}{r} 14 \\ -7 \\ \hline \end{array}$$

Subtract. Use the add-to-check fact to help.

3.
9	14
+ 5	− 5

4.
5	11
+ 6	− 6

5.
8	15
+ 7	− 7

Finish each fact family.

6. $5 + 8 = $ ____
   $8 + 5 = $ ____
   $13 - $ ____ $ = $ ____
   $13 - $ ____ $ = $ ____

7. $8 + 9 = $ ____
   $9 + 8 = $ ____
   $17 - $ ____ $ = $ ____
   $17 - $ ____ $ = $ ____

8. 3 big tigers come to play with 5 little tigers. How many more little ones are there?

____ ⬭ ____ = ____

Ring to finish the story.

____ tigers in all.

____ more little ones.

ENRICHMENT
Using a Number Line to Add or Subtract

$$8 - 2 = \underline{6}$$ $$11 + 3 = \underline{14}$$

Add or subtract.
Use the number line.

1. $6 + 2 = \underline{}$ $16 - 5 = \underline{}$ $8 + 3 = \underline{}$

2. $5 + 5 = \underline{}$ $8 + 8 = \underline{}$ $12 - 6 = \underline{}$

3. $18 - 9 = \underline{}$ $17 - 8 = \underline{}$ $9 + 5 = \underline{}$

4. $9 + 4 = \underline{}$ $13 - 4 = \underline{}$ $8 + 6 = \underline{}$

5. $3 + 7 = \underline{}$ $10 - 3 = \underline{}$ $13 - 7 = \underline{}$

6. $15 - 7 = \underline{}$ $17 - 7 = \underline{}$ $9 + 8 = \underline{}$

Name _____

CUMULATIVE REVIEW

1. Where is the hour hand?

- ○ 9
- ○ 12
- ○ 10

2. Where is the minute hand?

- ○ 4
- ○ 12
- ○ 1

3. What is the time?

- ○ 4:30
- ○ 2:30
- ○ 3:30

4. Which class comes first?

math class 11:00

reading class 10:30

art class 9:30

- ○ math
- ○ art
- ○ reading

Add.

5. $9 + 9 = $ ____

- ○ 17
- ○ 18
- ○ 19

6. $\begin{array}{r} 4 \\ + 9 \\ \hline \end{array}$

- ○ 12
- ○ 13
- ○ 14

7. $\begin{array}{r} 6 \\ 6 \\ + 1 \\ \hline \end{array}$

- ○ 12
- ○ 13
- ○ 14

8. Find the double-plus-one fact for $7 + 7 = 14$.

- ○ $6 + 7 = 13$
- ○ $8 + 9 = 17$
- ○ $8 + 7 = 15$

9. Choose the correct number sentence.

There are 9 .

We need 15 to play.

How many more do we need?

- ○ $15 - 8 = 7$
- ○ $15 - 7 = 8$
- ○ $15 - 9 = 6$

Chapter 16 Cumulative Review

17
Understanding 2-Digit Addition and Subtraction

Workmat

Theme: Physical Exercise

Counting On by Ones

Work with a partner. Use blocks. Lay out blocks for the blue number. Count on as you lay out blocks for the yellow number. Write the sum.

1. $\boxed{31} + \boxed{2} = \underline{}$

2. $\boxed{16} + \boxed{3} = \underline{}$

3. $\boxed{28} + \boxed{3} = \underline{}$

4. $\boxed{39} + \boxed{1} = \underline{}$

Write the numbers as you count on. Write the sum.

5.

40, $\underline{}$, $\underline{}$

$40 + 2 = \underline{}$

6.

22, $\underline{}$, $\underline{}$, $\underline{}$

$22 + 3 = \underline{}$

USE MENTAL MATH

41, 42, 43, 44

Count on to find the sum.

7. $41 + 3 = \underline{}$

8. $54 + 3 = \underline{}$

Making a Ten

17 is I ten, 7 ones.
3 more makes a ten.
That is 2 tens and
3 extra, 23 in all.

Work in a group. Use ▦ and counters.
Put counters in the ▦ to show the first
number. Put counters outside the ▦
to show the second number. Then
make a ten. Write how many in all.

$$17$$
$$+\ 6$$
$$23$$

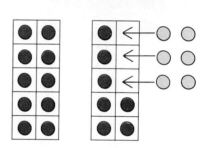

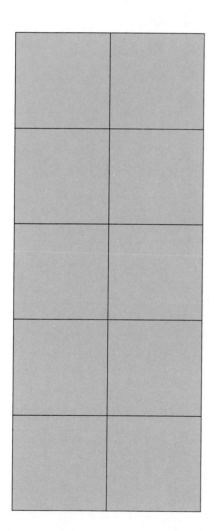

$$18$$
$$+\ 4$$

$$19$$
$$+\ 5$$

$$16$$
$$+\ 6$$

$$15$$
$$+\ 8$$

$$14$$
$$+\ 4$$

$$17$$
$$+\ 7$$

Draw lines to make a ten.
Write how many in all.

1.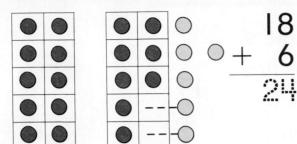
$$\begin{array}{r} 18 \\ + \ 6 \\ \hline 24 \end{array}$$

2.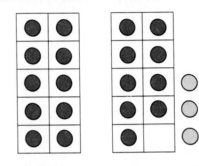
$$\begin{array}{r} 15 \\ + \ 7 \\ \hline \end{array}$$

3.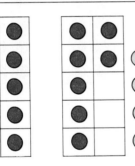
$$\begin{array}{r} 16 \\ + \ 4 \\ \hline \end{array}$$

4.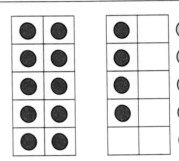
$$\begin{array}{r} 19 \\ + \ 3 \\ \hline \end{array}$$

5.
$$\begin{array}{r} 17 \\ + \ 4 \\ \hline \end{array}$$

6.
$$\begin{array}{r} 14 \\ + \ 5 \\ \hline \end{array}$$

PROBLEM SOLVING

7. I have

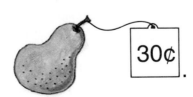

The pear costs

30¢.

How much more do I need?

_____ ¢

Problem Solving
Understanding the Operations

UNDERSTAND
FIND DATA
PLAN
ESTIMATE
SOLVE
CHECK

Count on or use a ⊞ to solve.
Write the answer.

1.

Lucy jumped 18 times.
She jumped 3 more times.
How many times did she
jump in all?

_____ times

$$\begin{array}{r} 18 \\ +\ 3 \\ \hline \end{array}$$

2.

Ruth bounced the ball 23 times.
She bounced it 3 more times.
How many times did she bounce
the ball in all?

_____ times

_____

3.

Sylvia hopped 5 times.
She hopped 16 more times.
How many times did she
hop in all?

_____ times

_____

4.

Peter did 26 toe touches.
He did 5 more.
How many toe touches
did he do in all?

_____ toe touches

_____

Data Analysis

Which sports do your classmates like best? Take a survey to find out.

1. Make a tally mark for each vote.

biking _____ total

softball _____ total

soccer _____ total

roller skating _____ total

2. Mark X on the graph for each tally.

3. Write **Sports Survey** to name the graph.

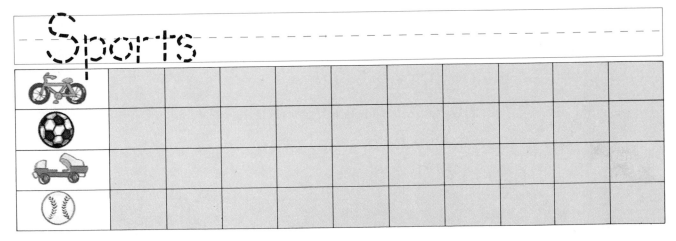

Sports

0   1   __   3   __   5   6   __   8   __   10

4. Write the missing numbers on the graph.
5. Ring what your classmates liked best. Cross out what they liked least.

Name _____

Adding Tens and Ones

Work in a group. Cut out
the score cards. Place cards
on the squares. Show each
number with blocks. Write
the numbers. Then add.

```
   13
+  25
-----
   38
```

Jump-a-Thon
Score Box

1.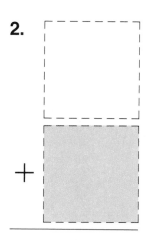

2.

3.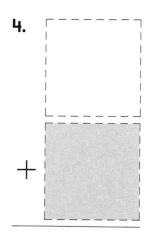

4.

| 31 | 13 | 24 | 32 | 20 | 15 | 25 | 14 |

Paste the score cards
on the squares below.
Draw tens and ones
to show each number.
Write how many in all.

23

+ 11

34

That is 3 tens
and 4 ones,
34.

1.

+

2.

+

3.

+

4.

+

 35 11 21 34 23 12 22 33

Name _____

Counting Back By Ones

| 24 Soccer Balls | 18 Balls | 36 Cones | 23 Jump Ropes |

Listen to the story. Use blocks. Write
the numbers as you count back.

1.

24

23 , ____ , ____

How many are left?

$24 - 3 =$ ____

2.

18

____ , ____

How many are left?

$18 - 2 =$ ____

3.

36

____ , ____ , ____

How many are left?

$36 - 3 =$ ____

4.

23

____ , ____

How many are left?

$23 - 2 =$ ____

Use blocks. Count back to
find the difference.

1.

_____ , _____

$35 - 2 =$ _____

2.

_____ , _____ , _____

$26 - 3 =$ _____

POWER PRACTICE/QUIZ

1. Draw lines to make a ten.
Write how many in all.

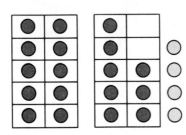

$$\begin{array}{r} 18 \\ + \ 4 \\ \hline \end{array}$$

2. Count on by tens. Write
the numbers. Then
write how many in all.

$$\begin{array}{r} 33 \\ + 20 \\ \hline \end{array}$$

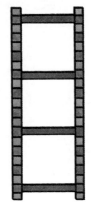

Write the numbers as you count on.
Write the sum.

3.

31, _____ , _____ , _____

$31 + 3 =$ _____

4.

23, _____ , _____

$23 + 2 =$ _____

WRAP UP

MATH WORDS

Match. Then add or subtract.

1. | Count on by ones. |

2. | Count on by tens. |

3. | Count back by ones. |

4. | Count back by tens. |

5. | Make ten, add extra. |

$29 - 2 = \underline{\quad}$

$87 - 50 = \underline{\quad}$

$35 + 3 = \underline{\quad}$

$46 + 20 = \underline{\quad}$

$25 + 7 = \underline{\quad}$

MATH REASONING

Write the missing numbers.

6.
$$
\begin{array}{r}
5 \quad 6 \\
- \ 3 \quad \square \\
\hline
2 \quad 1
\end{array}
$$

$$
\begin{array}{r}
8 \quad \square \\
- \ 4 \quad 3 \\
\hline
4 \quad 2
\end{array}
$$

$$
\begin{array}{r}
\square \quad 9 \\
- \ 5 \quad 5 \\
\hline
2 \quad 4
\end{array}
$$

7.
$$
\begin{array}{r}
6 \quad 3 \\
- \ \square \quad 2 \\
\hline
1 \quad 1
\end{array}
$$

$$
\begin{array}{r}
\square \quad \square \\
- \ 3 \quad 4 \\
\hline
6 \quad 2
\end{array}
$$

$$
\begin{array}{r}
8 \quad \square \\
- \ 5 \quad 5 \\
\hline
3 \quad 2
\end{array}
$$

POWER PRACTICE/TEST

1. Write the number as you count on. Write the sum.

    22, ___ , ___ , ___

    22 + 3 = ___

2. Write the number as you count back. Write the difference.

    38, ___ , ___

    38 − 2 = ___

3. Count on by tens. Then write how many in all.

    27
    + 20
    ———

    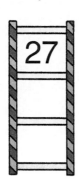

4. Count back by tens. Then write the difference.

    62
    − 30
    ———

    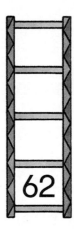

5. Draw tens and ones to show the sum. Add.

    12
    + 13
    ———

6. Cross out tens and ones to subtract.

    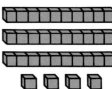

    34
    − 21
    ———

7. Josh found 9 balls. Nancy found 20 balls. How many balls did Josh and Nancy find?

    ___ balls

ENRICHMENT
Finding Another Solution

Sara sold 1 seashell on Monday.
She sold 2 seashells on Tuesday.
She sold 4 seashells on Wednesday.
She sold 8 seashells on Thursday.

How many seashells did she sell
on Friday? Fill in the table to find
the answer.

Day	Monday	Tuesday	Wednesday	Thursday	Friday
Shells Sold	1	2	4	8	

Sara sold _____ seashells on Friday.
Now do the problem another way.

Draw a picture.	or	Use counters.

Did you get the same answer?
Ring one.   yes   no

CUMULATIVE REVIEW

Add.

1.
$$\begin{array}{r} 8 \\ +\ 8 \\ \hline \end{array}$$
○ 15
○ 16
○ 17

Subtract.

5.
$$\begin{array}{r} 17 \\ -\ 9 \\ \hline \end{array}$$
○ 9
○ 8
○ 7

2.
$$\begin{array}{r} 9 \\ 7 \\ +\ 2 \\ \hline \end{array}$$
○ 18
○ 17
○ 19

6.
$$\begin{array}{r} 16 \\ -\ 8 \\ \hline \end{array}$$
○ 7
○ 8
○ 9

7. Find the add-to-check
   fact for $12 - 5 = 7$.
   ○ $7 + 6 = 13$
   ○ $7 - 5 = 2$
   ○ $5 + 7 = 12$

3.
$$\begin{array}{r} 8 \\ +\ 6 \\ \hline \end{array}$$
○ 14
○ 15
○ 16

8. Find the related
   subtraction fact.

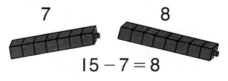

7   8

$15 - 7 = 8$

4. Find the
   double-plus-one fact.
   ○ $7 + 3 = 10$
   ○ $7 + 8 = 15$
   ○ $7 + 7 = 14$

   ○ $15 - 15 = 0$
   ○ $8 - 7 = 1$
   ○ $15 - 8 = 7$

9. Choose the correct answer.
   Glenn has 11 books.
   He has read 6 of them.
   How many does he have left to read?

   ○ 5 books
   ○ 17 books
   ○ 6 books

18
Extending Number Ideas

Workmat

Theme: Gardening

Multiplying Equal Groups of Two

Circle groups of two. Count by twos.
Write how many in all.

1.

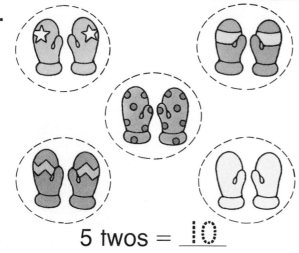

5 twos = 10

2.

3 twos = ____

3.

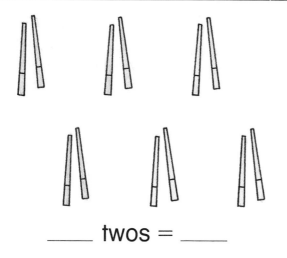

____ twos = ____

4.

____ twos = ____

USE MENTAL MATH

Look at the picture. Use mental
math to answer the questions.

5. How many ears are there?   ____ ears

6. How many eyes are there?   ____ eyes

Name _____

Multiplying Equal Groups of Five

Cut out the flower cards.

Put them in the gardens below. Paste.

Count by fives. Write how many in all.

1.

4 fives = _____

2.

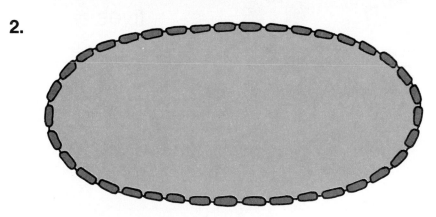

3 fives = _____

3.

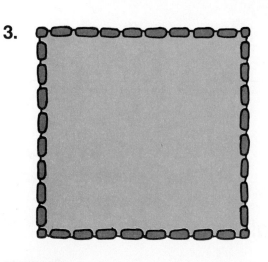

2 fives = _____

Count by fives. Write how many in all.

1.

__2__ fives = __10__

2.

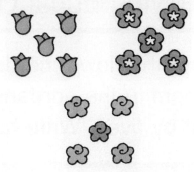

____ fives = ____

3.

____ fives = ____

4.

____ fives = ____

SHOW WITH COUNTERS

5. Use counters to solve. How many flowers did he plant?

He planted ____ flowers in all.

Jimmy,
Use 3 large flower pots.
Plant 5 flowers in each.
Plant 2 flowers in a small pot.

Name _____

Problem Solving
Understanding the Operations

UNDERSTAND
FIND DATA
PLAN
ESTIMATE
SOLVE
CHECK

Color the apples to show the story.
Finish the subtraction sentence.
Answer the question.

Kenyan Bag
and Basket

1. 12 apples are in the basket.
   7 are yellow.
   The others are red.
   How many apples are red?

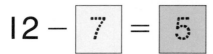

$12 - \boxed{7} = \boxed{5}$ __5__ apples are red.

2. 10 apples are in the basket.
   4 are yellow.
   The others are red.
   How many apples are red?

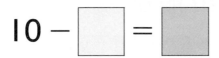

$10 - \square = \square$ _____ apples are red.

3. 12 apples are in the basket.
   8 are red.
   The others are yellow.
   How many apples are yellow?

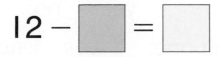

$12 - \square = \square$ _____ apples are yellow.

Probability

Work with a partner. Use 5 red and 5 yellow cubes. Fill a bag with the numbers given.

1. 5 cubes are in the bag.
   4 are red. 1 is yellow.

   Are you more likely to pick a red or a yellow cube? Ring one.

   red   yellow

2. Try it. Shake the bag. Pick a cube. Tally. Put the cube back in the bag. Do this 10 times.

Red	Yellow

3. 6 cubes are in the bag.
   4 are yellow. 2 are red.

   Are you more likely to pick a red or a yellow cube? Ring one.

   red   yellow

4. Try it. Shake the bag. Pick a cube. Tally. Put the cube back in the bag. Do this 10 times.

Red	Yellow

5. Talk about what you picked out of the bag.

   Was your first guess correct? Ring one.   yes   no

   Was your second guess correct? Ring one.   yes   no

Name _____

Understanding Division
Sharing

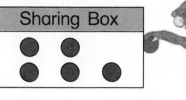
I more for you,
I more for you,
and I more for you.

Work with a partner. Use counters.
Share the number of seeds. Make an
equal group for each person. Write
how many are in each group.

Sharing Box

1.  6 bean seeds   3 people

Each gets

__2__ seeds.

2. 9 carrot seeds   3 people

Each gets

____ seeds.

3. 10 marigold seeds   2 people

Each gets

____ seeds.

4.  12 pumpkin seeds   3 people

Each gets

____ seeds.

5.  14 tomato seeds   2 people

Each gets

____ seeds.

6.  12 lettuce seeds   2 people

Each gets

____ seeds.

Sharing Box

Use counters. Share the number of seeds.
Make an equal group for each person.
Write how many are in each group.

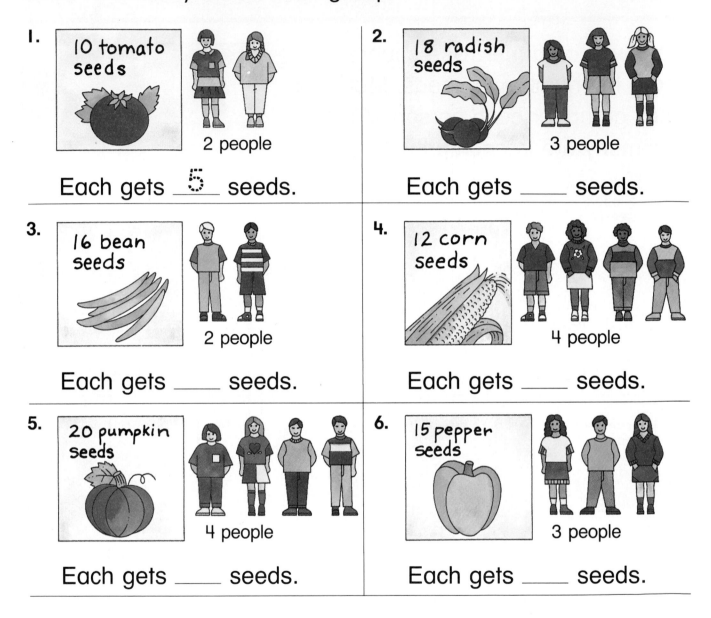

1. 10 tomato seeds
   2 people
   Each gets __5__ seeds.

2. 18 radish seeds
   3 people
   Each gets ____ seeds.

3. 16 bean seeds
   2 people
   Each gets ____ seeds.

4. 12 corn seeds
   4 people
   Each gets ____ seeds.

5. 20 pumpkin seeds
   4 people
   Each gets ____ seeds.

6. 15 pepper seeds
   3 people
   Each gets ____ seeds.

PROBLEM SOLVING

Solve. Use punchout coins to help.

7. Fran has 20¢ in nickels. How many nickels does she have? ____ nickels

8. Will has 25¢ in nickels. How many nickels does he have? ____ nickels

Understanding Division
Separating

Work with a partner. Use counters. Show the amount of fruit in the box. Make equal groups for each bag. Write how many bags are full.

3 in one bag and 3 in another bag. 2 bags are full.

Grouping Box

1.  6 oranges 3 in each bag

   __2__ bags are full.

2.  18 oranges 3 in each bag

   _____ bags are full.

3.  16 pears 2 in each bag

   _____ bags are full.

4.  20 apples 4 in each bag

   _____ bags are full.

Grouping Box

Use counters. Show the amount of fruit.
Make equal groups for each bag.
Write how many bags are full.

1.

12 apples   4 in each bag

_3_ bags are full.

2.

14 apples   2 in each bag

____ bags are full.

3.

10 oranges   2 in each bag

____ bags are full.

4.

18 oranges   6 in each bag

____ bags are full.

POWER PRACTICE/QUIZ

Tell how many in all.

1. Count by twos.

3 twos = ____

2. Count by fives.

2 fives = ____

Use counters. Show the number of seeds.
Make an equal group for each person.
Write how many are in each group.

3.

15 onion seeds   3 people

Each gets ____ seeds.

4.

12 carrot seeds   6 people

Each gets ____ seeds.

Fractions
Halves

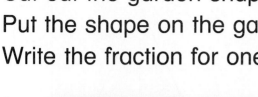

Cut out the garden shapes below.
Put the shape on the garden. Paste.
Write the fraction for one part.

1.

one half planted $\dfrac{1}{2}$

2.

one half
planted $\dfrac{1}{2}$

3.

one half planted $\dfrac{1}{2}$

4.

one half
planted $\dfrac{1}{2}$

Color one half of each shape.
Write the fraction.

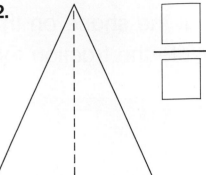

I out of 2 is shaded. That is $\frac{1}{2}$.

1.

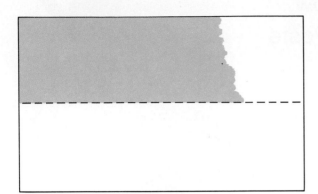

$\frac{1}{2}$

2.

3.

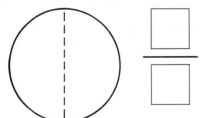

4.

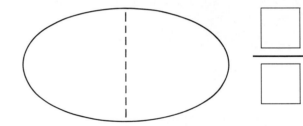

5.

6.

7.

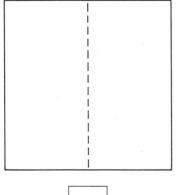
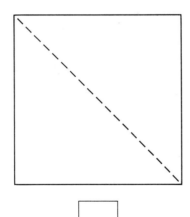
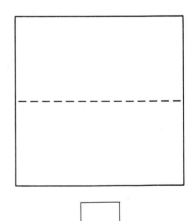

More Practice, page 432, set A

Fractions
Thirds and Fourths

These gardens are divided into equal parts.

Use your fraction pieces. Show the part of the garden to be planted. Color a smaller circle to match.

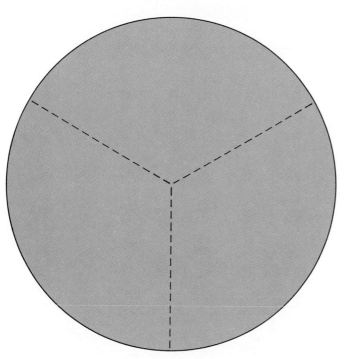

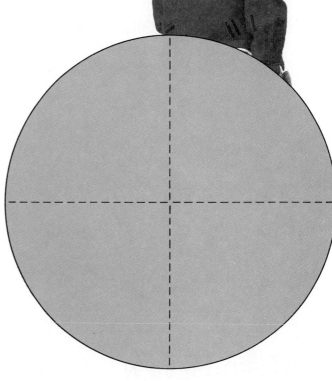

1. Plant 1 part.
3 parts in all.

one third
$\frac{1}{3}$ of the
equal parts

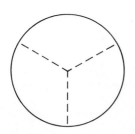

2. Plant 2 parts.
3 parts in all.

two thirds
$\frac{2}{3}$ of the
equal parts

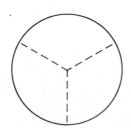

3. Plant 1 part.
4 parts in all.

one fourth
$\frac{1}{4}$ of the
equal parts

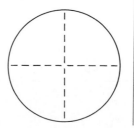

4. Plant 3 parts.
4 parts in all.

three fourths
$\frac{3}{4}$ of the
equal parts

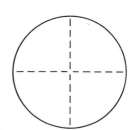

Color the garden.
Show how much has been planted.

1.

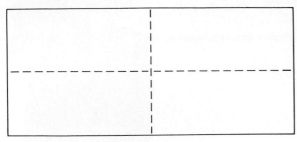

three fourths planted $\dfrac{3}{4}$

2.

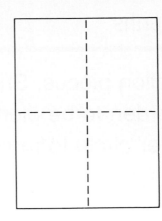

one fourth planted $\dfrac{1}{4}$

3.

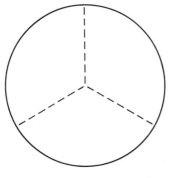

one third planted $\dfrac{1}{3}$

4.

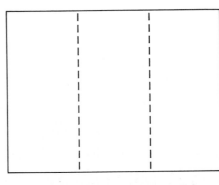

two thirds planted $\dfrac{2}{3}$

MIXED REVIEW

5. Count the money.

_____ ¢

6. Write the time.

_____

7. Add.

$$\begin{array}{r} 7 \\ + 7 \\ \hline \end{array} \qquad \begin{array}{r} 9 \\ + 6 \\ \hline \end{array} \qquad \begin{array}{r} 8 \\ + 8 \\ \hline \end{array}$$

8. Subtract.

$$\begin{array}{r} 18 \\ - 9 \\ \hline \end{array} \qquad \begin{array}{r} 16 \\ - 8 \\ \hline \end{array} \qquad \begin{array}{r} 14 \\ - 9 \\ \hline \end{array}$$

Fractions
Using Sets

I of the 4 is red.
I fourth is red.

Work with a partner. Lay out two-color counters to show the tomatoes. Color to match. Say the fraction.

I. I of 2 is red.

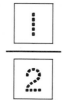 one half

2. I of 3 is yellow.

 one third

3. I of 4 is red.

one fourth

4. 2 of 3 are red.

 two thirds

5. 2 of 4 are red.

two fourths

6. 3 of 4 are yellow.

three fourths

Color to match.

1.

one half $\dfrac{1}{2}$
red

2.

two thirds $\dfrac{2}{3}$
green

3.

two fourths green $\dfrac{2}{4}$

4.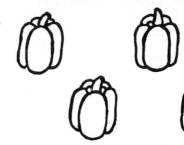

one fourth red $\dfrac{1}{4}$

5.

one third $\dfrac{1}{3}$
yellow

6.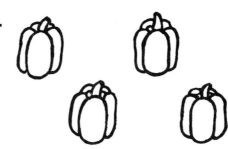

three fourths red $\dfrac{3}{4}$

PROBLEM SOLVING

7. Solve. Color to show the story.

10 peppers are in the bag. 6 are green. The others are red. How many peppers are red?

$10 - \boxed{} = \boxed{}$

_____ peppers are red.

Problem Solving
Finding Missing Data

UNDERSTAND
FIND DATA
PLAN
ESTIMATE
SOLVE
CHECK

 zinnia seeds 10¢

 bean seeds 5¢

 corn seeds 20¢

 sunflower seeds 30¢

 marigold seeds 15¢

 tomato seeds 25¢

Solve. Use the data from
the seed packets to help.

1. Alice bought 1 packet of snow peas for
   15¢ and 1 packet of sunflower seeds.
   How much did she spend?

   She spent _____.

$$\begin{array}{r} 15¢ \\ +\ 30¢ \\ \hline 45¢ \end{array}$$

2. Eric bought 1 packet of peppers for
   20¢ and 1 packet of zinnia seeds.
   How much did he spend?

   He spent _____.

3. Jon bought 1 packet of cabbage seeds
   for 10¢ and 1 packet of corn seeds.
   How much did he spend?

   He spent _____.

4. Kristina bought 1 packet of carrot seeds
   for 40¢ and 1 packet of bean seeds.
   How much did she spend?

   She spent _____.

Problem Solving Strategy
Use Logical Reasoning

UNDERSTAND
FIND DATA
PLAN
ESTIMATE
SOLVE
CHECK

Read the clues. Write each name.

Bruce laughed at Sue's .

Sara is wearing a .

Dick is wearing a .

Joan gave Eric a .

_____
_____

_____
_____

_____
_____

_____
_____

_____
_____

_____
_____

WRAP UP

MATH WORDS

1.

   How many groups of two are there?   _____

   How many groups of five are there?   _____

   How many are there in all?   _____

2.

   Share the berries so each bird
   gets the same number. Use
   counters to help.   Each gets _____ berries.

3. Color one half.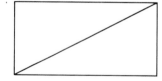

4. Color one fourth.

MATH REASONING

5. Tammy has 10 marbles. Hans
   has 5 marbles. Jane has
   6 marbles. To play a game,
   each needs the same number
   of marbles. Share the marbles
   so each has the same number.
   Use counters to help.

   Each gets _____ marbles.

POWER PRACTICE/TEST

Tell how many in all.

1. Count by twos.

4 twos = _____

2. Count by fives.

2 fives = _____

3. Make an equal group for each person. Write how many in each group. 5 people

Each gets _____ apples.

4. Make an equal group for each bag. Write how many bags are full. 3 in each bag

_____ bags are full.

Match.

5.

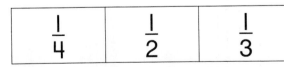

$\frac{1}{4}$ $\frac{1}{2}$ $\frac{1}{3}$

6.

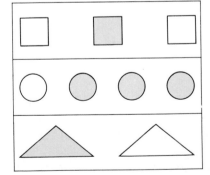

$\frac{3}{4}$

$\frac{1}{2}$

$\frac{1}{3}$

7. Zoe bought 1 packet of corn seeds for 15¢ and 1 packet of lettuce seeds. How much did she spend?

$+$ _____
_____

She spent _____.

Chapter 18   Power Practice/Test

ENRICHMENT
Relating Multiplication and Division

Work in a group. Use cubes to show each train below. Fill in the blanks to match. Then snap off each group of cubes. Fill in the blanks to match.

1.

   _____ twos = _____

   _____ shown in _____ groups of _____

2.

   _____ twos = _____

   _____ shown in _____ groups of _____

3.

   _____ fives = _____

   _____ shown in _____ groups of _____

CUMULATIVE REVIEW

1. Subtract.

$$\begin{array}{r} 18 \\ -\ 9 \\ \hline \end{array}$$

○ 9
○ 8
○ 7

2. Find the add-to-check
fact.

$$\begin{array}{r} 17 \\ -\ 8 \\ \hline 9 \end{array}$$

○ $7 + 8 = 15$
○ $9 + 8 = 17$
○ $9 + 7 = 16$

3. Which belongs in the
same fact family?

$7 + 7 = 14$

○ $14 - 8 = 6$
○ $14 - 7 = 7$
○ $7 - 7 = 0$

4. Subtract.

$14 - 9 =$ ___

○ 5
○ 7
○ 6

Add.

5.
$$\begin{array}{r} 43 \\ +\ 30 \\ \hline \end{array}$$

○ 83
○ 63
○ 73

6.
$$\begin{array}{r} 15 \\ +\ 22 \\ \hline \end{array}$$

○ 27
○ 37
○ 39

7. Count back by tens.
Choose the answer.

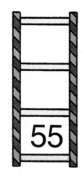

○ 75
○ 53
○ 35

$55 - 20 =$ ___

8. Subtract.
$$\begin{array}{r} 67 \\ -\ 34 \\ \hline \end{array}$$

○ 42
○ 33
○ 34

9. Choose the correct number sentence.

There were 28 🍓 in the basket.
Conchita ate 15. How many 🍓
are left?

○ $28 - 15 = 13$
○ $27 - 14 = 13$
○ $28 + 15 = 43$

Resource Bank and Glossary

Data Bank

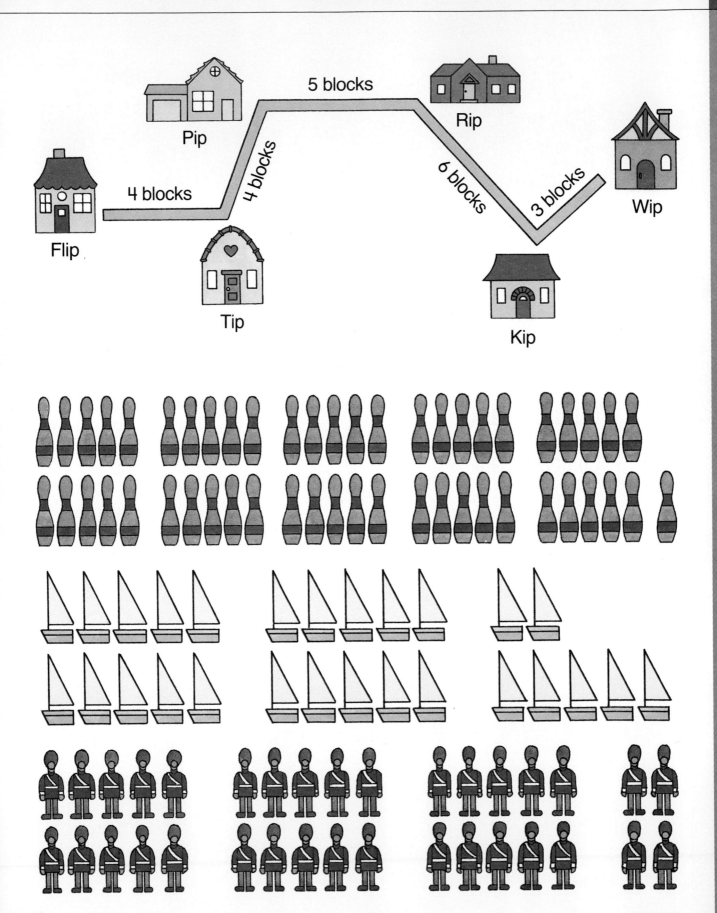

March, Year 2000

Sunday	Monday	Tuesday	Wednesday	Thursday	Friday	Saturday
			1	2	3	4
5	6	7	8	9	10	11
12	13	14	15	16	17	18
19	20	21	22	23	24	25
26	27	28	29	30	31	

Data Bank

5¢

8¢

6¢

Dinosaur Lengths

40 feet

20 feet

30 feet

Name _____

Getting Ready to Calculate

1. Press the keys shown. Write what you see.

Press	See
ON/C	
I	
ON/C	
I2	
ON/C	
I234	
5	
6	
ON/C	

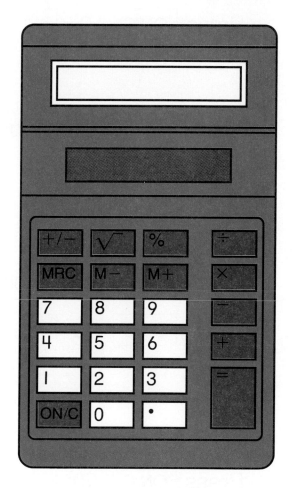

ACTIVITY

2. Press ON/C .

Press I 2 3 4 5 6 7 8 9.

Ring the last digit you see.

Name _____

Counting On and Back

1. Start at 0. Count on by 1s. Write what you see.

    Press │ ON/C │ 0 │ + │ 1 │ = │ │ = │ │ = │ │ = │ │ = │ │ = │

    ⋮
    ____ , ____ , ____ , ____ , ____ , ____

2. Start at 10. Count on by 10s. Write what you see.

    Press │ ON/C │ 10 │ + │ 10 │ = │ │ = │ │ = │ │ = │ │ = │ │ = │

    ____ , ____ , ____ , ____ , ____ , ____

3. Start at 20. Count back by 2s. Write what you see.

    Press │ ON/C │ 20 │ − │ 2 │ = │ │ = │ │ = │ │ = │ │ = │ │ = │

    ____ , ____ , ____ , ____ , ____ , ____

4. Start at 50. Count back by 5s. Write what you see.

    Press │ ON/C │ 50 │ − │ 5 │ = │ │ = │ │ = │ │ = │ │ = │ │ = │

    ____ , ____ , ____ , ____ , ____ , ____

ACTIVITY

5. Ring the numbers that do not belong.
    Start at 12. Count by 4s.

    8   12   16   20   22   28   32   36   41   44

Name _____

Adding Whole Numbers

Say each addition sentence as you
press the keys. Write the sum.

1. Say   "Five   plus   three   equals."

   Press   ON/C   5   +   3   =   [   ]

2. Say   "Ten   plus   four   equals."

   Press   ON/C   10   +   4   =   [   ]

3. Say   "Twenty   plus   seventy   equals."

   Press   ON/C   20   +   70   =   [   ]

4. Say   "Six   plus   four   plus   five   equals."

   Press   ON/C   6   +   4   +   5   =   [   ]

ACTIVITY

| 9 | 5 | 8 |

5. Work with a partner.

   Use two 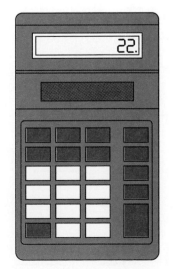 and one set
   of punchout number cards.
   Mix the cards. Each player
   takes three cards. Find the sum.
   The player with the greater sum
   wins. The first player to win six
   games is the champion.

Name _____

Subtracting Whole Numbers

Say each subtraction sentence as you
press the keys. Write the difference.

1. Say   "Nine minus four equals."

    Press ON/C   9   –   4   =

2. Say   "Fifteen minus eight equals."

    Press ON/C   15   –   8   =

3. Say   "Twenty minus   six equals."

    Press ON/C   20   –   6   =

ACTIVITY

Write each difference.
Connect the answers in order.

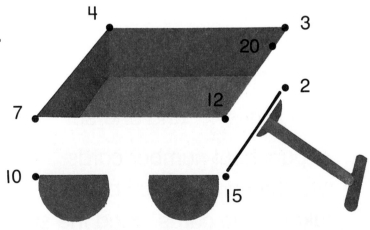

4. $9 - 7 =$ _____

5. $6 - 3 =$ _____

6. $11 - 7 =$ _____

7. $10 - 3 =$ _____

8. $18 - 8 =$ _____   9. $30 - 15 =$ _____

10. $24 - 12 =$ _____   11. $32 - 12 =$ _____

Name _____

Turtle Marathon

Write the number of corner turns each
turtle needs to make to finish the race.

Turtle 3 _____   Turtle 2 _____   Turtle 6 _____   Turtle 5 _____

Turtle 7 _____   Turtle 1 _____   Turtle 4 _____

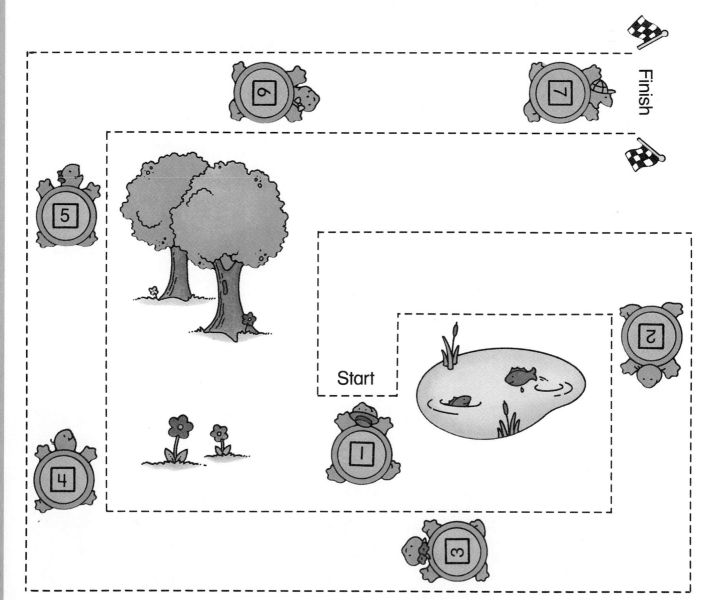

Name

Turtle Village

Cut out the turtle. Start in the HOME box. Follow the directions. Color each picture where the turtle stops.

1. FORWARD 3

2. RIGHT 90
FORWARD 3

3. RIGHT 90
FORWARD 5

4. RIGHT 90
FORWARD 6

5. RIGHT 90
FORWARD 4

6. RIGHT 90
FORWARD 5

Name _____

My Square

A square has 4 equal sides. □

Draw your own square.

1. Draw a △ at any dot to start.
2. Connect some dots to make a straight line.
3. Count the spaces between the dots.
4. Draw the other three sides.

Write your directions on another sheet of paper.

•   •   •   •   •   •   •   •

•   •   •   •   •   •   •   •

•   •   •   •   •   •   •   •

•   •   •   •   •   •   •   •

•   •   •   •   •   •   •   •

•   •   •   •   •   •   •   •

•   •   •   •   •   •   •   •

Name _____

Turtle Goes Fishing

The turtle is fishing. Follow the directions.
Connect the dots to help the turtle catch
the fish. Cut out the turtle above to help.

1. BACK 2	5. BACK 3
2. LEFT 90	6. RIGHT 90
3. BACK 4	7. FORWARD 1
4. RIGHT 90	

408 (four hundred eight)

Name _____

Set A   For use after page 2.

Ring the bird that does not belong.

1.

2.

Set B   For use after page 4.

Color to continue the pattern.

1.

2.

Set C   For use after page 12.

Write numbers to show the pattern.

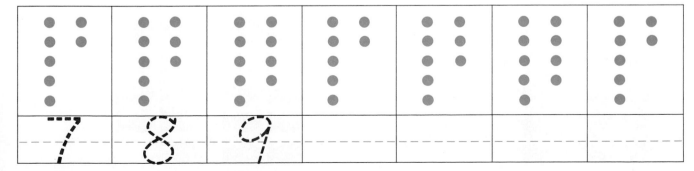

More Practice Bank

Name _____

Set A   For use after page 18.

1. Count on. Write the missing numbers.

2. Count back. Write the missing numbers.

Set B   For use after page 20.

Barry had his toy cars lined up on
his shelf as shown. Continue his pattern.
Ring the car that comes next.

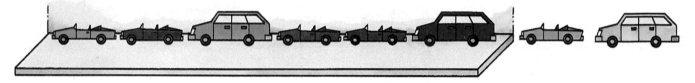

Set C   For use after page 30.

Write the number in all.

1.

2.

More Practice Bank

Name _____

Set A   For use after page 32.

Ring enough coins to pay.

1.

2.

Set B   For use after page 38.

1. Count. Write how many.

Alex ~~IIII~~ I _____   Marty ~~IIII~~ _____   Silvia III _____

2. Color the graph to show the tallies.

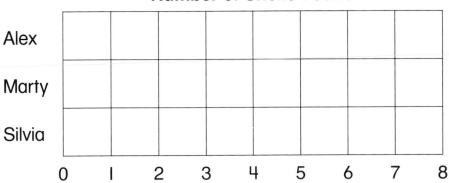

Number of Shells Found

3. How many more shells did
   Alex find than Silvia?   _____ more

4. How many fewer shells did
   Marty find than Alex?   _____ fewer

More Practice Bank

Name _____

Set A   For use after page 50.

Write the sum.

1.

   $3 + 2 =$ ___

2.

   $2 + 4 =$ ___

3.

   $3 + 3 =$ ___

4.

   $5 + 1 =$ ___

Set B   For use after page 60.

Write what you see. Add.

1.

2.

3.

Set C   For use after page 62.

Add.

1. $3¢ + 4¢ = $ ___ ¢
   in all

   $2¢ + 5¢ = $ ___ ¢
   in all

   $2¢ + 2¢ = $ ___ ¢
   in all

More Practice Bank

Name _____

Set A　For use after page 72.

Subtract.

1.

2.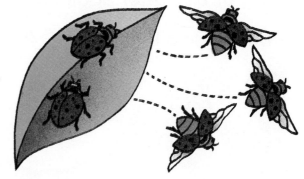

$3 - 1 =$ _____　　　$5 - 3 =$ _____

Set B　For use after page 76.

Subtract.

1. $\begin{array}{r} 3 \\ -\ 2 \\ \hline \end{array}$

2. $\begin{array}{r} 6 \\ -\ 3 \\ \hline \end{array}$

Set C　For use after page 82.

Subtract.

1.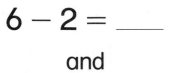

2.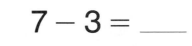

3.

$6 - 2 =$ _____　　　$7 - 3 =$ _____　　　$8 - 2 =$ _____

and　　　　　　and　　　　　　and

$6 - 4 =$ _____　　　$7 - 4 =$ _____　　　$8 - 6 =$ _____

Name _____

Set A For use after page 85.

4 owls sit in a tree.   2 fly away.

Ring the question you would ask.   Finish the
                                          number sentence.
How many owls are there in all?

How many owls are left?   _____ ◯ _____ = _____

Set B For use after page 92.

Add zero or count on.

$$\begin{array}{c} 5 \\ +\ 1 \\ \hline \end{array} \qquad \begin{array}{c} 0 \\ +\ 7 \\ \hline \end{array} \qquad \begin{array}{c} 2 \\ +\ 6 \\ \hline \end{array} \qquad \begin{array}{c} 8 \\ +\ 2 \\ \hline \end{array} \qquad \begin{array}{c} 1 \\ +\ 8 \\ \hline \end{array} \qquad \begin{array}{c} 9 \\ +\ 0 \\ \hline \end{array}$$

Set C For use after page 96.

Add.

$$\begin{array}{c} 2¢ \\ +\ 6¢ \\ \hline \end{array} \qquad \begin{array}{c} 9¢ \\ +\ 3¢ \\ \hline \end{array} \qquad \begin{array}{c} 7¢ \\ +\ 3¢ \\ \hline \end{array} \qquad \begin{array}{c} 0¢ \\ +\ 8¢ \\ \hline \end{array} \qquad \begin{array}{c} 3¢ \\ +\ 4¢ \\ \hline \end{array} \qquad \begin{array}{c} 8¢ \\ +\ 1¢ \\ \hline \end{array}$$

More Practice Bank

Name _____

Set A   For use after page 114.

Add. Ring sums of 10.

$$\begin{array}{r} 4 \\ +\ 6 \\ \hline \end{array} \qquad \begin{array}{r} 8 \\ +\ 2 \\ \hline \end{array} \qquad \begin{array}{r} 4 \\ +\ 4 \\ \hline \end{array} \qquad \begin{array}{r} 1 \\ +\ 9 \\ \hline \end{array} \qquad \begin{array}{r} 5 \\ +\ 5 \\ \hline \end{array} \qquad \begin{array}{r} 6 \\ +\ 6 \\ \hline \end{array}$$

Set B   For use after page 124.

Add.

1.
$$\begin{array}{r} 8 \\ +\ 4 \\ \hline \end{array} \qquad \begin{array}{r} 4 \\ +\ 5 \\ \hline \end{array} \qquad \begin{array}{r} 5 \\ +\ 7 \\ \hline \end{array} \qquad \begin{array}{r} 0 \\ +\ 9 \\ \hline \end{array} \qquad \begin{array}{r} 7 \\ +\ 4 \\ \hline \end{array} \qquad \begin{array}{r} 5 \\ +\ 6 \\ \hline \end{array}$$

2.
$$\begin{array}{r} 7 \\ +\ 5 \\ \hline \end{array} \qquad \begin{array}{r} 6 \\ +\ 6 \\ \hline \end{array} \qquad \begin{array}{r} 5 \\ +\ 2 \\ \hline \end{array} \qquad \begin{array}{r} 4 \\ +\ 8 \\ \hline \end{array} \qquad \begin{array}{r} 6 \\ +\ 0 \\ \hline \end{array} \qquad \begin{array}{r} 5 \\ +\ 4 \\ \hline \end{array}$$

Set C   For use after page 126.

Add.

$$\begin{array}{r} 3 \\ 4 \\ +\ 2 \\ \hline \end{array} \qquad \begin{array}{r} 6 \\ 3 \\ +\ 2 \\ \hline \end{array} \qquad \begin{array}{r} 2 \\ 0 \\ +\ 5 \\ \hline \end{array} \qquad \begin{array}{r} 5 \\ 2 \\ +\ 2 \\ \hline \end{array} \qquad \begin{array}{r} 1 \\ 4 \\ +\ 3 \\ \hline \end{array} \qquad \begin{array}{r} 5 \\ 3 \\ +\ 3 \\ \hline \end{array}$$

Name _____

Set A   For use after page 128.

Use the table to answer the question.

How much do 3 cost?

snails
4¢
each

snails	1	2	3
cost	4¢	8¢	____¢

3 snails cost ____ ¢.

Set B   For use after page 134.

Estimate how many units long.

Use 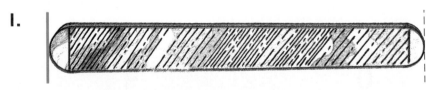 to measure.

1.

estimate ____ units

measure ____ units

2.

estimate ____ units

measure ____ units

More Practice Bank

Name _____

Set A For use after page 138.

Use your ruler. Measure.
Write the length or height.

1.

____ inches

2.

____ inches

3.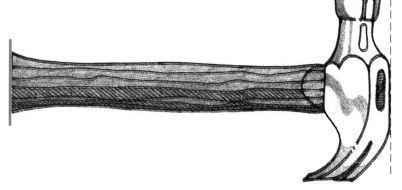

____ inches

Set B For use after page 140.

Use your foot ruler. Measure.
Ring the best answer.

1. your chair height

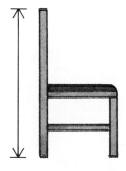

longer than 2 [ruler]

2 [ruler]

shorter than 2 [ruler]

2. your chair width

longer than 2 [ruler]

2 [ruler]

shorter than 2 [ruler]

Name _____

Set A   For use after page 142.

Ring 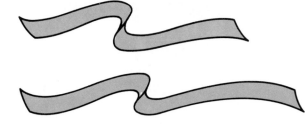 the longer one.
Ring 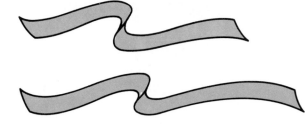 the shorter one.

1.

2.

Set B   For use after page 151.

Ring the answer if it makes sense. Cross
out if it does not make sense. Make
an estimate that does make sense.

1.

The baby snake is
10 centimeters long.

How long is the
snake's mother?

__12__ centimeters

_____ centimeters

2.

The puppy weighs
6 pounds.

How much does the
puppy's mother weigh?

__24__ pounds

_____ pounds

More Practice Bank

Name _____

Set A   For use after page 162.

Subtract.

1.
$$\begin{array}{r} 7 \\ -1 \\ \hline \end{array} \qquad \begin{array}{r} 9 \\ -2 \\ \hline \end{array} \qquad \begin{array}{r} 8 \\ -1 \\ \hline \end{array} \qquad \begin{array}{r} 10 \\ -2 \\ \hline \end{array} \qquad \begin{array}{r} 11 \\ -2 \\ \hline \end{array} \qquad \begin{array}{r} 5 \\ -2 \\ \hline \end{array}$$

2.
$$\begin{array}{r} 6 \\ -1 \\ \hline \end{array} \qquad \begin{array}{r} 11 \\ -2 \\ \hline \end{array} \qquad \begin{array}{r} 9 \\ -3 \\ \hline \end{array} \qquad \begin{array}{r} 10 \\ -3 \\ \hline \end{array} \qquad \begin{array}{r} 7 \\ -2 \\ \hline \end{array} \qquad \begin{array}{r} 8 \\ -2 \\ \hline \end{array}$$

Set B   For use after page 170.

Subtract.

$$\begin{array}{r} 8 \\ -4 \\ \hline \end{array} \qquad \begin{array}{r} 9 \\ -9 \\ \hline \end{array} \qquad \begin{array}{r} 10 \\ -5 \\ \hline \end{array} \qquad \begin{array}{r} 5 \\ -0 \\ \hline \end{array} \qquad \begin{array}{r} 7 \\ -3 \\ \hline \end{array} \qquad \begin{array}{r} 6 \\ -3 \\ \hline \end{array}$$

Set C   For use after page 186.

Write how many.

1.
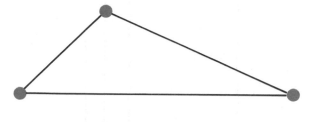

_____ sides

_____ corners

2.
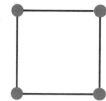

_____ sides

_____ corners

Name _____

Set A   For use after page 192.

Write how many pegs inside, outside, and on.

1.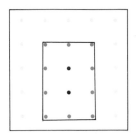

_____ inside

_____ outside

_____ on

2.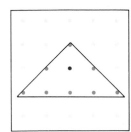

_____ inside

_____ outside

_____ on

Set B   For use after page 194.

Draw a line to make
two matching parts.

1.

2.

3.

Set C   For use after page 196.

Ring the one that is the same size and shape.

Name _____

Set A   For use after page 197.

Use your inch ruler.
Write how many inches.

1. How far is it from
   home to the library?

   _____ inches

2. How far is it from
   home to the store
   by way of the bank?

   _____ inches

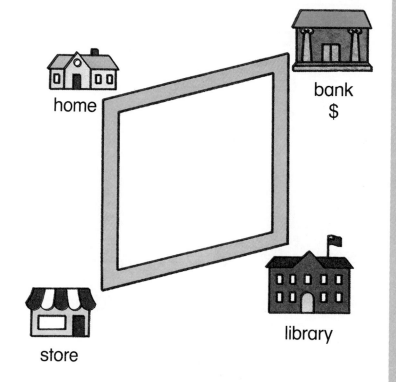

Set B   For use after page 198.

Color the one that comes next.

1.
   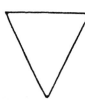 

2.

More Practice Bank

Name _____

Set A   For use after page 204.

Subtract.

9	10	9	10	9	10
− 5	− 6	− 4	− 8	− 6	− 7

Set B   For use after page 216.

Finish the fact family. Add or subtract.

1. $9 + 3 =$ ___
   $3 + 9 =$ ___
   $12 - 3 =$ ___
   $12 - 9 =$ ___

2. $7 + 2 =$ ___
   $2 + 7 =$ ___
   $9 - 2 =$ ___
   $9 - 7 =$ ___

3. $6 + 4 =$ ___
   $4 + 6 =$ ___
   $10 - 4 =$ ___
   $10 - 6 =$ ___

Set C   For use after page 218.

Subtract.

11	11	12	10	6	8
− 8	− 5	− 9	− 8	− 4	− 6

More Practice Bank

Name _____

Set A   For use after page 226.

Ring groups of ten. Write how
many tens and ones.

1.

Tens	Ones

2.

Tens	Ones

Set B   For use after page 240.

Show how much money. Color
enough dimes. Color
enough pennies.

1.

2.

Name _____

Set A   For use after page 248.

Count. Write how many.

1.

_____ , _____ , _____ , _____ , _____

2.

_____ , _____ , _____ , _____ , _____

Set B   For use after page 260.

Start at the top of the ladder.
Write as you count ten more.

1.    2.    3. 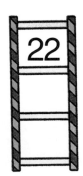   4.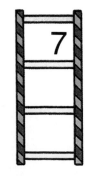

Set C   For use after page 264.

Count and color the frogs.

 second  fifth

More Practice Bank

Name _____

Set A   For use after page 272.

Use coin punchouts. Cover each
coin as you count. Write the amount.

1.   2.

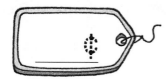   

Set B   For use after page 276.

Count the money. Write the amount.

_____, _____, _____, _____, _____, _____

Set C   For use after page 284.

Count the money. Write the amount.

1.

_____, _____, _____, _____, _____

2.

_____, _____, _____, _____, _____

Name _____

Set A For use after page 294.

Show the time on each clock.

1.

8 o'clock

2.

10 o'clock

Set B For use after page 298.

Write the times.

1.

____ : ____

2.

____ : ____

3.

____ : ____

Set C For use after page 302.

Ring the answer.

1. Valentine's Day is

   on a _____.

   Tuesday   Friday

2. Washington's Birthday

   is on February _____.

   12   15   22   29

FEBRUARY						
Sun.	Mon.	Tues.	Wed.	Thurs.	Fri.	Sat.
			1	2	3	4
5	6	7	8	9	10	11
12	13	♡14	15	16	17	18
19	20	21	22	23	24	25
26	27	28				

More Practice Bank

Name _____

Set A   For use after page 310.

Add.

8	9	9	4	7	9
+9	+6	+9	+9	+9	+5

Set B   For use after page 316.

Add.

5	9	2	4	9	4
3	4	8	6	9	0
+5	+5	+7	+5	+2	+4

Set C   For use after page 325.

Ring the number if it is correct.
Cross out if it is wrong. Write the
correct number sentence.

7 koalas are playing.
3 koalas are eating.
How many more koalas
are playing?

<u>10</u> more koalas are playing.

_____ ◯ _____ = _____

Name _____

Set A   For use after page 332.

Ring the subtraction doubles.
Then subtract all.

1. $10 - 5 =$ ___ $9 - 6 =$ ___ $16 - 8 =$ ___

2. $8 - 4 =$ ___ $18 - 9 =$ ___ $10 - 4 =$ ___

Set B   For use after page 340.

Subtract. Use the
add-to-check fact to help.

1.
5	12
+ 7	− 5

2.
7	13
+ 6	− 6

3.
4	11
+ 7	− 4

Set C   For use after page 347.

Write the number sentence for
the story. Write the answer.
Ring to finish the story.

7 dinosaurs are eating.
2 dinosaurs are sleeping.
How many more are eating?

___ ◯ ___ = ___

___ more are eating.

___ dinosaurs in all.

More Practice Bank

Name _____

Set A   For use after page 356.

Draw lines to make a ten.
Write how many in all.

1.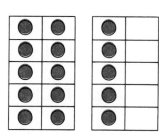
$$\begin{array}{r} 17 \\ + \ 5 \\ \hline \end{array}$$

2.
$$\begin{array}{r} 15 \\ + \ 6 \\ \hline \end{array}$$

Set B   For use after page 360.

Count on by tens.
Write how many in all.

1.
$$\begin{array}{r} 15 \\ + 20 \\ \hline \end{array}$$

2.
$$\begin{array}{r} 28 \\ + 30 \\ \hline \end{array}$$
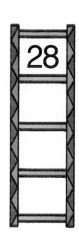

3.
$$\begin{array}{r} 32 \\ + 10 \\ \hline \end{array}$$

Set C   For use after page 368.

Find the difference. Cross out
tens and ones to show it.

1.
$$\begin{array}{r} 36 \\ - 14 \\ \hline \end{array}$$
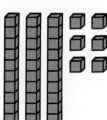

2.
$$\begin{array}{r} 48 \\ - 25 \\ \hline \end{array}$$
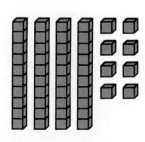

Name _____

Set A   For use after page 369.

Use mental math, blocks and paper

and pencil, or a to solve the

problem. ✔ the method you used.

Ian brought home 29 rocks.   _____
He gave 14 to his sister.   _____
How many rocks does he
have left?   _____

                                 _____

_____ left

I used

☐ mental math

☐ calculator

☐ blocks and
   paper and
   pencil

Set B   For use after page 370.

Draw a picture. Show the order
they finished the race.

Tommy finished first.
Tina finished before
Elena. Rocky finished
after Elena.

Elena   Rocky   Tommy   Tina

More Practice Bank

Name _____

Set A   For use after page 378.

Write how many in all.

1.

_____ fives = _____

2.

_____ fives = _____

Set B   For use after page 379.

Finish the subtraction sentence.

1. 13 apples are in the bag.
   8 are red. The others
   are yellow. How many
   are yellow?

   13 − ▢ = ▢

   _____ apples are yellow.

2. 11 apples are in the bag.
   6 are yellow. The others
   are red. How many are
   red?

   11 − ▢ = ▢

   _____ apples are red.

Set C   For use after page 382.

Share the fruit. Make an equal group for each
person. Write how many are in each group.

1.

   10 apples   5 people

   Each gets _____ apples.

2.

   25 berries   5 people

   Each gets _____ berries.

Name _____

Set A   For use after page 386.

Ring the shapes that show halves.

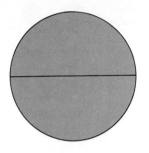 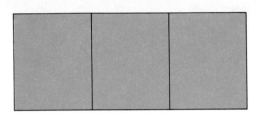 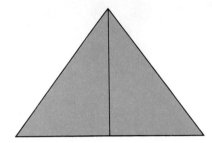

Set B   For use after page 388.

Ring the shapes that show fourths.

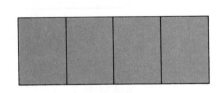 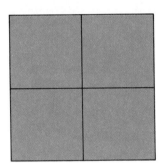 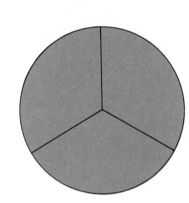

Set C   For use after page 390.

Ring the sets that show $\frac{1}{3}$ red.

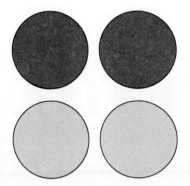 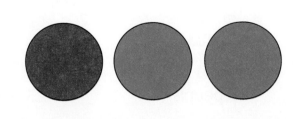 

Glossary

Add

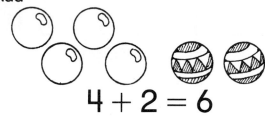

$$4 + 2 = 6$$

Addition sentence

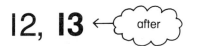

$$3 + 6 = 9$$

After

12, 13 ← after

Area

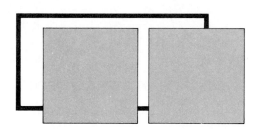

The **area** of this shape is 2 tiles.

Bar graph

Sea Animals We Like

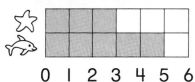

0 1 2 3 4 5 6

Before

before → **12,** 13

Between

9, 10, 11 between

Box

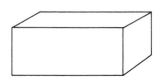

Calculator

Calendar

MAY

Sun.	Mon.	Tue.	Wed.	Thu.	Fri.	Sat.
	1	2	3	4	5	6
7	8	9	10	11	12	13
14	15	16	17	18	19	20
21	22	23	24	25	26	27
28	29	30	31			

Capacity

The **capacity** of this glass is 1 cup.

Centimeter

1 centimeter

0 1 2 3 4 5 6 7 8

centimeter ruler

Glossary

Circle

Cone

Congruent figures

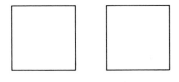

Corner

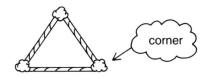

corner

Cube

Cylinder

Decimeter

I decimeter

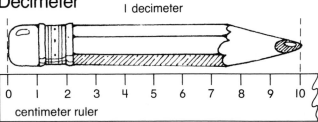

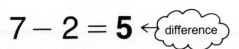

centimeter ruler

Difference

$$7 - 2 = 5$$ ← difference

Digit

0 1 2 3 4 5 6 7 8 9

There are ten **digits.**

Dime

10¢ or 10 cents

Divide

3 people

6 bean seeds

Each person gets 2 seeds.

Dollar bill

$1.00 or 100¢ or 100 cents

Dozen

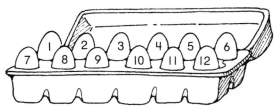

Even

2   4   6   8

Even numbers make pairs.

Glossary

Fact family

$$2 + 4 = 6 \qquad 6 - 4 = 2$$
$$4 + 2 = 6 \qquad 6 - 2 = 4$$

Fewer

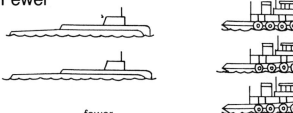

fewer

Foot

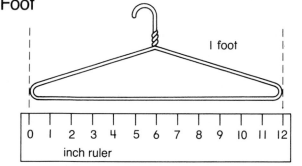

1 foot

inch ruler

Fractions

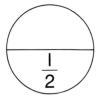 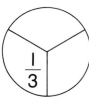 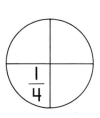

$\dfrac{1}{2}$ $\dfrac{1}{3}$ $\dfrac{1}{4}$

one half   one third   one fourth

Geoboard

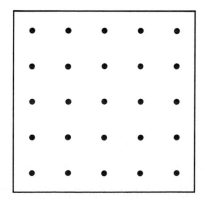

Greater than

 17   13

Half hour

2:00 to 2:30

Hour

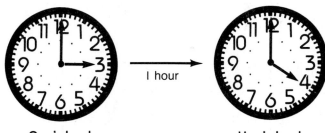

3 o'clock   1 hour   4 o'clock

Hour hand

The **hour hand** is pointing to the 9.

Inch

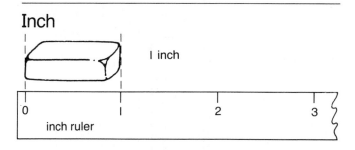

1 inch

inch ruler

Glossary

Inside

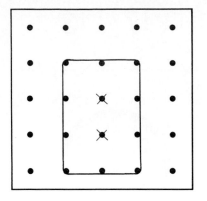

The Xs are **inside**.

Less than

Minute hand

The **minute hand** is pointing to the 12.

More

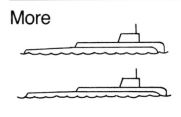 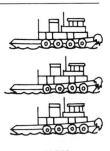

more

Multiply

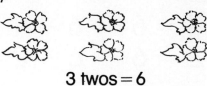

3 twos = 6

Nickel

5¢ or 5 cents

Number line

Number sentence

$5 + 3 = 8$ or $7 - 4 = 3$

Odd

1   3   5   7

Odd numbers of objects cannot be paired.

On

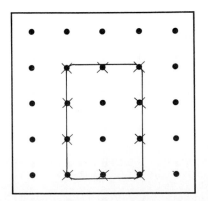

The Xs are **on** the rubber band.

Glossary

Ordinal numbers

first   second   third

Outside

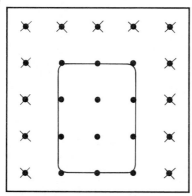

The Xs are **outside**.

Oval

Pattern

Penny

1¢ or 1 cent

Pictograph

Boats

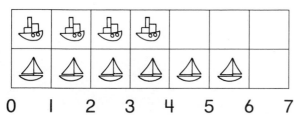

0   1   2   3   4   5   6   7

Quarter

25¢ or 25 cents

Rectangle

Ruler

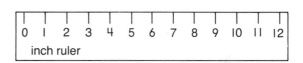

inch ruler

Side

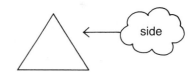

side

Sphere

Square

Subtract

$4 - 1 = 3$

Subtraction sentence

$7 - 5 = 2$

Glossary

Sum

$$1 + 3 = 4 \leftarrow \text{sum}$$

Survey

Do you like cats or dogs better?

Tally

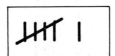

Temperature

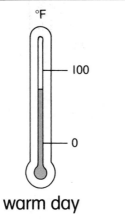

warm day

Ten-frame

Triangle

Turnaround fact

$$3 + 4 = 7 \qquad 4 + 3 = 7$$

Week

JUNE

Sun.	Mon.	Tue.	Wed.	Thu.	Fri.	Sat.
1	2	3	4	5	6	7
8	9	10	11	12	13	14

I **week** is 7 days.

Weight

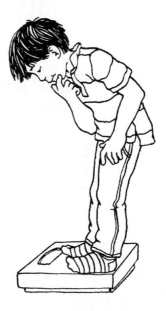

Counting Board

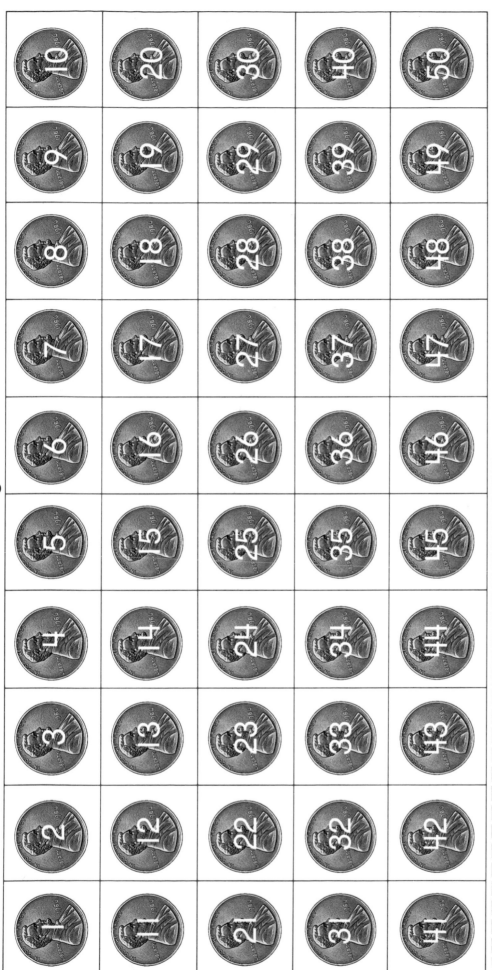

1	2	3	4	5	6	7	8	9	10
11	12	13	14	15	16	17	18	19	20
21	22	23	24	25	26	27	28	29	30
31	32	33	34	35	36	37	38	39	40
41	42	43	44	45	46	47	48	49	50

Money Cover-Ups

Punch out.

Punch out.

Punch out.

Money Cover-Up

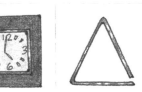

Use with pages 144 and 187.

Use with page 51.

Punch out.

Clocks

Use with page 104.

 1: 00

2: 00

 3: 00

 4: 30

 5: 30

6: 30

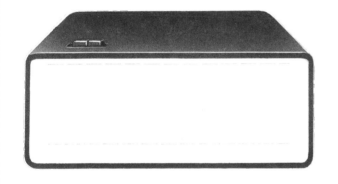

7: 00

8: 00

9: 00

10: 30

11: 30

12: 30

6 + 4	7 + 2	3 + 6	8 + 2	2 + 8

Say the
number **after.**

10

4 + 4	3 + 7	8 + 2	6 + 2	2 + 6

15

6 + 6	3 + 5	6 + 2	7 + 2	2 + 7

11

4 + 5	2 + 4	5 + 1	2 + 9	9 + 2

9

5 + 6	9 + 2	3 + 8	1 + 7	7 + 1

14

5 + 5	5 + 2	6 + 1	3 + 2	2 + 3

12

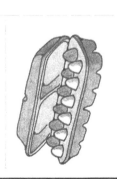

Ladder Punchout

Say the
number **before.**

11	10	9	10
16	8	10	8
12	9	8	12
10	11	6	9
15	8	11	11
13	5	7	10

$$\begin{array}{r} 4 \\ + 8 \\ \hline \end{array} \qquad \begin{array}{r} 5 \\ + 5 \\ \hline 10 \end{array} \qquad \begin{array}{r} 6 \\ + 6 \\ \hline 12 \end{array}$$

9 − 6	10 − 8	9 − 3	7 − 3
11 − 9	9 − 4	7 − 2	10 − 3
12 − 9	10 − 6	8 − 3	8 − 3
9 − 7	10 − 9	6 − 6	11 − 3
8 − 6	10 − 7	8 − 2	9 − 3
8 − 5	9 − 5	7 − 3	12 − 3

6
+ 5

4
+ 5

5
+ 6

5
+ 4

4	$\begin{array}{r} 3 \\ +\ 6 \\ \hline 9 \end{array}$	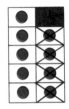	3
7	$\begin{array}{r} 2 \\ +\ 5 \\ \hline 7 \end{array}$	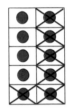	2
5	$\begin{array}{r} 3 \\ +\ 5 \\ \hline 8 \end{array}$	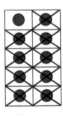	3
8	$\begin{array}{r} 6 \\ +\ 0 \\ \hline 6 \end{array}$	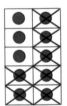	2
6	$\begin{array}{r} 2 \\ +\ 6 \\ \hline 8 \end{array}$	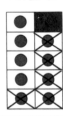	2
9	$\begin{array}{r} 3 \\ +\ 4 \\ \hline 7 \end{array}$		3

Add-to-Check
Facts

$$\begin{array}{r} 6 \\ + 7 \\ \hline 13 \end{array}$$

$$\begin{array}{r} 4 \\ + 9 \\ \hline 13 \end{array}$$

$$\begin{array}{r} 6 \\ + 8 \\ \hline 14 \end{array}$$

$$\begin{array}{r} 5 \\ + 8 \\ \hline 13 \end{array}$$

$$\begin{array}{r} 6 \\ + 9 \\ \hline 15 \end{array}$$

$$\begin{array}{r} 5 \\ + 9 \\ \hline 14 \end{array}$$

$$\begin{array}{r} 6 \\ + 7 \\ \hline \end{array}$$

$$\begin{array}{r} 7 \\ + 8 \\ \hline \end{array}$$

$$\begin{array}{r} 7 \\ + 6 \\ \hline \end{array}$$

$$\begin{array}{r} 8 \\ + 7 \\ \hline \end{array}$$

$$\begin{array}{r} 8 \\ + 9 \\ \hline \end{array}$$

$$\begin{array}{r} 9 \\ + 8 \\ \hline \end{array}$$

Say the number.

$$\begin{array}{r} 12 \\ - 5 \\ \hline \end{array}$$

$$\begin{array}{r} 11 \\ - 4 \\ \hline \end{array}$$

$$\begin{array}{r} 12 \\ - 7 \\ \hline \end{array}$$

$$\begin{array}{r} 12 \\ - 4 \\ \hline \end{array}$$

$$\begin{array}{r} 11 \\ - 5 \\ \hline \end{array}$$

$$\begin{array}{r} 11 \\ - 7 \\ \hline \end{array}$$

$$\begin{array}{r} 6 \\ + 6 \\ \hline \end{array}$$

$$\begin{array}{r} 7 \\ + 7 \\ \hline \end{array}$$

$$\begin{array}{r} 8 \\ + 8 \\ \hline \end{array}$$

$$\begin{array}{r} 9 \\ + 9 \\ \hline \end{array}$$

$\begin{array}{r} 5 \\ +\ 7 \\ \hline 12 \end{array}$	Say the tens. Say the ones. **40**		$\begin{array}{r} 13 \\ -\ 6 \\ \hline \end{array}$
$\begin{array}{r} 4 \\ +\ 7 \\ \hline 11 \end{array}$	**26**	FEBRUARY calendar (1–28) rows 1–7 and 8–14 circled	$\begin{array}{r} 13 \\ -\ 4 \\ \hline \end{array}$
$\begin{array}{r} 7 \\ +\ 5 \\ \hline 12 \end{array}$	**17**		$\begin{array}{r} 14 \\ -\ 6 \\ \hline \end{array}$
$\begin{array}{r} 4 \\ +\ 8 \\ \hline 12 \end{array}$	**22**	FEBRUARY calendar (1–28) rows 1–7 and 8–14 circled	$\begin{array}{r} 13 \\ -\ 5 \\ \hline \end{array}$
$\begin{array}{r} 5 \\ +\ 6 \\ \hline 11 \end{array}$	**32**		$\begin{array}{r} 15 \\ -\ 6 \\ \hline \end{array}$
$\begin{array}{r} 7 \\ +\ 4 \\ \hline 11 \end{array}$	**14**	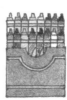	$\begin{array}{r} 14 \\ -\ 5 \\ \hline \end{array}$

Related Subtraction Facts

$$13 - 4 = 9$$

$$15 - 6 = 9$$

$$14 - 5 = 9$$

$$17 - 8 = 9$$

$$12 - 3 = 9$$

$$16 - 7 = 9$$

Add-to-Check Facts

$$7 + 8 = 15$$

$$8 + 5 = 13$$

$$7 + 9 = 16$$

$$8 + 6 = 14$$

$$8 + 9 = 17$$

$$8 + 7 = 15$$

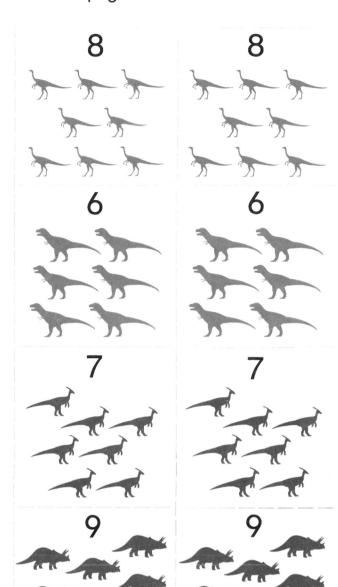

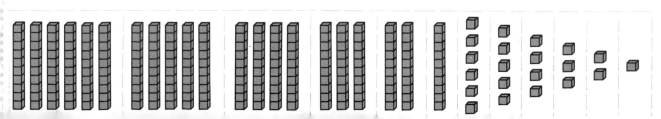

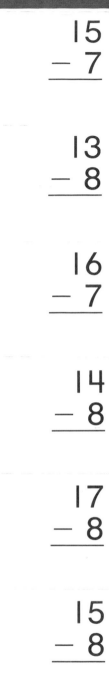

15
− 7

13
− 8

16
− 7

14
− 8

17
− 8

15
− 8

Related
Subtraction
Facts

13
− 9

15
− 9

14
− 9

17
− 9

12
− 9

16
− 9